Far Horizons

A HISTORY OF THE AIR SQUADRON

THE AIR SQUADRON
UNA

Far

Alex Martin

Horizons

A HISTORY OF THE AIR SQUADRON

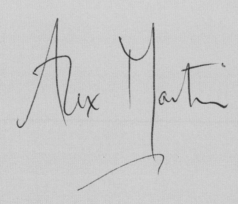

BENE FACTUM PUBLISHING
LONDON

Far Horizons – A history of the Air Squadron
First published in 2009 by
Bene Factum Publishing Ltd
PO Box 58122
London
sw8 5wz

Email: inquiries@bene-factum.co.uk
www.bene-factum.co.uk

ISBN: 978-1-903071-21-2
Text © Alex Martin

A CIP catalogue record of this is available from the
British Library

Design by Anikst Design, London
Printed and bound by Printer Trento, Italy

Cover photograph by Martin Barraclough

CONTENTS

WINDSOR CASTLE

I was invited to become Honorary Air Commodore of the Air Squadron in 1983, but before accepting, I did a little research. It was obviously a very successful club, but I was delighted, and very impressed, to find that, since its foundation, the members had shown an impressive commitment to the promotion of aviation in Britain. They had sponsored aerobatic and home-build competitions; they had encouraged support for the armed forces, and for the collections of historic aircraft. In addition they had supported international relief work through the Mission Aviation Fellowship, and had instituted awards and scholarships for aspiring young pilots and engineers. These have continued to increase in number and value through their stewardship of the Geoffrey de Havilland Flying Foundation.

With this remarkable record of achievements, I had no hesitation in accepting the invitation. Now that I have seen this splendid book, admired the photographs, and read about the magnificent aeroplanes owned by the members, and their adventurous flying expeditions, I am even more delighted to be associated with the Squadron.

I am sure that anyone interested in aircraft and aviation will find this book a very rewarding read.

Philip

Introduction

It is now just over forty years since a group of friends met in London to found the Air Squadron; ten pilots, gathered around a dinner table, with a shared ambition, a passion for flying, and that special English gift of doing things to the highest standard without appearing to make any effort at all. Since then, the organisation they created has grown vigorously: it now numbers 130 members, of whom about 60 regularly take part in its flying events. In recent years many younger pilots have joined, creating a bridge to the future. The Squadron's sorties have evolved from social weekends in France to transcontinental expeditions of two to three weeks' duration. The purpose of these trips has broadened too, and now includes a diplomatic and cultural dimension, sowing the seeds of friendship and goodwill around the world.

Charitable work plays an ever more significant part in the Squadron's activities. The Geoffrey de Havilland Flying Foundation is administered and financed by the Air Squadron, offering flying scholarships and awards for excellence to air cadets. A Sword of Honour is presented annually to cadets in Britain, South Africa, Poland and the USA. Contacts with the armed forces are flourishing. An annual lecture at Coutts, the Squadron's bank since 1966, is the latest addition to a varied and lively programme of events.

In 1966 the Air Squadron had no 'tedious things like rules or subscriptions', but with time these became necessary. Today there is a written constitution and a formal committee, guided and administered by the Honorary Secretary. It is a smooth-running machine, yet it retains the special quality of friendship that inspired it from the start.

At the Winter Dinner of 2008, the Air Squadron welcomed its Honorary Air Commodore, His Royal Highness the Duke of Edinburgh, at the Cavalry and Guards Club in London. The Duke presented medals to David Hare and Bruno Schroder for their outstanding achievements and contributions over many years. In a series of short speeches, members of the Squadron sketched out the range of its activities – John Steel on the recent Balkans trip, Nicholas Parkhouse on a plan to visit Airbus Industries in France, Ian Macfadyen on the work of the de Havilland Flying Foundation, and Sir Jock Stirrup on the forthcoming visit to the helicopter squadrons of the armed forces. Listening to these presentations, and reviewing the story that unfolds in the pages of this book, members may feel justly proud of their achievements. In the words of the chairman, Sir Michael Graydon, 'Those free spirits who founded the Air Squadron nearly fifty years ago could never have imagined what has been accomplished since then. Our foundations are strong; we will continue to encourage and assist young people to fly. Over the next half century we can look forward to more aerial expeditions, with some going even further afield. For an organisation whose members are united in a love of flying, the far horizons beckon.'

Chapter 1   The Early Years   1966-80

1

January 7, 1971
8 JAN 1971

Dear David,

I have just been looking through the list of
Air Squadron Members and no doubt individuals will
be sending you any relevant corrections but I have
noticed the following errors or omissions:-

1. James Baring has an aircraft and a landing field.

2. Winston Churchill has an aircraft.

3. David Constable Maxwell has a landing field.

4. John Houlder has I think replaced his Cessna with
    an Aero Commander.

5. Patrick Lindsay has an aircraft.

6. Adrian Swire has a Spitfire.

7. Tommy Sopwith has a Jet Ranger.

8. Whitney Straight is a "Companion" not a "Dame".

9. John Williams-Wynne has an aircraft and a landing
    strip.

10. Gerald Ward has a helicopter.

11. Dugdale and Shelburne both have Cessnas.

Yours ever,

D.B. Eaden, Esq.,
Norfolk House,
187 High Street,
GUILDFORD,
Surrey.

2

1 Hugh Astor (1920-99) grew up at Hever Castle in Kent, went to Eton and New College, Oxford, and had a distinguished war career in MI5, feeding false information to the Germans through double agents, particularly over the D-Day landings of 1944. After two further years' intelligence work in French Indo-China, he retired with the rank of Lieutenant-Colonel and joined *The Times* (owned by his father since 1922) as Assistant Middle East Correspondent in 1947. He subsequently worked in all the departments, including printing, management and editorial, before becoming a director in 1956. While his father ran the paper from tax exile in the South of France, Hugh and his elder brother Gavin worked hard to persuade the board to diversify into commercial television, a move which would have guaranteed the newspaper's financial independence. This was resisted by older members of the board, and in 1967 the Astors, unwilling to continue losing money, sold their shareholding to Roy Thomson (who had profited handsomely from his own investment in commercial TV). At the time of founding the Air Squadron, Hugh's entry in *Who's Who* gave the following information: Deputy-Chairman The Times Publishing Co. Ltd; Chairman The Times Bookshop; Director: Hambro's Bank; Phoenix Assurance; Hutchinson's & Co. Ltd; Winterbottom Trust Ltd. Governor: Middlesex Hospital; Bradfield College; Trustee, Trust Houses Ltd. J.P. Berks, 1953; High Sheriff of Berkshire, 1963. *Recreations*: sailing, flying, shooting, diving. *Clubs*: Brooks's, Buck's, Royal Aero, Royal Yacht Squadron, Royal Ocean Racing. He also competed in the London-Sydney and London-Victoria air races.

2 An early attempt to produce a list of members, their aircraft and airfields contained plenty of inaccuracies, which Hugh Astor was at pains to correct. David Eaden, a Battle of Britain pilot, was Joint Honorary Secretary of the Air Squadron 1970-72.

3 Anthony Cayzer (1920-99) was the second son of Lord Rotherwick, whose family had risen to prominence as shipowners in Victorian England. After Eton and Sandhurst, he served with the Royal Scots Greys from 1939 to 1944. In 1966 he was Deputy-Chairman of British & Commonwealth Shipping Co. and Union-Castle Steamship Co., as well as a director of Cayzer, Irvine & Co, Clan Line Steamers, British United Airways, Martins Bank, Caledonia Investments, and Greenock Dockyard Co. He was a keen flyer and yachtsman, and the originator of the idea of the Air Squadron.

4 Anthony Cayzer's aviator's certificate, issued in 1946

The Early Years   1966-80

The Air Squadron was born on 1st February 1966, at 2 Ilchester Place, London W14. The occasion was a black-tie dinner given by Anthony Cayzer – shipowner, yachtsman and keen amateur pilot – for a group of eight friends at his London home. His guests were Hugh Astor, Douglas Bader, James Baring, Ivor Faulconer, John Houlder, Peter Vanneck, John Verulam and Caryll Waterpark. Three were members of the Royal Yacht Squadron, Britain's most prestigious sailing club. All had aeroplanes and loved flying. They decided to found a club of their own, with the proviso that the word 'club' was never to be used. It would instead be a 'Squadron' – a word with a bolder, brisker, more martial ring - and they would call it the Air Squadron.

Credit for the idea belongs squarely with Anthony Cayzer. John Houlder remembers him calling into his office in Liverpool (they were on different floors of the Royal Liver Building, and often had coffee together) to ask what he thought of forming an Air Squadron. Hugh Astor recalled 'a chance remark made when Tony Cayzer was staying to shoot over the weekend of 11 December 1965. We were both members of the Royal Yacht Squadron and were attracted by the idea of forming a similar organisation for those interested in aviation. We met to discuss the idea further a week or two later over lunch at Tony's office in the City, where we were joined by Peter Vanneck... The three of us agreed that the idea was worth pursuing.'

Memories of that dinner at Ilchester Place are now hazy, but James Baring, who was managing

a recording studio in Soho at the time, remembers a man running in from the street with the words, 'James, there's a posh geezer in a Roller wants to see you,' before he was chauffeured luxuriously away to Kensington. 'It must have been an extremely good dinner,' he says, 'because I came out of it with the job of Secretary.'

A handwritten note on Cayzer's blue headed paper records the occasion for posterity in a matter-of-fact way. A more vivid account survives in this letter:

St Albans, February 15th 1966

My dear Tony,

I went to a dinner the other day given by Tony Cayzer at which there were a number of elderly aviators and a few young ones.

They decided to call themselves The Air Squadron, partly to provoke other elderly aviators who were not present and partly to put themselves on a level with the Yacht Squadron.

The idea was to have a nucleus of people who could call on an aeroplane, which might in some conceivable emergency be useful, but probably more important to be a rather snob club dining together occasionally and prepared to make a nuisance of themselves from time to time against officialdom, for example, to cut down the restrictions on the use of RAF aerodromes.

It was decided to hold another dinner on May 17th at which each person present would ask a guest who might like to join and would be suitable to do so.

1

2

1 John Grimston (6th Earl of Verulam, 1912-1973), on the steps of his de Havilland Dove in 1963, as Hon. Air Commodore, No 1 (County of Hertford) Maritime Headquarters Unit, Royal Auxiliary Air Force. During the war he served with Coastal Command as a pilot. He was one of the founding members of the Air Squadron, Chairman of Enfield Rolling Mills and President of the London Chamber of Commerce, 1963–66. He was also Conservative MP for St Albans and Mid Herts (1943–45 and 1950–1959).

2 Whitney Straight (1912-1979), racing driver, Battle of Britain pilot and businessman, described in his *Times* obituary as 'a man whose remarkable versatility was matched only by his energy and the breadth of his interests'. The son of Dorothy Elmhirst, founder of Dartington Hall, he studied at Trinity College, Cambridge and combined motor racing and flying with a dynamic business career: he started the Straight Corporation in the 1930s, operating flying clubs and airfields across Britain, joined Rolls-Royce in 1955, and later became chairman. He was also Deputy Chairman of BEA and Managing Director of BOAC. As a pilot officer in 601 Squadron, he had an adventurous war: he was wounded in Norway, shot down over the Channel, and escaped through France and Spain to serve again in Egypt and England.

This letter is to ask if you would like to be my guest on that day, whether or not you might like to join.

The Air Squadron has at the moment no tedious things like rules or subscriptions, though no doubt these will come one day. The last evening was very enjoyable and I would expect the next one to be so too.

The dinner is at Brooks's. I do not know the time but will let you know later if you can come.

Yours ever

"J.G."

[John Grimston, Earl of Verulam]

Verulam was one of the 'elderly aviators' (he was born in 1912). There is respect as well as amusement in his description of the new project - and a glimpse of the irritation that free-spirited pilots were already feeling at the encroachments of the regulators. Those who know the Air Squadron today will immediately recognize the style: urbane, light-hearted, yet with a glint of steel.

A second dinner was held, as promised, at Brooks's Club, on May 17th. The host on this occasion was Peter Vanneck. Besides Tony Savile (the recipient of the letter quoted above), there were seven guests: Max Aitken (like Bader a famous wartime fighter pilot, in 1966 leading a less tranquil life at the top of his father Lord Beaverbrook's newspaper empire), Derek Dempster, David Eaden, Tony Everard, Osborne King, Julian Salmond and Tommy Sopwith (son of the founder of the Sopwith Aviation Company). 'Tedious things like rules' were quick to appear. They agreed to pay a subscription of 2 guineas per

annum, hold two dinners a year in London, meet from time to time 'to further members' interests in private aviation', and volunteer for service in a national emergency. They would also invite a further 16 friends to a 'third and final inaugural dinner' at Boodle's Club on July 25th.

No formal minutes survive of this third gathering, although the menu does: Sole Farcie Vieille France, Filet de Boeuf Rôti, and Soufflé Fromage. The only named wine was 1959 Taittinger – an early indication of the Squadron's predilection for champagne. Newcomers that night were Tom Brook Smith, Winston Churchill (grandson of the wartime Prime Minister), David Constable Maxwell, Robin D'Erlanger, Hugh Dundas, Clive Francis, Jimmy Gardner, Desmond Norman, Torquil Norman, Ian Ponsford, David Smiley, Euan Strathcona, Whitney Straight, Luke White, John Williams-Wynne and Philip Wills. Most were to become members, either on the spot or in later years. A committee was formed (Astor, Cayzer and Vanneck, with James Baring as Secretary), and a first 'cross-channel dinner' was planned.

This was a fly-in to le Touquet on 24th September, with dinner at the Club de la Forêt, returning to England the next day. Caryll Waterpark remembers arriving in a brand-new Piper Aztec, Tommy Sopwith in a de Havilland Dove 'with two very pretty girls on board', Hugh Astor in a Beechcraft twin and Tony Cayzer in a four-engined de Havilland Heron. On that first French outing, members dined, as they had in London, on sole and fillet of beef, followed by

1

> "First turning point: MTB at Brighton pier?
> (Occasion on finishing, when I took away 2 fishing
> lines from the end of the pier — one broke: O.K. — the other
> ran out and nearly set the fisherman's reel on fire — a
> lot of aggro, apology and a £1 quietener.)

5.45		
.55		
.25		
1.10		
.50		
1.10		
.45		
1.15		
1.00		
.15		

2

1   Peter Vanneck (1922-99) was the most flamboyant of the three founders of the Air Squadron. He spent his formative years in Australia, where his father, Lord Huntingfield, was Governor of the State of Victoria from 1934 to 1939. He served in the Royal Navy during the war, first in the Atlantic, then on MTBs in the North Sea, where he took up the lifelong habit of the 'Motor Torpedo Boat Breakfast' - a bowl of cornflakes with milk and brandy (or whisky), to be taken before going out in the evening. He learned to fly with the Navy in 1945, and despite an examiner's comment that he was 'inclined to over-confidence', flew successfully and stylishly for the rest of his life. After the war he studied at Cambridge and Harvard, then worked for the Norwich engineering firm of Ransome, Simms and Jeffries before finding his vocation in the City of London – first at Phillips and Drew, then at Rowe and Pitman, where he later became a partner. He served in the Royal Auxiliary Air Force from 1950 to 1987, commanding 601 Squadron and rising to the rank of Air Commodore. His second wife, Elizabeth,

remembers meeting him for the first time at Cowes in 1963 - 'a wonderfully glamorous man - good-looking, dashing, utterly captivating.' He was Gentleman Usher to the Queen from 1967 to 1979, Lord Mayor of London 1977-8, and Member of the European Parliament for Cleveland and North Yorkshire (his 'retirement job') 1979-89. Friends remember him as a man of infectious high spirits, who loved grand occasions, sailing, flying, uniforms of every kind, and champagne. 'When Peter walked into a room, the party started.'

2   Peter Vanneck's log book records the race at Brighton in 1963 when he flew so close to the pier that he caught two fishing lines with his wings.

3   Lieutenant Peter Vanneck arrives at the South African Air Force base at Zwartkop, near Pretoria, in a Sea Fury. Vanneck was serving with 807 Squadron on the aircraft carrier HMS *Theseus*, on a mission to collect Bank of England gold deposited in South Africa for safe keeping during the war.

3

4

5

4   Tony Savile joined the Air Squadron at its second inaugural dinner in May 1966 at the invitation of Lord Verulam. He is pictured here with members of his family and his last aircraft, a Piper 260 Comanche C. 'My flying,' he says, 'was entirely for pleasure, with approximately 2,000 hours throughout Europe, the Middle East and to Cape Town.'

5   Osborne (Ossie) King, a member from Northern Ireland, was Captain of the Motor Torpedo Boat in which Euan Strathcona and Peter Vanneck served in World War II. A shrewd businessman, he also loved company, and was a keen and active member of the Squadron. He owned a real estate business in Ireland, and invited friends and fellow members to come in on property investments with him – always, recalls Euan Strathcona, with very positive results. He is seen here on the Air Squadron visit to Colonsay in 1973.

6

6   HRH The Duke of Edinburgh watching a helicopter competition at Oxford Airport with Tommy Sopwith (left) and Caryll Waterpark (right).

1 The Tiger Club flew a special diamond nine formation over St Alban's Cathedral for Sir Geoffrey de Havilland's memorial service in 1965. There were four future Air Squadron pilots in the formation – James Baring, Martin Barraclough, Tony Haig-Thomas, and John Thomson.

2 Norman Jones gave the aerobatic Tiger Moths ecclesiastical names as a tribute to his friend and co-founder of the Tiger Club, the flying instructor C.A. Nepean-Bishop (known to everyone as 'Bish'). Four aircraft - 'the Bishop', 'the Archbishop', 'the Canon' and 'the Deacon' – were converted to single-seaters, with an inverted fuel system, a repositioned fuel tank, and wooden leading edges to the wings.

3 As well as half a dozen Tiger Moths based at Redhill and Fairoaks for members' use ('half a crown in the box if you bent one'), Norman Jones's Tiger Club fitted a Tiger Moth with floats at Lee-on-Solent, where it was used by Martin Barraclough, Ivor Faulconer and others.

4 A Tiger Club display briefing, 1965. Three Air Squadron members can be seen here: James Baring (2nd from left), Martin Barraclough (4th from left) and Robin D'Erlanger (far right). In the centre, doing the talking, is Bill Innes, a leading Tiger Club member and BEA pilot. Founded by Norman Jones in 1956, the Tiger Club was devoted to 'good sporting flying at high standards and at the lowest possible costs'. Several other Air Squadron members came from the Club – Prince Philip, Peter Vanneck, Simon Ames, Tom Storey, Adrian Swire, Ivor Faulconer, Winston Churchill, Tony Haig-Thomas, Charles Masefield, Philip Meeson, and latterly Nick Parkhouse and Maxi Gainza.

cheeses from a local farm and *Pêches Flambées Monte Carlo*. Sancerre, Pomerol and Champagne were served. Nothing has survived from that dinner but the menu and a note of its cost - £4 a head (roughly double the annual subscription). The details, and many of the participants, have long gone. It was, however, the start of a long and happy association between the Air Squadron and le Touquet. There were to be many more visits in the years to come.

On December 1st James Baring wrote to members with a draft Constitution and Rules.

1. *The Air Squadron is an association of friends who are aviation enthusiasts.*
2. *Membership is limited to a maximum of 50.*
3. *Members must have qualified as aviators.*
4. *Candidates for Election will be circulated by the Secretary together with the names of six sponsors to all members of the Squadron in time for them to be considered at an election meeting to be held twice yearly in London. It is suggested that a member, before proposing a candidate, should mention his name at a meeting or dinner preceding the election at which the candidate will be considered. There will be two candidature dinners a year, to be held in London.*
5. *By a two-thirds majority vote of the members present at such a dinner, membership may be terminated.*
6. *Members' subscription to be 2 guineas a year payable annually by bankers order.*

A committee and secretary will be re-elected annually.

1

The circular also contained the following announcement:

The Squadron has been asked by the Tiger Club, who in conjunction with the Royal Aero Club are organising a new aerobatic competition, if we would consider presenting a trophy for the competition, and also supplying a Judge. The Committee felt this was a good idea, and P. Vanneck is organising. The competition will be called the Air Squadron Trophy and will be open to all comers in aeroplanes without inverted fuel systems (including jets!).

As this letter implies, things were becoming both more organised and more serious. By the end of its first year, the Air Squadron had recruited 33 members, four of them highly decorated World War II fighter pilots (Aitken, Bader, Dundas and Straight). They had high-level links with Government, commercial and military aviation, finance, television and the press, as well as the engineering, shipping and petroleum industries.

2

4

3

They had a bank account at Coutts. Their social networks reached out through the Tiger Club, the Royal Aero Club and Royal Aeronautical Society, the Royal Auxiliary Air Force (particularly 601 Squadron), veterans of the Army, Navy and Air Force, the Royal Yacht Squadron, the City of London and its Livery Companies, the gentlemen's clubs of St James's, various country shoots and hunts, and the St Moritz Tobogganing Club. There was a healthy sprinkling of grand family names, which even in London of the Swinging Sixties still counted for a lot. With one foreign trip completed, three London dinners, and a new aerobatic competition in its name, the Air Squadron had made a promising start.

The first Annual General Meeting was held at Boodle's Club on March 22nd 1967, immediately after the Spring Dinner. The rules were adopted, a membership list was published, and the year's programme announced. This would include a three-day visit to the champagne houses at Epernay on May 5-7, the presentation of the first Air Squadron Trophy, a fly-in buffet lunch hosted by David Constable Maxwell at Market Bosworth, and a film show on Flight Safety at the Royal Aeronautical Society. Air Squadron insignia had been produced by Tommy Sopwith, and Douglas Bader volunteered to check the design with the College of Heralds.

With members planning to fly in to Epernay and Bosworth from airfields around Britain, instructions had to be issued. James Baring took care of Epernay, listing the radio frequencies, runway dimensions and grades of fuel available. He painted a vivid picture of the weekend's activities: 'On Sunday we are invited by the House of Bollinger to visit their establishment in the morning, and Madame Bollinger has invited any members of the Squadron still on their feet by this time to a buffet lunch at her home.' An application form asked members to specify 'Number of wives, lady friends, etc. accompanying you (NB Maximum allowed: ONE)'.

The weekend was a triumph, and a silver

1

1 Colonel John Williams-Wynne (1908-1998) at the time of joining the Air Squadron was HM Lord-Lieutenant of Merioneth and Constable of Harlech Castle. After graduating from Cambridge in Mechanical Sciences he was commissioned in the Royal Artillery in 1929, serving in India and Ceylon during the war, where he won a DSO in 1945. After retiring from the Army in 1948, he farmed in Merioneth, where he kept a Rallye Commodore 150 on his farm airstrip notoriously vulnerable to sea-mists. He founded the Flying Farmers Association, with help and encouragement from Douglas Bader, who spoke at two of the FFA's early meetings. A devoted public servant, John Williams-Wynne sat on many committees and boards, including the Ministry of Agriculture Experimental Husbandry Farm,

Merseyside and North Wales Electricity Board, the Forestry Commission, the National Parks Commission, and the Gwynedd River Board. He listed his recreations in 1966 as 'almost anything except golf and cricket'.

2 The letter of invitation to a fly-in lunch sent to members in March 1969 by John Williams-Wynne.

3 A map of the farm airstrip at Peniarth drawn by John Williams-Wynne for his Air Squadron guests.

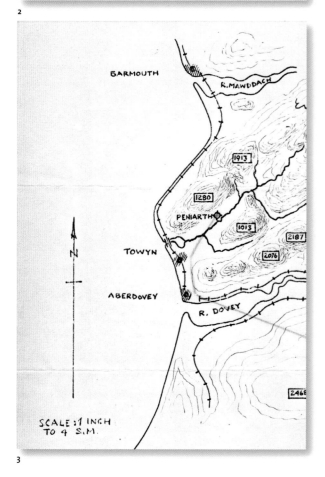

salver engraved with the signatures of all who attended was presented to Moët et Chandon by way of thanks.

The joining instructions for lunch at Bosworth were much more complicated. David Constable Maxwell's military training is evident in every line of the three pages detailing Location, Identification, Signals Area, Altitude, Runway, Radio Facilities, Navigational Facilities, Procedures, Warnings, Alternatives and Comments for Pilots Flying "Contact". These conclude with the fateful words: 'the airfield cannot be missed.' Despite the extraordinary thoroughness of the directions (or possibly because of it), at least one member had serious difficulties. John Williams-Wynne wrote to the Honorary Secretary afterwards: 'I want to find out from some of you experts how the hell you found H. Bosworth Hall the other day. I did it by creeping along below the cloud, or going round it, and staying well under the Airway Amber One - but I felt there was probably another way - especially when the canal which I was following so carefully disappeared into a tunnel!'

The Air Squadron Trophy was presented on July 1st by Douglas Bader at Staverton. It was won by David Allen, an Australian, whose name was duly engraved on its base. The trophy itself, a silver-gilt George III sauce tureen, had been bought in Bond Street by James Baring and Peter Vanneck. Members contributed £4 each to the cost of £120.

At the Autumn Dinner, held at the Turf Club on December 7th, Peter Vanneck was able to look back over a highly successful second year. Adrian Swire was elected, and Douglas Bader suggested that the membership should now be limited to 35 or thereabouts. If the Squadron grew too fast, he thought, 'it could become impersonal and lose its point.'

After two hectic years, 1968 was much quieter. A visit to the British Aircraft Corporation at Filton gave members their first glimpse of Concorde on May 25. At the Spring Dinner, membership was closed at 36 after the admission of Martin Barraclough, Patrick Lindsay and Sam Clutton. There was a trip to Cognac in the autumn at the invitation of René Martell, and David Constable Maxwell was appointed historian to the Squadron - a trifle prematurely, one might have thought, given that there were barely two years of activity to record, but a sign of the self-confidence of the organisation that they were already thinking about posterity.

The Air Squadron Trophy competition was held at the Central Flying School, RAF Little Rissington, on June 22nd, its purpose now more carefully defined: 'to encourage promising aerobatic pilots and assist in building a strong national aerobatic team for the World Aerobatic Championships which will be held in this country in 1970.'

Martin Barraclough remembers judging the competition with Douglas Bader. As they climbed the steps to the control tower, Bader asked how many pilots were flying British aeroplanes.

'Just one,' said Barraclough.

'Right,' said Bader, 'we know who's going to win, don't we?'

1

2

3

1–2 Martin Barraclough in the Tiger Cub's Arrow Active, of which he was the display pilot for the 1965-66 seasons. He had learnt to fly in Kenya in 1953, and flew for Steel Brothers (Tanganyika Forests) before returning to England in 1958 to join his family's ship-owning business. He joined the Tiger Club, where he spent 'a decade of wonderful and stimulating sport flying'. With James Baring, Tony Haig-Thomas and John Thomson (all future members of the Air Squadron) he flew in the Tiger Club Diamond Nine memorial flypast over St Alban's Cathedral for Sir Geoffrey de Havilland on 21st July 1965. Martin bought his first aeroplane in 1970, quickly becoming a passionate vintage aircraft enthusiast. He joined the Air Squadron in 1968, and has been one of its most active members ever since, earning the unofficial title of 'Paparazzo' for his photography.

3 Martin Barraclough in the Tiger club's Jodel Ambassadeur after having flown to a ball at Kidlington on 19th June 1964, danced all night and flown back to Redhill with the dawn.

Sir Douglas Bader

Group Captain Sir Douglas Bader CBE, DSO, DFC, was born in 1910 and educated at St. Edward's School, Oxford, and the Royal Air Force College, Cranwell. He was commissioned in June 1930 and posted to 23 Fighter Squadron. On 14 December 1931, he crashed in a Bristol Bulldog single-seater fighter, losing both legs as a result. In May 1933 he was invalided from the RAF and in June joined the Shell Company. He rejoined the RAF in November 1939. His promotion was rapid and his success spectacular. Starting with his retired rank of Flying Officer, he became Flight Lieutenant in April 1940, Squadron Leader in June, and Wing Commander in March 1941. Bader's official score was 22 German aircraft destroyed. On 9 August 1941 he was shot down over France and taken prisoner. After escaping for 24 hours from his hospital in St. Omer, he was taken to Germany under heavy escort. In his first twelve months as a prisoner, he was transferred through six POW camps, from two of which he made abortive attempts to escape. In August 1942 he arrived at Colditz where he remained until his release by the US First Army on 15 April 1945.

Douglas Bader retired from the Royal Air Force as a Group Captain in 1946 and rejoined the Shell International Petroleum Company. He was Director of Shell Aaircraft 1958-69. He was a member of the Board of the Civil Aviation Authority 1972-78, and worked tirelessly for the disabled, both civilian and military, until his death in 1982. He was a founding member of the Air Squadron and contributed greatly to its identity and principles in the early years. He flew friends and fellow members in his own light aircraft, a Beech Travelair, on numerous Air Squadron visits. A patriot to the last, he took care to mispronounce all foreign names, and had little time for bureaucrats of any nationality. In Dinard once on an Air Squadron visit, he was angered when Ground Control refused to let him take off during the lunch hour. He took off anyway, and was told that he would be shot down by the French Air Force unless he returned immediately. He replied, 'Bugger you,' and flew on. Finally his friends persuaded him to come back and the purpose of the authorities' firmness was revealed: the Mayor of Dinard had planned a surprise ceremony in his honour. Douglas Bader became a figure of worldwide fame with the release of the film *Reach for the Sky* (1956) based on Paul Brickhill's book of the same name. He was knighted in 1976.

4

4   Douglas Bader climbs into his Spitfire for the Victory Flypast in 1945.

5   Douglas Bader and Peter Vanneck at a reception in the late 1970s.

5

VISITES

Service : Mr. René F.M.   N° :   Date de la note 20/I0/69

Pays d'origine GDE BRETAGNE   Langue ~~Britannique~~ombre
                                       anglaise

Noms

            RALLYE

☒ M. A. Martin
☒ Madame Depeux
☐ Service
☒ Chanteloup
☒ M. Berruer
☒ Visite Mise en Bouteilles
☒ Visite Chais
☒ Publicité ✓
☐ Introducteurs
☐ Salle Dégustation
☒ Salle d'Attente

ARIVÉE PRÉVUE à COGNAC - Date : 23/I0/69   Heure : I7 H° 00
DEPART PRÉVU de COGNAC - Date : 25/I0/69   Heure : dans la
                                                    matinée

VISITE MARTELL :   Date   Heure
— Chais . . . . 24/I0/69   I5 H° 30
— Mise en Bouteilles .   ☒   d°
— Distillerie . GALLIENNE dans la matinée
— Chai Saint-Martin . .   ☒   d°
— Salle Dégustation . .   ☒   I7 H° 00

CADEAUX SOUVENIRS : Nombre : 25   Composition :

MODE DE TRANSPORT DU VISITEUR : Avions personnels

☒ Mr. René F.M.
x Mr. Michel F.M.
x Mr. André F.M.
x Mr. Edouard F.M.
x Mr. Patrick F.M.

TERRASSE & PARADIS

(Affaire traitée directement entre
Mr. A. FORT & Melle POURET)

VOITURES MARTELL :   Nombre :   Date   Heure   Lieu
                      Minicar &
— à l'arrivée . . . .   ☒   23/I0/69   I7 H° 00   LE PARVEAU
— au départ Minicar + ☒   25/I0/69   08 H° 30   CHANTELOUP
— à disposition . . . . . .

CARS :   Nombre   Date   Heure   Lieu
— à l'arrivée . . . .
— au départ . . . .
— à disposition   I   24/I0/69   ⌀ 9 H° 00   (toute la journée) Maison MARTELL

REPAS :   Déjeuner /Dîner   Couverts   Date   Heure   Lieu
           Dîner   23/I0/69   CHANTELOUP
           Déj/Dîner   24/I0/69   d°

CHAMBRES :   1 Lit   2 Lits
— Lieu : CHANTELOUP   Nombre : en totalité   du 23/I0/69   soir au 25/I0/69 matin

OBSERVATIONS :   LIVRE D'OR   PHOTOGRAPHE

1 René Firino Martell (1927-1995) worked for the family firm of Martell & Co for 40 years. After studies in Bordeaux and the USA, he joined the commercial department in 1949, and quickly rose to positions of responsibility, becoming a Director in 1955, Vice-President in 1972 and President in 1977. A *New York Times* article in 1995 spoke of his skill in developing the reach of the company, and his brilliant manoeuvring of rival takeover bids to increase its value from $500 million in July 1987 to $850 million ('a staggering 36 times Martell's annual earnings') at the time of its sale to Seagram in January 1988. René Martell was Honorary President of the Aéro-Club de Cognac and himself flew an Aero Commander; he welcomed the Air Squadron personally to the town in 1968 and 1969. He was made an Honorary Member of the Air Squadron in 1969 and a Chevalier de la Légion d'Honneur by decree of the French President in 1981.

The headquarters of Martell & Co in Cognac, visited by the Air Squadron in 1968, 1969 and 2002.

When the Air Squadron visited in October 1969, members flew in for a tour of the Martell establishment (presses, distillery, warehouse, blending, bottling, tasting) before dinner at Château Chanteloup with René Martell and his family. A description of the trip by David Constable Maxwell made special mention of 'superbly comfortable bedrooms each not only with its own bathroom but also a bottle of Martell in case of emergency'.

1969 produced a torrent of events: as well as the Spring and Autumn dinners, there was a second visit to le Touquet in May, a fly-in lunch with Colonel and Mrs Williams-Wynne at Peniarth in June 8, the aerobatics competition at Little Rissington (July 19), a visit to the Stamford Game Show followed by tea at Bosworth Hall with the Constable Maxwells (July 26), a trip to the Isle of Wight to see Britten-Norman Aircraft, the British Hovercraft Corporation and the Royal Yacht Squadron (October 4-5), and a second expedition to Cognac, featuring a 'conducted tour round vineyards, factory, bottling plant, stores, etc', with dinner both nights as guests of the Martells (October 23-5). Hugh Astor also found time to compete in the London to Sydney Air Race in December, flying a Britten-Norman Islander and finishing sixth.

Meanwhile the potential for involvement in public events was growing. Members were invited to attend a 'Flying for Fun' rally at Sywell on September 13-14 'to encourage interest among young people and introduce them to the most economic examples of powered aircraft, gliders, rotocraft, etc., including home building and model flying.' In partnership with the Air League and the British Gliding Association, the Committee of the Air Squadron had agreed to underwrite some of the expenses of this rally, although the day was 'expected to cover its costs completely'. Presumably this prediction was fulfilled, as no further mention was made of it. Again, one notes the seriousness of the intent. The encouragement

of young aviators was later to become a major part of the Squadron's *raison d'être*.

A heavier financial undertaking loomed in the shape of the forthcoming World Aerobatic Championships, for which the Royal Aero Club was seeking to raise £12,000. A cautious note in the minutes of the Spring Dinner and AGM records: 'it was thought that the Committee should keep in touch with the situation in the event that the Squadron might lend its moral support to the fund raising.'

At the 1969 Autumn Dinner, Comte Frédéric Chandon and René Martell were made honorary members in recognition of their services to the Air Squadron. James Baring announced that he and his wife Nini were about to start a family; he would therefore need help with the job of Honorary Secretary. David Constable Maxwell, who had already organised several trips, and David Eaden, a Surrey solicitor and ex-fighter pilot, agreed to divide the work between them. Part-time help from a typist would be provided at the rate of 10 shillings an hour.

After four vigorous and expansive years, 1970 was something of an anti-climax. This may have been a necessary relaxation of the pace, or one of those critical phases in the growth of an organism when it must prepare itself seriously for survival. The year began with optimistic plans, most of them never to be realised. The Committee met in January and announced visits to Sardinia, Switzerland, Ostend and Southampton, where the Chairman of Cunard, Sir Basil Smallpiece, had invited the Squadron for lunch on the *Queen*

1

2

1 Caryll Waterpark with his first aircraft, a Piper Cruiser, Kenya 1949.

2 Gerald Ward (1938-2008) was an early member of the Air Squadron, and one of its first helicopter pilots. 'We were definitely the poor relations on outings,' he recalled, 'and we pretended there was a mystique about helicopter flying. In fact it's a lot easier, because you land at 0 miles per hour.' He is pictured here in 1974 with his Brantly B2B, 'which cost new in 1969 £18,000. I got my PPL on Tiger Moths in 1957. I was taught by Joan Hughes, legendary ferry pilot in the war who flew every plane, single, twin and 4-engined, alongside the likes of Amy Johnson and Diana Barnato Walker. I converted to rotary in 1968, when I was taught by another flying legend, Peter Peckowski, who did all the amazing helicopter flying in one of the early James Bond films, ostensibly inside a volcano. I have been a member of the Air Squadron longer than I can remember, and was greeted at the first dinner I went to as a member by the likes of Douglas Bader, Max Aitken, Hugh Dundas, Patrick Lindsay, Hugh Astor and Tony Cayzer. What fun it all was!'

3 Tommy Sopwith showing Caryll Waterpark the controls of his Jet Ranger helicopter. Both were directors and shareholders of CSE Aviation in Oxford.

3

4

4   Tony Everard with his Brantly B2 on the lawn of his Leicestershire home in 1963. Born in 1922, Tony Everard served in the Household Cavalry during the war, and was wounded in France in 1944. Although he planned a career in the army after the war, his father's early death propelled him into the family brewing business. He resisted buyout offers ('I feared for the jobs of my employees, who were marvellous people, and I said "I've got a car and a set of golf clubs, I don't need five cars and five sets of golf clubs," so we managed to keep it in the family.') Everard's has remained a private company, and is now run by Tony's nephew Richard, also a keen helicopter pilot and member of the Air Squadron. Tony Everard joined the Air Squadron at the invitation of John Houlder in 1966. He founded the Helicopter Club of Great Britain in a hotel room in Deauville on 3rd July 1966, and recruited the first President in an unusual way. 'I walked into Buckingham Palace, which you could still do in those days, and said I would like to invite Prince Philip to be our President. An equerry said, "Take a seat, I'll go and ask him." He came back a few minutes later and said the Prince thought it was a great idea and he would be delighted.'

Elizabeth II. At the Spring Dinner, an increased subscription was agreed (from 2 guineas to £5), together with the creation of an ambitious set of committees. The first, consisting of Max Aitken, Hugh Dundas and Luke White, was to run 'the Spitfire project' (a Mark IX recently bought by Adrian Swire). The second was to be an Aerobatics Committee, with Martin Barraclough, Robin D'Erlanger, Anthony Steel, and Douglas Bader. The third was a Vintage Aircraft Committee, with Kenneth McAlpine, Patrick Lindsay and Tony Haig-Thomas (who was not actually a member yet, although he stood fair to become one). Finally, there was to be a Helicopter Sub-Committee, with Tommy Sopwith, Gerald Ward, and Kenneth McAlpine in the Chair.

Whatever the enthusiasm around the dinner table, it quickly vanished in the chilly spring air. Tommy Sopwith wrote to David Eaden on 20 April: 'Our original objective was to have a couple of fully licensed dinners and the same number of flying expeditions per year, purely as a group of friends who were keen on flying, but we appear to

be running the risk of drifting into a conventional club full of committees, sub-committees, good causes and so forth which might, God forbid, turn into an awful bore.' He was supported by a forceful letter from Kenneth McAlpine, reporting on the first meeting of the Helicopter Sub-Committee: 'We discussed the subject very fully and came to the conclusion that there was nothing that the Squadron could or should do in regard to helicopters as we felt that the social side of the helicopter interests were looked after fully by the Helicopter Club and that the legal and operating side of helicopters were looked after by the British Helicopter Advisory Board. Therefore if the Squadron started to become involved in either of these fields it would only be at the expense of the efforts of other organisations' (Letter to David Eaden, 7 May 1970).

Max Aitken, who had not been present when his name was put forward for the Spitfire Committee, interpreted the project as a disguised attempt to sell him the aircraft, and had to be carefully pacified. Hugh Astor was unenthusiastic

1

Year 1968 Month/Date	AIRCRAFT		Commander	Holder's Operating Capacity	Journey or Nature of Flight		
	Type	Registration			From (Dep)	(Times)	To (Arr)
—	—	—	—	—	— Totals brought forward		
JUL 27	Fournier RF4	G-AVNX	SELF	P1	Stapleford - Redhill Redhill - S'ford		
JUN - AUG	Cherokee, Jodel, Mascaret, Aricorpe · SIAI 260			P1			
AUG 2	MASCARET	G-ASKL	SELF	P1	REDHILL - STAPLEFORD - MIDDLETON ST GEORGE		
AUG 4	..	..	..	P1	MIDDLETON ST G - DAGENHA		
1969							
FEB 11	Cessna 150	1920-2	SELF		Nassau - Normans Cay VV		
MAY 11	Rollason Beta	G-ATLY	..		Redhill		
MAY - JULY	Tiub·Cub· Jodel · Aricorpe · Beta · Condor· Active			P1	Redhill & Stapleford		
JULY 5	ARROW ACTIVE	G-ABVE	SELF	P1	REDHILL		
JULY 26	SIAI MARCHETTI	G— ?	J. BARING	P1/P2	CRANFIELD		
AUG 6 - 13	HARVARD	G-AXCR	OSBORNE · SELF	P2/C. P1	BLACKBUSHE		
AUG 8 - 10	APACHE	G-ASMY	SELF	P1/P2/C	STAPLEFORD · LE TOUQUET GATWICK		
SEPT 13	CESSNA 402	AUST.	MASLING	P2/C	SYDNEY - COOTAMUNDRA		
SEPT 28	MUSTANG	N851D	BARRON / AUSTIN	P2/C	Miami / Sarasota / Miami Sarasota Miami		
OCTOBER	Jodel · Islander · Marchetti	Cessna.		P1/P2/C	Redhill Brombridge		
NOV 1st	SPITFIRE IX	GASJV · MH434	SELF	P1	BLACKBUSHE		

118   Grand Total: **536** hrs. **50** mins   Totals Carried forward

2

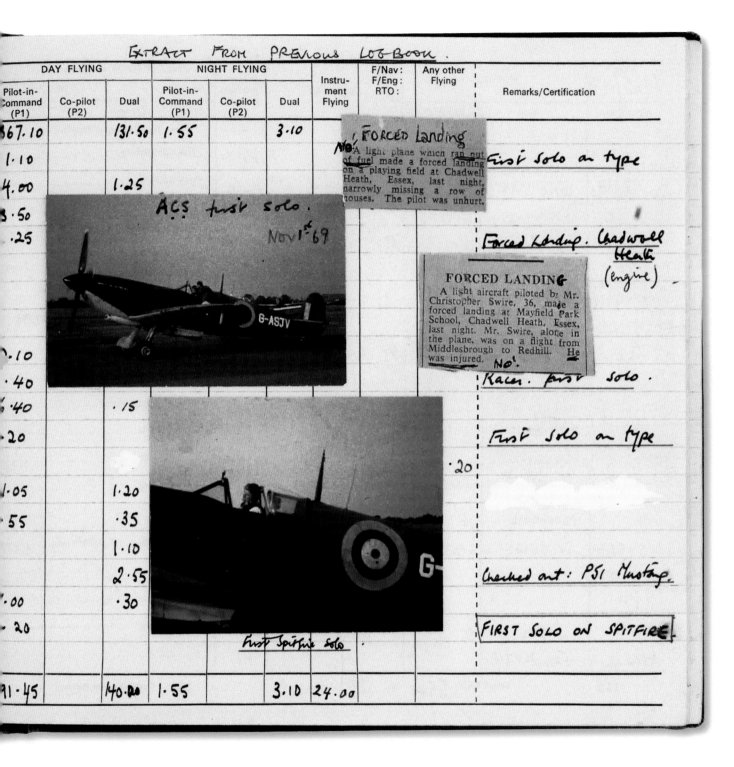

EXTRACT FROM PREVIOUS LOG BOOK.

DAY FLYING			NIGHT FLYING			Instrument Flying	F/Nav: F/Eng: RTO:	Any other Flying	Remarks/Certification
Pilot-in-Command (P1)	Co-pilot (P2)	Dual	Pilot-in-Command (P1)	Co-pilot (P2)	Dual				
367.10		131.50	1.55		3.10				FORCED Landing
1.10									First solo on type
4.00		1.25							
3.50									ACS first solo. Nov 1st '69
.25									Forced Landing. Chadwell Heath (engine)
									FORCED LANDING
.10									
.40									Racer. first solo.
.40		.15							
.20									First solo on type
							.20		
1.05		1.20							
55		.35							
		1.10							
		2.55							Checked out : P51 Mustang
.00		.30							
.20									FIRST SOLO ON SPITFIRE
									First Spitfire solo .
91.45		140.20	1.55		3.10	24.00			

Within photograph: ACS first solo. Nov 1st '69

Within photograph: First Spitfire solo

Newspaper clipping: FORCED Landing — A light plane which ran out of fuel made a forced landing on a playing field at Chadwell Heath, Essex, last night, narrowly missing a row of houses. The pilot was unhurt.

Newspaper clipping: FORCED LANDING — A light aircraft piloted by Mr. Christopher Swire, 36, made a forced landing at Mayfield Park School, Chadwell Heath, Essex, last night. Mr. Swire, alone in the plane, was on a flight from Middlesbrough to Redhill. He was injured.

1 Adrian Swire learned to fly in the Oxford University Air Squadron after serving in the Coldstream Guards (1950-1952). His business career, with the family firms of Butterfield & Swire, John Swire & Sons, and Cathay Pacific Airways, has been combined with service on many public bodies (among them the International Chamber of Shipping, the RAF Benevolent Fund, and the Board of Trustees of the RAF Museum) as well as active membership of the Tiger Club and the Air Squadron. He was a Visiting Fellow at Nuffield College, Oxford (1981–89) and Pro-Chancellor of Southampton University 1995–2004. He was knighted in 1982 and received the Air League Founders' Medal in 2006. The Spitfire Mark IX in this photograph by Arthur Gibson was the first aeroplane he owned.

2 Summarised extracts from Adrian Swire's log recording his first solo flight on a Spitfire.

2 David Constable Maxwell (far left) with his brothers Gerald, Ian, Andrew and Michael as Gold Staff Officers at the coronation of Queen Elizabeth II in 1953. Gerald and Michael were both highly-decorated fighter pilots – Gerald in the war of 1914-18, Michael in 1939-45. David Constable Maxwell was Joint Honorary Secretary of the Air Squadron 1970-72 and first suggested to James Baring in 1972 that it should be made clear at Winter Dinners whether a proposed new member was 'a licensed puddle-jumper in a hired Auster or an all weather chap like you'.

about the new committees, as was David Constable Maxwell: 'meetings mean agendas and minutes and bumf to use a venerable Army expression. The idea of the various committees was I think an endeavour to instil in the various Chairmen a blazing enthusiasm for the work entrusted to them, but owing to the difficulty of extracting from some of the members a simple "yes" or "no" on a post card I fear the original conception was a false one.' (Letter to Hugh Astor, 16 May 1970).

The new Joint Honorary Secretaries were starting to find life difficult in other ways too. In a letter to Caryll Waterpark, David Eaden complained: 'It seems incredible that half the members have not even bothered to reply over the QE2 visit, although a stamped addressed envelope was enclosed' (30 April 1970). In fact the QE2 visit went reasonably well, with ten members and ten guests attending, and photographs of the occasion appearing in the newspapers. Despite the ambitious plans, the only Air Squadron event that summer was the aerobatic competition.

At the end of August David Constable Maxwell was forced to cancel the Squadron's trip to Switzerland, scheduled for the first weekend in October. The visit had been inspired by his brother Andrew's recent purchase of Château de Villamand, near Vaud, where the Members were invited to dinner after visiting the local sights. Unfortunately local labour problems meant that building work would not be completed in time for the party. Cancelling, even when it is called 'postponement' (as this was), never looks

good. Maxwell must have been embarrassed and annoyed. He had other things on his mind too - such as the wedding of his daughter Jennifer on September 12th. It may be that his hectic private life affected his judgement, but he wrote to Hugh Astor in low spirits on August 27th: 'I am afraid I am a little bit despondent about the future of the Air Squadron. With the exception of you, Tony, Peter and David Eaden, the members are largely dormant. They never reply, answer invitations or push the boat out in any aeronautical sense. I said I would write the history but my efforts to get help from members of the Squadron to do this has been quite unavailing and I rather feel it is not worth doing unless there is a certain future for the Squadron. I am beginning to wonder whether there is.'

The trips to Sardinia and Ostend also collapsed, although there was cheering news at the end of August when Tommy Sopwith won the Daily Express International Offshore Power Boat Race, with Jimmy Gardner coming third.

Yet if individuals were doing well, the Squadron as an organisation was struggling to meet its own high standards. One of the members (Gerald Ward) never received his invitation to the Autumn Dinner, and the business of that evening, held at the Turf Club on November 4, was chaotically conducted. Three new members (William Dugdale, Tony Haig-Thomas, and the Earl of Shelburne) were elected - or possibly not. No-one seemed to know. Letters went back and forth in an effort to find someone who could remember exactly

2

2 Max Aitken (right) presents a double magnum of champagne to Tommy Sopwith for circumnavigating the Isle of Wight by powerboat in under an hour. Both were keen pilots and yachtsmen. Max Aitken (1910-1985) had worked as a test pilot for Lockheed in the 1930s, and had a distinguished career as a fighter pilot in World War II, winning the DFC in 1940 and the DSO as commander of a night-fighter squadron in 1942. After the war he was Conservative MP for Holborn (1945-50) and later became chairman of his father Lord Beaverbrook's press empire, Express Newspapers. He disclaimed his father's title in 1964.

Tommy Sopwith, son of Sir Thomas Sopwith, founder of the Sopwith and Hawker aircraft companies, was a leading powerboat racer, winning the Cowes-Torquay race in 1961 and 1968, and finishing second in the World Championships in 1970.

what had been decided. Eventually Tony Cayzer reassured everyone that he remembered it all quite clearly: three new members *had* been elected. But Hugh Astor had another query: had anyone troubled to ask if they wished to join? Did they even know what the Air Squadron was?

In answer to his own questions Hugh Astor produced an introductory letter for newcomers. This was sent out on 16 December 1970, and constitutes the first official description of the Air Squadron by one of its founders.

It is simply an association of some three dozen individuals who share a common interest in aviation in some form or another - aeroplanes, helicoptering, gliding, balloons, parachuting, etc. It is really a social group and we try to hold two dinners a year in London,

generally at Brooks's or Boodle's, and also to make one or two airborne sorties in the summer months. For example, recent sorties have included trips to Cognac as the guests of the Martells, another to Epernay as the guests of the Champagne producers. This year a visit to the Costa Smeralda, Sardinia, had to be cancelled at short notice and instead we were entertained to lunch aboard the Queen Elizabeth by Cunard. Although the number who can go on these sorties generally has to be limited, the Members who do take part are encouraged to bring wives, daughters, etc.

For your information I enclose herewith a list of the existing Members and have no doubt that many of them are already known to you. The annual subscription is £5 a year and there is of course the additional cost of any annual dinners which you may attend.

In addition to these social activities the Air Squadron has presented trophies for aerobatics, and for the best home-built aircraft. The intention of these trophies, which are competed for annually, is to promote an interest in aviation generally.

It will give great pleasure to our Members if you feel able to join us.

The reference to a trophy 'for the best home-built aircraft' is intriguing. This is the first explicit mention of it in the Air Squadron papers. The next is a letter sent in July 1971 by Air Commodore Christopher Paul, President of the Popular Flying Association, expressing gratitude for the provision of funds for a trophy ('a very beautiful solid silver cup on a polished light oak base... about ten inches high... hallmarked George V. It is engraved *The Air*

1   Group Captain Sir Hugh Dundas (1920-1995), CBE, DSO, DFC was one of the most distinguished fighter pilots of World War II. He wrote with unusual eloquence and candour about his wartime experiences and inner conflicts in his book *Flying Start*.

He was born in Barnborough in 1920 and joined the South Yorkshire Squadron, Auxiliary Air Force in 1939. Shot down in the Battle of Britain, trapped in a spinning and disabled plane to escape only seconds before it crashed in flames, he experienced his first brush with death. After discharge from hospital he rejoined his squadron and saw more action in the Battle of Britain. In 1941 he flew more than sixty missions over northern France with Douglas Bader, before Bader was shot down and taken prisoner. Promoted to Squadron Leader at twenty-one and to Wing Commander at twenty-two, he was posted to North Africa and took part in fighting which culminated in the liberation of Tunisia. He led his Spitfire wing in the invasions of Sicily and Italy. By the end of 1943 the unbroken years of danger and exhaustion were taking their toll

and, after a spell in hospital with jaundice, he was removed from operations and posted to staff college in Haifa. However, the posting was cancelled when he was recalled to replace an officer who had been killed in Italy, where he led a fighter-bomber wing supporting the Eighth Army in its advance to the Alps. Hugh Dundas ended the war a Group Captain – at twenty-four, the youngest ever in the RAF, and one of the most highly respected officers in the service.

After leaving the Air Force he joined Beaverbrook Newspapers. In 1961 he moved to the BET Group of which he became managing director in 1973 and chairman in 1982. He was also chairman of Thames Television from 1981 to 1987. He was knighted in 1987.

2   HRH Prince Charles on a visit to RAF Valley in October 1972, the year he joined the Air Squadron. The prince is in conversation with Flight Lieutenant Peter Squire, who would go on to lead No 1 Squadron and win a DFC flying Harriers in the Falklands War, later becoming C-in-C Strike Command (1999-2000) and Chief of the Air Staff (2000-2003). Peter Squire recalls, 'I was explaining some of the external features of a two-seat Hunter aircraft to HRH prior to flying with him in the same aircraft. Behind the Prince is Flt Lt Frank Hall, the squadron's engineering officer. I was an instructor on the Hunter Squadron, whose role at that time was predominantly that of training Foreign and Commonwealth students

on the Hunter. The Prince had shown interest in flying in a fast jet aircraft and this was the RAF's response - Operation Golden Eagle 72. The sortie passed uneventfully but I regret that the profile had been overly prescribed by higher authority and specifically ruled out low flying, which was precisely what HRH wanted to see. High level loops at 30,000 ft did not hold quite the same appeal! I was the unit display pilot at the time and so we did do some aerobatics slightly closer to the ground than the ordained high level manoeuvering'.

3

3 HRH Prince William of Gloucester (1941-1972) studied at Cambridge and Stanford before embarking on a diplomatic career, serving in Lagos and Tokyo. He was a keen pilot who joined the Air Squadron in 1972 and often invited Simon Ames to fly with him. After attending the aerobatic competition for the Air Squadron Trophy at Rochester that year, he died in a flying race in August. This photograph was given to Simon Ames by Princess Alice in her son's memory.

Squadron Trophy for the best home built aeroplane present at the P.F.A. Annual Rally'). This was first awarded in 1970, to Roy Watling Greenwood for a Turbulent 'which was quite unbelievably good … far better than Rollason or any of the commercial firms have ever turned out'. The competition attracted 40 entries in 1970, and has continued to run successfully ever since.

In 1971, the affairs of the Air Squadron began to pick up. On May 1 there was a visit to the Redifon Flight Simulator at Crawley, arranged by Hugh Dundas, who was Chairman of the parent company, Rediffusion. Guests were warned: 'Some of this will be quite technical and perhaps involve a bit of climbing up and down... We aim to have a car driving simulator there with which to amuse the ladies who don't want the full tour. There will also be a form of "poker" against the computer.' This was a demonstration of what Harold Wilson had called 'the white heat of technology'. The visit, which included an excellent lunch, was much enjoyed.

This was another occasion for a display of Douglas Bader's celebrated patriotism. Martin Barraclough, in his book *Fifty Years Have Flown*, recalls:

When we were being shown around the model of the countryside surrounding Gatwick, that was photographed by a suspended camera and projected onto a screen for the benefit of the pilot in the simulated cockpit – these were the days before computerised imagery – Douglas asked who was in the simulator and was told that it was a Lufthansa

pilot. Nearly choking on his pipe, which he smoked incessantly, he bellowed, 'My God, has anyone got a revolver?' You almost believed that he meant it!

On June 5th the Air Squadron Trophy competition was held once again at Little Rissington. There was low cloud, the competitors were outnumbered by the officials, and Peter Vanneck, who presented the Trophy, was the only member who managed to turn up. 'We really must do something about this,' he wrote, suggesting a 'three-line whip' next year.

There were no such problems with a return visit to Epernay (1-3 October), where the house of Moët et Chandon worked its old magic, with a tour of the 18th-century cellars of Maison Ruinart (converted from ancient Roman chalk quarries), and the usual gastronomic, viticultural and social delights. On one such visit Peter Vanneck was heard to remark, 'Isn't it marvellous to have your back teeth awash with champagne!'

The Autumn Dinner, held at the Penthouse Club on November 17th, was less appreciated. A rival to the Playboy Club, it offered similar attractions of half-naked waitresses and gambling tables in plush surroundings. Letters to the Secretary afterwards describe the occasion as 'awful', although several younger members clearly enjoyed it as a joke. One newly elected member resigned. For the art of damning with faint praise it would be hard to beat John Williams-Wynne's comment: 'it was an interesting experience and an opportunity to visit premises which I would never otherwise have occasion to enter.'

Morale began noticeably to improve in 1972,

when Prince Charles was invited to join the Squadron and, to everyone's delight, accepted. (He had turned down the first offer in 1969 on the grounds that he was too inexperienced a pilot.) Royal connections, expertly handled by John Williams-Wynne and Peter Vanneck, were further developed when Prince William of Gloucester presented the Air Squadron Trophy at Rochester in August. Less than a month later, however, Prince William and his co-pilot Vyrell Mitchell crashed in an air race from Halfpenny Green airfield near Wolverhampton. Both were killed. Simon Ames, who had often flown with the Prince, witnessed the accident, caused by a 'classic error' - a steep turn too soon after take-off - and had the unenviable task of telephoning Kensington Palace with the news.

Earlier that summer, another member had disappeared from view in circumstances almost as dramatic. David Eaden, Joint Honorary Secretary for the past two years, first suffered the death of his wife after a long illness, and then went bankrupt. A letter was written to Coutts rescinding his authorisation to sign Air Squadron cheques, and his fellow Secretary, David Constable Maxwell, commented: 'Poor chap he must have fallen very hard.' In the cruel way of such things, his name never appeared again in the Squadron's correspondence. He is remembered affectionately by Ivor Faulconer, who trained with him in the Fleet Air Arm in 1940, and recalls him as 'a delightful man and an excellent fighter pilot who was a good friend of Douglas Bader's and mine. It was very sad.'

James Baring once again took up the role of

Secretary, and in the new year (1973) produced a *coup de théâtre.*

I had just purchased a corner house in Elgin Crescent, London for the princely sum of £11,000. This was before the value of such properties was understood… I decided to hold the next dinner there rather than at Brooks's or White's or Boodle's. I had to put down a new parquet floor, wallpaper, doorways, curtains, and in the basement install a kitchen where there was none. The Friday before the week of the dinner my brother-in-law Martin Barraclough came round to check that all was ready. Due to the usual problems (work started weeks late and got delayed while builders went back to fix old jobs elsewhere), it was still a building site. No wallpaper, doorways but no floor, no curtains, the entrance hall was done but there was no kitchen. "I'll book a hotel!" said Martin. I told him all would be all right on the night, but he went away shaking his head.

Over the weekend, unknown to the builders, Andrew Chadwick, architect extraordinaire, got in some professionals who specialised in exhibitions. Six guys who worked so fast you had to keep moving just to stay out of the way. A friend of my wife Nini who was a professional caterer took charge of planning and preparing the food.

By the afternoon of the day of the dinner the pictures were on the walls and nobody, providing they didn't go upstairs or down, could have guessed it had not been there for years.

But my ever thoughtful brother-in-law, unaware of this, had decided he had better do something to soften what he feared would be a disaster and came

1

dressed as a builder in white overalls and a hard hat. He arrived to find an already assembled company of about 20 drinking champagne in evening dress in spectacularly beautiful surroundings.

"Martin, have you come by parachute?" and other remarks came from bemused members. Fortunately, before he left home, his wife Zaza had prevailed on him to put on proper dress underneath just in case. Unable to explain, he slipped out of his garb to emerge like James Bond from a wet suit in a scarcely rumpled DJ. They still didn't get it, so eventually I decided to help him out and admitted guests to the basement where the kitchen had just been assembled in a relatively free association of equipment on bare concrete, and the amazing Annie Barratt was producing dinner for 50. Everything went like clockwork and nobody guessed that the pictures on the walls were Athena prints behind non-reflecting glass, bought and framed for a few pounds the week before. It was a great evening!

The spontaneous, theatrical nature of the occasion brought a flood of enthusiastic letters to the Secretary. '*Much* more fun than those dreaded clubs,' wrote Ivor Faulconer. Hugh Astor thought it 'one of the most successful dinners ever - congratulations to you and Nini and those charming helpers on a superhuman achievement.'

A few months later, the Squadron had another outstanding success with a visit to Colonsay. This was the home of Euan Strathcona, an ex-Motor Torpedo Boat officer who had served in the war with Peter Vanneck and Ossie King. Genial, black-bearded, famously hospitable, with interests that ranged from sailing to contemporary music to

1

2

1 A windswept Bruno Schroder on the Isle of Colonsay, May 1973 – his first outing with the Air Squadron. His adventures that weekend 'completely persuaded me that an aircraft was needed to enjoy the Inner and Outer Hebrides (and many other things too).' He then learnt to fly on a fortnight's holiday in Nairobi: 'It was hard work, I did nothing but ground studies and three flights a day. The instructor didn't have a day off for two weeks. He said he'd never do it again.' Back in England he took twin, night and instrument ratings, and remembers his instructor Eric Thurston telling him, 'This is a licence to learn.' Since then he has flown to Australia, the Falklands, the South Pacific, North and South America, South Africa, Russia, and across the North Pole and around the world in 1988.

2 John Houlder (right) on a North Sea oil rig in the early 1970s. With him is Henri Delauze, President of the deep sea diving and engineering firm Comex. John Houlder has become a legend in the Air Squadron, a founding member still flying his Aero Commander at the age of 92, seventy-one years after he bought his first aeroplane in 1937. (See Chapter 6 for a longer account of John Houlder's life.)

3 Euan Strathcona (4th Baron Strathcona and Mount Royal) served in a Royal Navy Motor Torpedo Boat during World War II with Peter Vanneck under the command of Ossie King. He was one of many members of both the Royal Yacht Squadron and the Air Squadron. After studies at Cambridge and McGill universities he became an industrial consultant, then took up a political career, serving as Minister of State (Ministry of Defence) in 1979-81. He encouraged and helped to forge the relationship between the Air Squadron and the armed forces in 1979-80. His charitable roles include Chairman of the Bath Festival Society, Deputy Chairman of the SS *Great Britain* Project, Founder Chairman of the Coastal Forces Heritage Trust, and President of the Falkland Islands Trust. The fly-in to his home on Colonsay in May 1973 was one of the most successful events of the Air Squadron's early years.

3

politics, he also had a big house and the staff to cope with an airborne invasion.

The Strathconas thought the Squadron should call on their friend Bruno Schroder on the way up. He had a place on the neighbouring island of Islay, and he gladly offered the aviators lunch. Winston Churchill then offered him a seat in his Piper Seneca from London. They set off early on May 12 from Gatwick, although not quite as early as they would have liked: Bruno Schroder, at his firm's insistence, had to take out life insurance for £2 million - a sum which impressed his fellow passengers enormously.

Bruno remembers the journey vividly: 'Off we went, beautiful weather, with Martin Barraclough co-pilot and Winston up front. I was relegated to the back. We were up at about 7000 feet over Liverpool, heading across the Irish Sea, and far below there was a ship with a streak of black three miles behind it. Winston said, "That ship must be cleaning its tanks. We must go and see who it is." (At the time he was an MP.) And so we dived down to about 100 feet and Winston, who is a great photographer, took out a huge camera, and as we hurtled past the stern he took photographs of what this offending boat was doing. We then climbed up again and reported that this ship was cleaning its tanks in the Irish Sea. About three minutes later, back over the radio came the fact that actually it was a sewage ship operating out of Winston's own constituency.'

'Winston,' recalls Martin Barraclough, 'went very pink.'

They arrived late on Islay, where the others had already arrived and were enjoying lunch. Hugh Astor was presiding – with his usual effortless grace, even at another man's table.

The plan was to fly that afternoon to the short grass airstrip at Oronsay, and continue to Colonsay by boat. During lunch, however, the weather turned nasty, with driving rain and cloud at 50 feet. Euan Strathcona remembers, 'Everyone was saying, "We might as well have a jolly good lunch because we're obviously not going to get to Colonsay tonight." But I said to Des Norman, "It's an interesting thing, Des. Oronsay is totally flat. The height of the strip is about 30 feet. There's nothing between Islay airport and Oronsay which is over 50 feet, and here we are with a 50 foot ceiling." "Oh well,' said Des, "I think we ought to go and have a look." I said, "I know the way quite well, it's not very difficult anyway." So we got into his Islander and we took off under these rather inauspicious conditions. We had no problem at all. We landed on the airstrip at Oronsay. Then to our astonishment everybody else started coming in - including John Houlder in his massive twin-engined Aero Commander. I was absolutely staggered. I thought Des and I were making a recce.'

Back on Islay, Bruno Schroder was getting into the spirit of things. While Winston Churchill worked out the course for Oronsay with a compass and circular slide rule, he offered a simpler solution. 'We'll go down the road, and when we get to the fork I'll shout from the back, *Turn right!*'

Landing at Oronsay was not entirely

1 Desmond Norman (1929-2002), who designed and built Britain's best-selling post-war transport aircraft, the Britten-Norman Islander. The eldest son of Sir Nigel Norman, CO of 601 Squadron, builder of airports and founder of Airwork, Desmond qualified as an engineer at the de Havilland Aeronautical Technical School, and with his fellow-graduate John 'Brains' Britten founded Britten-Norman at Bembridge on the Isle of Wight in 1954. They also started a crop-spraying company, Crop Culture, developing a rotary atomiser, the Micronair, which is still in use all over the world. Starting with three war-surplus Tiger Moths, Crop Culture grew to 70 aircraft with a vast

international business. Desmond's adventures as a pilot are legendary - whether displaying Meteors with 601 Squadron, spraying crops in Sudan, or flying down to Italy with a cigar and a bottle of 'readimix' (whisky and soda) in his Tiger Moth's luggage compartment . His brother Torquil, his son Alex, and his nephew Casey are all members of the Air Squadron.

2 James Baring, first Honorary Secretary of the Air Squadron (1966-70), ran Regent Sound Recording Studios in Denmark Street, London, frequented by artists including The Rolling Stones, The Who, Rolf Harris, Shirley Bassey and the Beatles. A keen competition and aerobatic pilot with The Tiger Club, he chaired the UK Aircraft Owners and Pilots Committee and represented private and sporting pilots for IAOPA and FAI on various international bodies.

straightforward. When James Baring landed, bumping across a windblown field, he felt bound to warn his friends about the rabbit holes on the runway which would snap off a wheel in an instant. A Pan Am pilot flying 30,000 feet above heard the radio conversation, commented on the madness of the British, and hurried off across the Atlantic towards saner shores.

(There are rival versions of this anecdote. Was it an American or British airliner high above? And sheep or rabbits? Euan Strathcona recalls: 'Young Winston came up on the radio saying, "Watch out, boys, my windscreen's become covered in rabbit shit." Whereupon a wonderful disembodied voice appeared saying, "This is BEA 234 at 30,000 feet. There's not much rabbit shit where I am."')

With late arrivals, and everyone drenched by the rain, dinner at Colonsay went on long past midnight. Yet the beauty of the surroundings, the delicious food (which included a perfectly-cooked chocolate soufflé), the excellent wine, and the relief after the sheer struggle of getting there, made the occasion magical. 'Everybody agrees,' wrote James Baring, 'that it was really a marvellous weekend and the most satisfactory exercise that the Air Squadron has undertaken to date.'

Bruno Schroder quickly decided that he must learn to fly. On May 24 he wrote to Baring: 'I so enjoyed the opportunity of meeting you and the other members of the Air Squadron. I had the most marvellous flight out to the Outer Hebrides with Winston and Minnie Churchill on Sunday night, ending up in Mull. It completely persuaded me that

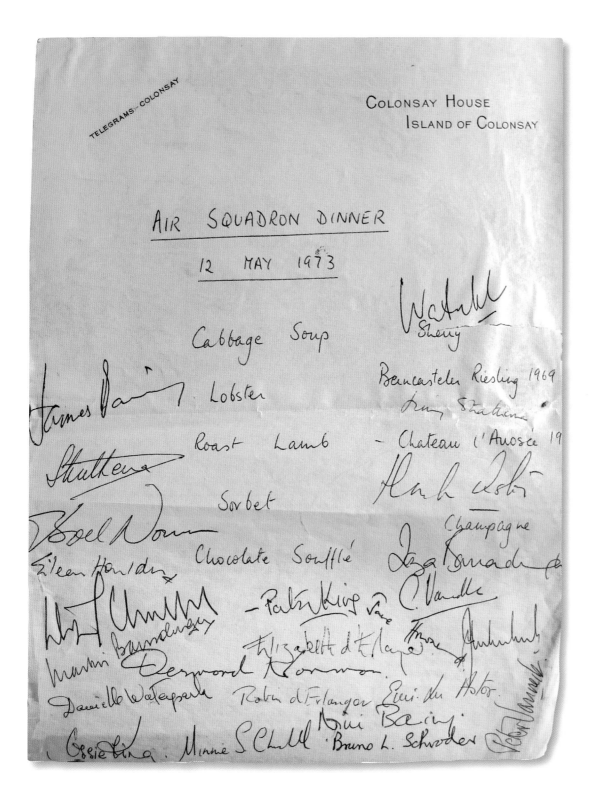

AIR SQUADRON DINNER

12 MAY 1973

Cabbage Soup

Lobster

Roast Lamb

Sorbet

Chocolate Soufflé

Sherry

Brauncasteler Riesling 1969

Chateau l'Anosée 19

Champagne

an aircraft was needed to enjoy the Inner and Outer Hebrides (and many other things too!)'

Later that year there was a trip to Bordeaux and four new members were elected: Tom Storey, David Somerset, the Earl of Erne, and Bluey Mavroleon.

In 1974, the Spring Dinner was held in the House of Commons, thanks to the efforts of Winston Churchill, who had retained his seat in the General Election earlier that year. In July James Baring announced that he was moving to France to become a *vigneron*, Hugh Astor was made temporary Treasurer, and Simon Ames (at that time Chief Executive of the British Light Aviation Centre, soon to be renamed the Aircraft Owners and Pilots Association) was invited to take over as Secretary. Simon, an ex-Fleet Air Arm pilot known and respected for his high standards, authority and expert knowledge of the press and PR, proved an inspired choice.

During the summer of 1974 a duplicate of the Air Squadron Trophy was ordered by Peter Vanneck from his favourite silversmiths, C J Vander of Hatton Garden. There was no more space on the original for winners' names. 'We must engrave the names at half the size and make this one last twice as long,' he announced. The duplicate would be presented at the annual aerobatics competition, while the original would be kept safe and displayed at Squadron dinners. Tony Cayzer was 'somewhat staggered' that the duplicate cost more than twice as much as the original (£302.50 versus £120), but after a few mild protests the matter was quickly forgotten.

At the Winter Dinner on 10th December, Simon

1

1 Bluey Mavroleon (1927-2009), shipowner and pilot who joined the Air Squadron in 1973. His father was from a distinguished Greek shipowning family, but his mother and upbringing were English - including Charterhouse and the Grenadier Guards. He learned to fly in 1970, bought a Cessna 182 and later switched to Squirrel helicopters. He often flew his twin engined Squirrel, G-OMAV, between his homes in England and Greece.

Ames was formally appointed Honorary Secretary, and Tom Storey Treasurer. Three new members were elected: Angus Hamilton, Bruno Schroder, and William Williams-Wynne. Determination was expressed to keep better minutes of meetings and to sort out certain 'mysteries' which had surfaced in the accounts.

In January 1975 Simon Ames wrote to his fellow committee members promising to straighten everything out. Last year's acting Treasurer, Hugh Astor, replied encouragingly, 'I am sure that the affairs of the Air Squadron are now getting on to a very much more business-like basis and that our affairs will run very much more smoothly in future.'

That summer an embarrassment occurred. A visit to HMS *Fearless*, anchored in the Thames at Greenwich, was cancelled at the last minute after only one member signed up. Simon Ames wrote apologetically to Captain J R Rumble of *Fearless*: 'Our circulation to members proved that Monday was an unpopular day - the last Monday in June more unpopular than many others.' The root of the problem seems to have been that the details of the visit were finalised by the ship's officers only a month before. Soothing letters were written, but the episode did not leave a happy memory in anyone's mind.

At the Winter Dinner at Buck's on 19th November, Micky Astor, Alex Bridport and Robin Neville were elected to the membership, and 'it was agreed that the Air Squadron should play a slightly more prominent role in promoting the interests of aviation'. In order to provide the necessary funds, subscriptions were raised from

£10 to £15. Meanwhile plans were outlined for visits to the Loire, the Air Traffic Control Centre at West Drayton, and RAF Kinloss. Flights to Marrakesh and the North of Norway were suggested, as was a trip to Baden Baden. This last was to become a standing joke: almost every year from 1975 onwards, David Constable Maxwell would propose a visit to this famous German spa, so popular among the royalty and nobility of Europe in the 19th century. Yet the curious fact is that despite several trips to Germany the Air Squadron has never made it to Baden Baden. And, as a point of honour, perhaps never will.

In 1976, in an effort to promote the interests of aviation, prize money for the Air Squadron Trophy for aerobatics was doubled to £200, with ten gallons of free fuel offered to all competitors. The event, held at Old Warden in June, was now restricted to pilots at Intermediate level, where it was felt that most encouragement was needed. The day was a great success. Thirteen members with fourteen guests turned up: an enormous improvement on previous years. Tony Smith in a Tiger Club Stampe won the 1st prize of £60, together with an Air Squadron Medallion and the Trophy. A grand picnic lunch, offered by Messrs Lindsay, Barraclough, Schroder, Swire and Haig-Thomas, helped the day go well.

Meanwhile, in the Queen's birthday honours, Douglas Bader was knighted - 'exactly the right chap for precisely the right reasons and very well deserved', as Simon Ames wrote in his letter of congratulation. A fortnight later, a party of 17 flew

2

to Angers to be regally entertained by the Duc and Duchesse de Brissac, the Marquis and Marquise de Brissac, M et Mme Cointreau, and the Prince and Princesse de Ligne. The weather was exceptionally hot (it was the summer of the Great Drought), and the visitors found welcome relief on a tour of caves containing a mushroom museum. This, said Ossie King, 'was the only cool place we had been in all weekend'. There was great delight when James and Nini Baring joined the party after a six hundred mile journey by car: 'Both were looking extremely well and we all look forward to drinking Château Baring after James has trodden his first crop of grapes.'

Four new members were elected (John Bagge, Ben Bledisloe, Charles Chelsea, and Charles Fergusson) and two resigned (David Smiley, and Whitney Straight). It was decided to fix the total at 50 active members, plus 12 who were currently inactive. With a firm hand on the administration from Simon Ames, Peter Vanneck felt glad to report that 'the show really seems to be on the right road'.

In 1977 Professor Edward 'Teddy' Hall (pioneer of radiocarbon dating, and father of the future Air Squadron Navigator, Bill Hall) was elected to the membership, together with Robert Lamplough and Christopher Tennant. In July cold winds and driving rain accompanied the aerobatic competition at Old Warden. Luckily Simon Ames had laid on a marquee for the occasion – or thought he had. A letter from his assistant Carolyn Evans to the contractors, W. Smith & Sons of Stotfold, tells its own tragi-comic tale:

1 Old Warden, 24 June 1978. Alex Henshaw (right) presents Martin Barraclough with the original log book of his Mew Gull G-AEXF, which had just been rebuilt by Tom Storey (left).

2 The remains of Alex Henshaw's Percival Mew Gull as Martin Barraclough and Tom Storey found it, Blackpool 1971.

3 Professor Edward 'Teddy' Hall (1924-2001), founded the Oxford University Research Laboratory for Archaeology and History of Art, and was renowned for his work in enhancing the reliability of accelerator mass spectrometry (or AMS dating), commonly known as radiocarbon dating. His scientific techniques of investigation enabled him to expose Piltdown Man as a hoax, and, in 1988, to date the Turin Shroud as a medieval artefact from the period 1260-1390. An avid balloonist and pilot, he is pictured here arriving with his wife Jeffie for a night at the opera in Glyndebourne.

3

1st August 1977

Dear Sirs,

I am in receipt of your invoice for a total of £27-00 for the hire of a Marquee at Old Warden Aerodrome on June 18th.

I must admit I was somewhat horrified at the size of this bill, in comparison to the service I received. On my arrival at Old Warden on the morning of June 18th, I could not even locate a Marquee, and on enquiring at the General Manager's office, I was directed to a point on the airfield where a few poles supporting a canvas roof stood. This I was told was a Marquee, it had one very dirty side to it, the other three sides being open to the strong winds and rain that prevailed on that day. Inside were some odd bits of canvas that did not bear any relation to the shape and size of the "Marquee" which after much effort and ingenuity I managed to drape around two other sides of the "Marquee" in order to keep our guests dry and reasonably warm. By which time I myself, acting as hostess at this meeting, was a rather soggy dishevelled hostess, and the day was not quite as I had planned.

I am enclosing your account, perhaps you would be so kind as to amend it suitably in the light of the above.

The proprietor of the marquee firm, Harold Smith, wrote back the next day:

Dear Sir,

In reply to yours of 1st August we are rather surprised at your remarks concerning our account for marquee hire at Old Warden.

When you asked for a marquee to be left on site for your use the following week in order to reduce the charge you can hardly expect first class service, as someone else had already used it and no doubt taken the sides off. However, these could have been put back in 20 minutes or so.

In the circumstances we will reduce the account to £21.60 on the understanding that it is settled at once.

Despite the foul weather, the competition was flown, and Brendan O'Brien won first prize among the eleven contestants. The day was glowingly reported in *Flight International* by Tony Smith, who wrote: 'One really refreshing aspect of the contest was the location. The atmosphere at Old Warden must surely recall, more than anywhere else in Great Britain, the era when sport flying really was a way to freedom.'

In 1978, Peter Vanneck became Lord Mayor of London, and on April 6th an exceptionally glamorous and well-attended Spring Dinner was held at his official residence, Mansion House.

Ten days later an old dream came true for Martin Barraclough and Tom Storey. They completed their six-year restoration of G-AEXF, the Percival Mew Gull flown by Alex Henshaw from London to Cape Town and back in record-breaking time in 1939. This historic aeroplane, which they had found rotting wingless in a shed in Blackpool in 1972, took to the air again on 16th April 1978.

On June 3rd, the Squadron's efforts to put on a successful aerobatics day at Old Warden were finally rewarded. John Harper, Contest Director, wrote, 'At long last it all came right. The venue was

1 Old Warden, home of the Shuttleworth Collection, where the Air Squadron held many events in the 1970s and 1980s. John Allison and Tony Haig-Thomas fly the historic Shuttleworth aircraft at displays, and Tony Haig-Thomas has played a leading role in the management of the Collection.

2 Charles Masefield at the controls of a DH60 Moth, G-EBLV, with his son Ashley in the front seat. This was the eighth DH60 off the production line, completed in August 1925 at Stag Lane. It was delivered to the Lancashire Aero Club, Woodford, by Alan Cobham on August 29th 1925. The aircraft was transferred to Avro ownership and subsequently remained with the company (Avro, Hawker Siddeley, BAE) - mostly based at Hatfield - for some 66 years until Charles delivered it to the Shuttleworth Trust at Old Warden in 1991. G-EBLV is the oldest surviving Moth aircraft in the world.

2

splendid, the flying good, the judges international, Air Squadron happy and the weather perfect.' Alan Dix, a Dan Air pilot, took the winner's prize in his first year of competition aerobatics.

The Air Squadron-Old Warden partnership was now thriving. The following year, 1979, they decided to hold a two-day event, with the Trophy competition on June 2nd and a display by Air Squadron members in their aeroplanes on June 3rd. Fifteen aircraft were made ready for the day, but the June weather proved treacherous again, with 8/8 cloud at 300 feet and 300 metres visibility in the morning, improving only marginally by the afternoon. 'If the weather had been good,' wrote Simon Ames in his report, 'the Air Squadron Flying Display would have been a tremendous success.... Let's try again in 1980.'

At the 1979 Winter Dinner Ian Macpherson, eldest son of Lord Strathcarron, was elected, and Simon Bostock nominated as a possible for next year. He was described to the members as 'a Squadron Leader in the Royal Air Force, also a shooting man with grouse moors in Yorkshire.' Whether it was the words 'Squadron Leader' or 'grouse moors' that endeared

him more to the membership is not recorded, but the following year he was in. It was a significant moment: this was the first serving RAF officer to join the Air Squadron, and the start of a long and happy friendship with the service.

Chapter 2   Spreading Wings   1981-1993

Tom Storey's Mew Gull and Martin
Barraclough's DH Rapide, Old Warden 1980.

1

1 Tony Haig-Thomas flying the Shuttleworth's DH51, previously VP-KAA, the first aircraft to be registered in Kenya. Tony served in the RAF from April 1956 to Dec 1963. He flew Vampires, Venoms, Meteors and Hunters operationally, but also Javelin, Canberra and Sea Hawk aircraft before leaving to join a merchant bank. In 1966 he flew in the world aerobatic championships in Moscow. During the 1970s he had a collection of seven different de Havilland Moth types. He became a Shuttleworth pilot in 1976 and then the Aviation Trustee of the Collection in 1996.

A memoir of his RAF days, *Fall out Roman Catholics and Jews*, was published in 2008. An extract from this can be found in Chapter 6.

2 Simon Bostock, the first serving officer in the Royal Air Force to be elected a member, and a key figure in setting up and running the Air Squadron Trophy for cadets. Simon graduated from Cranwell with the Queen's Medal in 1965 and went on to fly Lightnings in Singapore and then Gnats at RAF Valley. Staff appointments followed, at MOD, the Central Flying School and RAF Cranwell, interspersed with 2 tours on No 11

Squadron (Lightnings) at RAF Binbrook, the latter as Squadron Commander. He then instructed at the RAF Staff College, before commanding RAF Bulmer. A year at Pakistan's National Defence College was followed by a tour at Headquarters Strike Command and finally appointment in 1993 as Commandant of the RAF Central Flying School, which included responsibility for the Red Arrows. The photograph shows him beside a Red Arrows Hawk. He retired in 1996 with the rank of Air Commodore and now manages his sporting estate in Yorkshire. [Photo by Phil Crow, RAF]

Spreading Wings   1981-1993

2

In April 1981, Simon Ames wrote to Peter Vanneck asking, 'Is the Air Squadron being sufficiently enterprising these days? Average attendance at functions is below 50%. Either we need a different style, or we need some more active members. What are your views?'

Peter Vanneck was by now well into his 'retirement job' as Member of the European Parliament for Cleveland. He was so busy shuttling between his constituency, his London office, the two European assemblies at Brussels and Strasbourg and his country house in Suffolk that he was unable to attend a single Air Squadron event that year.

Looking at the record of events, one can see why Simon Ames was concerned. The period between 1977 and 1983 was remarkably quiet, with only the aerobatics event at Old Warden and two annual dinners on the card, year after year. Compared with earlier times, the programme looked unadventurous. Clubs inevitably go through quiet times – they are not necessarily bad times – when members are busy making a living, having families, pursuing other interests, and everyone is content to chug along at an easy pace. Then the feeling grows that some novelty is needed. Change comes, and the club is renewed. As it happened, the entire country was going through a slump in the late 1970s. As the tired Labour Government of James Callaghan muddled its way to its demise in 1979, a pall was cast over enterprise of every kind. Then came the struggles of the early 1980s, when British society seemed at war with itself, while the harsh medicine of monetarism was unflinchingly

administered by Britain's first female Prime Minister. It was not an easy time, and a happy outcome was far from certain.

As it turned out, Simon Ames need not have worried. The seeds of new growth had been sown. Within five years, there would be a new vigour, self-confidence and sense of purpose about the Air Squadron. They would be making longer and more challenging trips, taking on an important charitable role, and becoming involved in interesting ways with the military. The change in their fortunes can be traced to a single cause: the election of members serving in the armed forces.

Simon Bostock had been the first to join. In 1982 he was followed by Denis 'Splinters' Smallwood, retired from the RAF but working as a Military Adviser to British Aerospace. Over the next ten years came John Allison, Christopher D'Oyly, and David Checketts, Equerry to Prince Charles (1983), then Ian Macfadyen and John Thomson (1985), David Cyster and Johnny Moss (1986), Marcus de Ferranti (1988), Alex Howard (1988), Peter Squire and Patrick Hine (1990), Michael Beetham (1991), and Peter Cameron (1992).

The first effect of this policy was to add a new and exciting event to each year's calendar. In March 1982, with the help of Euan Strathcona, Minister of State for Defence, permission was given for a two-day tour of RAF Gutersloh in Germany. Built for the Luftwaffe in 1934-6, Gutersloh had been a favourite haunt of Hermann Goering; it was now a front-line Cold War base equipped with Harriers and Puma helicopters providing close air

1 The Air Squadron at RAF Marham, September 1988. Left to right: Raymond Salisbury-Jones, RAF host, Denis Smallwood, Raymond Baxter, Tony Savile, Bill Hall, Caryll Waterpark, Thomas Noel, David Corbett, unidentified, Ossie King, Kenneth McAlpine, unidentified, John Bagge, unidentified, David Strathcarron, Robs Lamplough, John Thomson, Simon Ames.

2 The Air Squadron at RAF Gutersloh, March 1982. Left to right: John Bagge, unknown, David Constable Maxwell, Denis Smallwood, Caryll Waterpark, 3 RAF hosts, Hugh Astor, Tom Storey, James Baring, Martin Barraclough, Ian Macpherson, Bruno Schroder.

3 David Wigan joined the Air Squadron in 1983. He flew Catalinas with the Royal Air Force in World War II, largely on anti U Boat operations over the North Atlantic from a base on Loch Earn in County Fermanagh. At the end of the war when stationed in Ceylon he contracted polio, which left him with a paralysed left arm. In 1972 he was inspired to take up flying again and passed a special

4

medical to prove that he could fly safely with one arm. He purchased a Cherokee 180, G-AZLN, obtained an Instrument Rating and flew many hundreds of hours around Europe until he gave up flying aged 70 in 1994. David was recognized as one of the finest shots in England, for which he was known as the "One-Armed Bandit". He was an enthusiastic and much liked member of The Air Squadron. He died in 2006 aged 82.

4 Johnny Moss flew helicopters with the Army Air Corps between 1973 and 1986 in Germany, Norway, Canada and Northern Ireland. He flew Bell 47, Scout, Gazelle and Lynx and amassed some 2000 hours, of which 1000 were in the Scout (pictured). Since leaving the Army he has worked in private banking. He was Secretary of the Cresta Run from 2002 to 2007.

support for the First British Army Corps. Caryll Waterpark flew a group of members from London in one of CSE's brand new Lear Jets, which one member recalled as being so fast that 'no sooner had we reached cruising height of 45,000 feet than we started our descent'. Photographs show the visitors in camouflage outfits, deeply absorbed in a spectacle that only the most powerful machines can provide. Martin Barraclough remembers learning to use the Rapier missile system, watching Harriers land on roads in the forest, and taking lunch in a tent with silver candelabra. In the words of John Bagge, 'Everything was perfect and most interesting.'

In the next ten years the Squadron went on to visit RAF stations at Brüggen, Leuchars, Brize Norton, Marham (where they had lunch on a VC10 while watching air-to-air refuelling over the North

Sea), Kinloss, Lossiemouth, Cosford, Scampton, Halton and Shawbury. They held Winter Dinners at the RAF Museum Hendon and at Bentley Priory, made two visits to the Army Air Corps, and enjoyed a memorable stay on HMS *Illustrious* as guests of the Fleet Air Arm.

The invitation to Brüggen had come through Simon Bostock. It was announced in a letter to Simon Ames:

Dear Simon, Just a very short note to say that I had Gp Capt John Thomson to lunch on Sunday and he made a rather nice offer. He commands RAF Brüggen in Germany (Jaguar Station) and he offered to host the Air Squadron at his station for a day or two, in similar style to your visit this year. John once toured France on James Baring's wing as part of a formation of Turbulents. He was also a Tiger Club member for a number of years, so he really does mean it when he says he would welcome us – especially if James Baring could make it. He promised to mention it to the CinC RAF Germany to clear the way so to speak and he is going to look at the chances of offering some Jaguar flights, though I must stress that the odds are by no means in favour. Could you let me know your reaction to the above before we go any further with fixing dates etc.

Simon Ames quickly replied that 'in view of the enormous popularity – and success – of the visit to RAF Germany in March this year,' he had 'absolutely no doubt' that members would be keen. 'Thank you for inspiring this project!' he concluded. 'These visits have [made] and will make the Air Squadron what it is. Your efforts are much

appreciated.'

Visits to RAF stations were soon being described by Simon Ames as 'business briefings' rather than 'jollies'. Although they were highly sociable occasions, much useful information was exchanged, and the Forces were quick to recognise the benefit of displaying their commitment and skill to a group of interested, knowledgeable and influential people. With governments on both right and left ever more keen on cost-cutting in the public sector, the military needed (and continue to need) a broad network of allies in civilian society.

The form of these visits was quickly established: two to three days packed with briefings on the work and equipment of the station, tours of the facilities, opportunities to fly (Air Squadron members in RAF aircraft, and, later, RAF personnel in Air Squadron aircraft); a formal dining-in night with speeches, toasts and the presentation of gifts; and a couple of good sessions in the bar. The letters that passed between Simon Ames and the station commanders are brimming with good will. When the Squadron visited RAF Brüggen in 1983, Group Captain John Thomson wrote to say, 'We thoroughly enjoyed having them here and I hope that they enjoyed the visit half as much as we.' Simon Ames replied: 'How I wish I had been there myself! All members who attended not only enjoyed themselves thoroughly, but were impressed by the spirit and motivation of all with whom they came into contact.'

Visits to stations in Germany carried the thrill of the front line, with Harriers emerging from

1

1 David Cyster at the controls of his DH82A Tiger Moth built in 1941. On 7th February 1978 he flew from London to Darwin in 32 days to commemorate the 50th Anniversary of the first solo flight to Australia by Bert Hinkler flying an Avro Avian. David's epic flight was the first time a Tiger Moth flew between the two countries. In 1979, he was the overall winner in the Famous Grouse Moth Rally from Hatfield to Strathallan.

2 Lt Colonel Christopher D'Oyly, a member from 1983 to 1999, was Commanding Officer of the Household Cavalry and organised a Winter Dinner for the Air Squadron at the Hyde Park Barracks in 1985. He owned a Prentice while serving with his regiment in Germany in the early 1960s, and later shared a Piper Cherokee and then a Comanche with Johnny Moss. He was for several years a flying instructor based at Fairoaks.

2

3

4

3   A Harrier demonstrates its capabilities on a forest road in West Germany, RAF Gutersloh 1982.

4   James Baring is shown the workings of the Rapier missile, RAF Brüggen 1983.

camouflaged netting in the woods and Jaguars firing rockets on practice ranges. On one occasion, it was suddenly announced that there would be a simulated attack by Warsaw Pact special forces. During the briefing for this exercise, no-one noticed that Caryll Waterpark was missing (he had wandered off for a few minutes into the trees). When the attack came, with some highly realistic explosions and machine-gun fire, Caryll was taken completely by surprise. 'He came staggering back into the camp,' James Baring recalls, 'looking much less dapper than usual.'

Nothing, however, could quite match the drama of the aircraft carrier HMS *Illustrious* and 814 Squadron on exercise in the North Sea in March 1988. Ian Sutherland wrote a detailed report of this visit, which began with lunchtime drinks in the ward room while the ship was still berthed at Newcastle. Outside 'the weather was blowing up, force eight gale, and there was concern about leaving harbour ... The Tyne is narrow so extra tugs were employed to make sure we didn't drift

to shore.' At 2 pm *Illustrious* sailed, despite the continuing high wind and waves surging over the breakwater. Their mission was to 'find, attack and destroy' HMS *Ark Royal*, which had left Edinburgh earlier that day. During dinner that evening, 'message was received that *Ark Royal* had been "found" and attack was imminent. Harriers were deployed around 9 pm – no doubt from the noise.'

After dinner they mustered on the bridge to see the aircraft return. It was now 11.15: 'it seemed a long sortie.' They were told that the Harriers had refuelled from an RAF VC10, then attacked *Ark Royal* from the least expected direction. 'Complete surprise was claimed and *Ark Royal* hit!' The return of the Harriers was an impressive sight: 'Moonlight with heavy snow showers – no lights on the ship until the Harriers arrived which added to the drama. Then you could see the snow flowing freely across the deck.' Down in the Operations Room, 'well away from the outside world', they dropped in on Captain Todd, who was busy fighting off a

1

2

counter-attack from *Ark Royal*. Again *Illustrious* came off best, taking out five Harriers with Sea Dart missiles.

The next day, *Ark Royal* joined them for naval manoeuvres: 'the sight of two aircraft carriers line astern at 5 cables and 25 knots in a rough sea is quite something.' Ian Sutherland added that 'all Air Squadron members showed excellent sea legs, as one would expect.'

At dinner on the second night Caryll Waterpark presented an engraved decanter to Captain Todd, who replied with an expression of his pleasure at having the chance to show the Navy at work. 'He then sang a few ditties.'

But the adventure was not over yet. At 5.30 the next morning the visitors were roused for a helicopter flight to Newcastle Airport. 'We were 105 nautical miles off shore. Survival suits were worn... We were lifted to the deck by the hangar lift, when the full force of the elements hit home. The wind was blowing some 50 knots, and you could hardly stand. It was drizzle, 1000 yards visibility with low cloud. After mounting the Sea King, we took off skimming the waves at 100 feet or so. After the first 30 minutes the weather began to clear and and we climbed to 500 feet at which height we progressed to Newcastle. On arrival we cleared Customs (tradition in the Navy so the Crown is not cheated by its Admirals, I presume) and the visit ended.'

War

Members of he Air Squadron were not alone in appreciating the courage, skill and commitment of Britain's armed forces in the 1980s. Just two weeks after the visit to RAF Gutersloh, on 2 April 1982, Argentinian forces invaded the Falkland Islands. The occupation lasted just over two months. A British Task Force reclaimed the islands in a determined and bravely-fought campaign, with considerable loss of life, aircraft and ships. Its stirring effect on the people of Britain was remarkable, and it helped the Conservative Party win two more terms in government.

The Air Squadron as an organisation was not directly affected by the conflict, although many individuals, like every British citizen at the time, followed the fortunes of the Task Force with passionate interest. Five future members of the Squadron, however, were deeply involved in the conduct of the war – two in the heat of battle, two in its aftermath, one at the highest level in London.

Michael Beetham was Chief of the Air Staff. At that time, he recalls, 'the Chiefs of Staff used to review the world situation every 6 to 12 months. We thought we should get rid of the Falklands. Defending them meant extending the runway at Stanley for big aeroplanes. That was going to cost £3 million. It's a trifling amount today, and it wasn't that big even then. But we couldn't spare it. So the government policy was to give priority to NATO. Any crisis – go to NATO. Then in January 1982 Nicholas Ridley and Richard Luce went to the UN in New York and talked to the Argentinians in the margins. The Argentinians went home and said the UK doesn't care about the Falklands. Ridley was that sort of chap, I'm afraid. He carries

3

responsibility for the Falklands War. He should have resigned, not Carrington or Luce.'

Earlier in his career, Beetham had commanded 214 Squadron, which pioneered air-to-air refuelling in Valiants. They had made the first non-stop flight to Cape Town in 1957, refuelling over the desert from Kano in Nigeria. His deep understanding of the subject was to be useful in the Falklands War.

'As Chief of the Air Staff I was there at all the critical times every day. The Royal Navy was in charge of the Task Force, the Army was in charge of the landings, the Royal Air Force provided air support. We had Harriers and could do air-to-air refuelling. There's a book called *Vulcan 607* by Rowland White that very accurately and readably tells the story of the bombing raid on Port Stanley. Critics don't appreciate the aim of that mission. We wanted to let the Argentinians know we could drop conventional bombs. It took fourteen tankers to get one Vulcan down to Stanley to drop twenty-one 1000lb bombs onto the runway. They did a cross cut, which gave a 90% chance of one bomb, and 60% chance of two bombs, hitting the runway. They got one practically in the middle. The Argentinians didn't repair the damage. It was a magnificent achievement. The Argentinians saw it and feared for the mainland. They withdrew their Mirages to defend it. That had a powerful psychological effect. And it was a relief to the Task Force not to face Mirage attacks.'

Peter Squire was commander of 1 Squadron of RAF Harriers. He remembers the war taking them completely by surprise. 'Nobody knew where the Falklands were. We had just got back from an Arctic deployment exercise in North Norway where we used to practise operating off snow. We were planning to take some aeroplanes for an exercise to Canada, when suddenly this invasion took place. So I got our Ground Liaison Officer to dig out some maps, find out where these islands were. They were a very very long way away, and it didn't seem possible that we could be involved, and yet in the back of my mind I knew that we were the most flexible offensive support unit within the Royal Air Force, we were trained and practised in air-to-air refuelling, so we could actually deploy long distances, and of course the Harrier can operate from a variety of platforms... But quite how we were going to be involved it was difficult to see at that stage.

'Just before Easter we got warning orders to be ready for operations in the South Atlantic, either from aircraft carriers or from forward land bases. That led us into a busy training period – a lot of low level flying, weapon delivery profiles, and modifying the aeroplanes so that they could be used from an aircraft carrier... Also we felt we needed an air-to-air missile. We got industry to design and make conversion kits and they did it all in three weeks. It was an extraordinary response. We also needed to qualify ourselves on the ski-jump, so we went down to Yeovilton and practised going off their static ski-jump down there.'

At the same time a container ship, the *Atlantic Conveyor,* was modified in Liverpool to carry

1 May 1982, Harriers on the deck of HMS *Hermes* in the Falklands War.

aircraft. Squire and his team of eight pilots and nineteen ground crew flew to Ascension Island where they loaded their eight Harriers onto the *Atlantic Conveyor*. On 18th May, about 100 miles from the Falklands, they transferred to the aircraft carrier *Hermes* and flew missions from there until the ceasefire in mid-June. (A week later the *Atlantic Conveyor* was sunk with several Wessex and Chinook helicopters still on board.) 1 Squadron lost three aircraft to enemy fire, but all pilots ejected safely. Peter Squire himself suffered an engine failure while hovering at San Carlos: 'I rode the aeroplane in, which wrote it off, but I managed to climb out of it without too many scars.'

Most aircraft were hit by ground to air weapons during the sorties. 'Towards the end, when we were going for targets in the hills to the west of Stanley, probably out of every pair of aircraft we sent out, one would come back with some sort of damage. On one particular sortie I had a bullet straight through the cockpit, in one side and out of the other. It made a very loud bang – but it didn't affect any of the systems, so it was possible to take it back to the carrier and get it repaired.'

Peter Squire was awarded the Distinguished Flying Cross for his part in the conflict. His Falklands diary is published on the RAF's website.

Peter Cameron had a different kind of war. He flew as a Royal Marine, commanding an air squadron of eighteen light helicopters in support of the land forces advancing from San Carlos to Port Stanley. Their main role was to fly weapons and ammunition into the battle zones, and bring

casualties out. Peter Cameron himself elected to fly Brigadier Julian Thompson, the Commander of 3 Commando Brigade, wherever he needed to go on the islands. 'In my view he was the Man of the Match. I flew him because I wanted to understand the strategy. I wanted to know what was in his mind, in order that I could anticipate and plan for future operations.' He often airlifted casualties to hospital. Frequently exposed to enemy fire, his squadron lost three helicopters and four crew during the landings at San Carlos and the Battle for Goose Green. The citation for his Military Cross states: 'From the first day of operations his squadron of Gazelle and Scout helicopters rendered outstanding service in support of the Brigade, often flying in appalling weather conditions by day and night, having to evade Argentine fighters and anti-aircraft fire... Throughout this most demanding period, Major Cameron led his Squadron with humour and compassion both on the ground and in the air. His fine example of courage and determination, in the face of severe losses, was an inspiration to all and his leadership ensured that no call for help went unanswered.'

At the conclusion of hostilities, Peter Cameron witnessed the Argentinian surrender, and remembers still with pained surprise the fact that the officers were allowed to keep their side-arms to protect themselves from attacks by their own men. 'They had treated the junior ranks appallingly. We picked up soldiers who had been shot through the ankles by their officers to stop them leaving their trenches.'

2

Peter Cameron's story is told in Max Arthur's book *Above All, Courage. The Falklands Front Line: First-Hand Accounts.* An extract is included in Chapter 6 of this book.

Ian Macfadyen was told that his squadron would be going to war with the Argentinians if their Phantom interceptor aircraft should ever become involved. As things stood, however, the runway at Port Stanley was too short. So they were assigned to the defence of Ascension Island. 'We were working on all sorts of new ideas and emergency requirements – night vision goggles, flares, chaff, new missiles – 9 Lima Sidewinder – and so on, a whole lot of stuff which was absolutely brand new... The ultimate aim for us was to go and land on the 4000-foot runway at Stanley, which for a Phantom was a very tall order, because it can easily get airborne in 4000 feet but it certainly can't land. So we needed to extend the runway by 2000 feet using aluminium matting purchased from the Unites States Marine Corps. We also had to install a series of arrestor wires as all landings would be as if on an aircraft carrier.'

The squadron continued to operate out of Ascension Island during the summer of 1982, but by October the runway at Stanley was ready. Ian had the privilege of flying the first Phantom to Stanley on Sunday 17 October 1982. Nineteen Victor tankers were in support, and he carried out eleven refuellings during a flight that lasted almost ten hours.

The squadron at Stanley quickly grew to ten aircraft. Conditions were cramped and often harsh. One half of the squadron was always at immediate readiness, living on a giant building site, with the other half on board a nearby ship in Port Stanley. 'I continued to fly in those remote but beautiful islands over the next nine months. It is hard to describe the difficulties involved in flying from a tiny airfield where the nearest diversion was Punta Arenas in Chile, well over 400 miles away, but day and night flying was conducted, with the odd moment of excitement.' In one of these he landed a Phantom in a race against incoming fog. By the time he touched down, the control tower had been completely enveloped.

In May 1983, when Ian returned to the UK, he had formed No 23 Squadron at Stanley and operations were settling down to a routine. The new airfield at Mount Pleasant was by then under construction, and eventually opened in 1984. RAF operations continue there to the present day.

Anthony Stansfeld watched Ian Macfadyen make the first Phantom landing at Stanley. He was commanding all the Army helicopters on the Falkland Islands at the time. 'I deployed south in a C130 as the war ended and took over the Army helicopters with 657 Sqn. We had an interesting time: tasks included running the postal service. finding the minefields, retrieving casualties, bodies etc, and general recce and resupply. I flew a captured Argentinean UH 1H with which we ran the postal service for about two months.'

Maxi Gainza found himself in an awkward position during the conflict. An Anglophile Argentinian living in London, he wrote articles for *La Prensa,* Argentina's leading newspaper, explaining the British view of the war to readers

1 Anthony Stansfeld flew Sioux and Scout helicopters with the British Army from 1970 to 1986, serving in Belize, Northern Ireland, Hong Kong, Canada, Germany and the Falkland Islands. He then commanded a Territorial Army Helicopter Squadron for six years. During this time he was Managing Director at Pilatus Britten-Norman, commuting to and from the Isle of Wight in a Grob 109B.

2 Ian Macfadyen as a Wing Commander in 1981. Air Marshal Ian Macfadyen has had a lifetime in aviation. He was taught to fly at White Waltham in 1959 by a famous ATA lady, Joan Hughes, on a Tiger Moth. He joined the RAF in 1960 as a Cranwell Cadet and spent most of his RAF flying life on fighters. He also trained as a flying instructor and spent two years back at Cranwell as the number 3 in The Poachers aerobatic team. He was later a Phantom solo aerobatic display pilot. Whilst commanding 29 Squadron, he flew the first Phantom into the Falkland Islands in 1982, where he spent the following 8 months. Later, he was Station Commander at RAF Leuchars. He served nearly 5 years in the Middle East, including the First Gulf War where he was Chief of Staff, and later Commander British Forces. In 2000 he began a 5-year spell as Lieutenant Governor of the Isle of Man. He was next the National President of the Royal British Legion, and he is now the Honorary Inspector General of the Royal Auxiliary Air Force. Today, he flies a Cirrus SR20 based at Filton. He is honoured to be Chairman of the Geoffrey de Havilland Flying Foundation, the Air Squadron's own charity. He has been a member since 1984.

3 Glenn Torpy joined the Royal Air Force in 1974 after graduating in Aeronautical Engineering at Imperial College London. He has flown Jet Provosts, Gnats, Jaguars, Hawks, Harriers, Tornados and Typhoons in a career that has included operations in Iraq and Kosovo and several UN missions, with a total of 4300 hours of fast-jet flying. He was PSO to John Thomson for 18 months, and remembers him as a man of 'great vision, ability and humanity; I was inspired by him, and still am.' Glenn Torpy was knighted in 2005 and joined the Air Squadron in 2006, the same year he was appointed Chief of the Air Staff (2006-9).

4

4 The Air Squadron visited the Battle of Britain Memorial Flight at RAF Coningsby in 1990 when several members were fortunate to fly in the Lancaster bomber. Front row, left to right: Johnny Moss, Eddie Liverpool, David Corbett, Tony Savile, Charles Chelsea, Gilbert Greenall, Alexander Haig-Thomas, Tom Storey, Simon Ames. Back row, left to right: RAF host, Ian Macfadyen, Alan Curtis, Thomas Noel, Charles Pearson, Leila Pearson, 4 Lancaster crew members, Tony Haig-Thomas, John Hogg, Simon Bostock, RAF host.

at home. His situation was further complicated in that his family owned the newspaper and had more than once been persecuted by dictators for pursuing a constitutionalist, democratic line. The Gainza family had spent the Peron years in exile in Uruguay, and part of Maxi's schooling had taken place in Montevideo. Since the Falklands invasion was known to be a desperate bid for prestige by the embattled dictator General Galtieri, these articles cannot have been easy to write.

There was one further civilian footnote to the Falklands War. Following Ian Macfadyen's 'first' with a Phantom, Bruno Schroder took the first British civil aircraft into Stanley in 1986, four years after the end of hostilities. Always one for a technical challenge, he was on a round-the-world trip in a Cessna Conquest II, which he flew in under the Argentinian radar, escorted by an RAF Phantom from the edge of the no-fly zone. Three years later he was there again, ferrying a Britten-Norman Islander from the Isle of Wight for the Falkland Islands Government Fishery Protection Service. Suzanne Maltzahn accompanied him in the co-pilot seat. Anthony Stansfeld, who was Managing Director of Pilatus Britten-Norman, describes this as 'a very remarkable flight indeed: a hell of a long way in a slow aeroplane, several very long-range legs across the sea, eight or nine hours each, and awful weather.'

After the Iraqi invasion of Kuwait on 2 August 1990 British forces were in action again. Operation Desert Storm, launched on January 16 1991, took five weeks to drive the Iraqis back

to their own borders. The swift military victory was followed by a dozen years of patrolling no-fly zones over northern and southern Iraq. Air Squadron members took part in these operations at several levels: John Thomson was Assistant Chief of the Air Staff and was often to be seen on the television news, taking press briefings at the Ministry of Defence. Ian Macfadyen was based in Riyadh as a Senior Staff Member with the British Military Command, and in the spring was appointed successor to General Sir Peter de la Billiere as Commander British Forces Middle East. Michael Graydon was Commander in Chief RAF Strike Command in the immediate aftermath of the war, with responsibility for the protection of the Kurdish minority in the North; he was subsequently Joint Commander Gulf Forces. Glenn Torpy flew Tornados with No 13 Squadron, specialising in low-level night-time reconnaissance at no more than 170 feet above the terrain to avoid SAM 8 missiles. It was, he recalls, 'exciting stuff'. He was awarded the Distinguished Service Order in the Gulf Honours List.

Non-military members caught a direct glimpse of the coming conflict when they visited RAF Coningsby in September 1990 and saw the chemical warfare protection suits that pilots were required to wear for flying in the desert campaign.

A new charitable role

During the early 1980s, an important change occurred in Air Squadron affairs. Simon Ames wrote to the British Aerobatic Association on 18

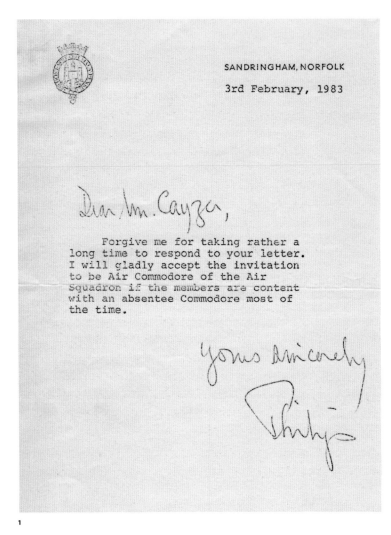

SANDRINGHAM, NORFOLK

3rd February, 1983

Dear Mr. Cayzer,

Forgive me for taking rather a
long time to respond to your letter.
I will gladly accept the invitation
to be Air Commodore of the Air
Squadron if the members are content
with an absentee Commodore most of
the time.

Yours sincerely

Philip

1 Prince Philip accepts the Squadron's
invitation to be Honorary Air Commodore.

November 1980: 'There is a feeling that there are
so many aerobatic competitions around these
days that the Air Squadron should consider
making 1981 a final year for sponsorship, and
consider some other aeronautical activity
for 1982.' The two organisations continued to
produce an annual air show for the next three
years, but their enthusiasm for joint ventures
was waning. In July 1981 the last combined
aerobatics competition and Air Squadron display
was held at Old Warden, with the traditional
lunch at the Hare and Hounds pub, and a fine
afternoon programme: a 50th Anniversary
challenge between the Oxford and Cambridge
University Air Squadrons in RAF Bulldog
aircraft, then displays by the Red Arrows, the
Rothmans Aerobatic Team, and members of the
Air Squadron in their vintage aeroplanes; pilots
included Patrick Lindsay, Martin Barraclough,
Tony Haig-Thomas and Robert Lamplough.
Proceeds from the gate and public joyrides would
go to the construction of a new de Havilland
hangar for the Shuttleworth Collection. £4,830
was raised.

In 1982, the aerobatics competition was
again held at Old Warden, but with no Air
Squadron display. The Squadron contributed
£300 towards cash prizes, fuel and insurance
costs for competitors. Only two members turned
up, however: Peter Vanneck, who presented the
Trophy, and Tony Haig-Thomas. This was felt to
be unfortunate but not particularly surprising.
Simon Ames reported that the British Aerobatic

Association 'would like to move from Old Warden
next year as the people there are not very helpful
any longer.' There had, it seems, been complaints
from locals about the noise. He added that in
his opinion 'we need a new venue and and a
revitalisation of the event.'

In July 1983 the aerobatics competition
was held at Fenland in Lincolnshire (where no
members attended), and in 1984 and 1985 at Audley
End. Air Squadron attendance was again very thin.
The owner of Audley End, Robin Neville, observed
that 'if so few are going to turn up it is really
rather a waste of time and effort on our part.' The
following year, the BAeA moved the competition to
Ipswich without discussing the matter with the Air
Squadron. There does not appear to have been any
ill will in the parting, and no objection was raised.
The two organisations just quietly drifted apart.

In 1984, Simon Bostock proposed a new format
for the Air Squadron Trophy. It was now to be a
prize 'for proficiency in CCF Air Sections'. His
proposal was enthusiastically taken up by the
members. The old trophy was mounted on a
mahogany plinth with a silver plate announcing its
new purpose. The first awards were made on 6 July
1985 at Old Warden, and have been supported with
undiminished zeal ever since. Simon Bostock tells
the full story of this award in Chapter 5.

Through the 1980s the membership increased
from 50 to almost 100. As well as military and
civilian aviators, the Squadron was delighted
in 1983 to welcome the Duke of Edinburgh as
Honorary Air Commodore. The Duke's acceptance

2

2 *The Times*, 6 February 1988. 'Smiles at Martell despite the ending of 273 years of independence - Seagram inherits a ruling dynasty.' René Martell, who engineered the £525 million sale of his family firm to Seagram, is on the right. He was a pilot, President of the Cognac Aero Club, and an honorary member of the Air Squadron. Patrick Martell is on the left, Edgar Bronfman of Seagram in the centre. Château Chanteloup, where Air Squadron visitors used to dine and stay, is in the background.

of the invitation was a powerful endorsement of the Squadron's status and a great boost to morale. Even if the Duke warned of almost permanent absenteeism (it was recently revealed that he is Patron of nearly 800 organisations) he has always offered encouragement and support to the Squadron's activities.

New honorary members were René Martell (1981), Sir Tom Sopwith, founder of the Sopwith and Hawker Aircraft Companies (1982), HRH Prince Andrew, Colonel Ozires Silva, Chairman of Embraer (1985), Friedrich Wilhelm Fürst von Hohenzollern and Comte Frédéric Chandon de Briailles (1987). Both René Martell and Frédéric Chandon had already been made Honorary Members in 1969, but no-one seems to have worried unduly about this.

As the Squadron and its commitments grew, a new Executive Committee was created, expanding the old informal 'triumvirate' of Astor, Cayzer and Vanneck assisted by Simon Ames. The new Executive now included Charles Chelsea, Eddie

Liverpool, Bruno Schroder and Adrian Swire. They held their first meeting in 1987.

The following year, the Honorary Secretary's life underwent a significant change: he became 'Simon Ames Corporate Communications and Marketing' after his job with British Caledonian was vaporised in the merger with British Airways. In another sign of the times, René Martell's venerable family firm was bought by the Canadian drinks conglomerate Seagram for £525 million. A smiling photograph in *The Times* Business Section suggested that both old and new owners were contented with the deal.

An important link with the past was severed with the death of Douglas Bader in November 1982. His patriotism, courage, forcefulness and support for the disabled were legendary, and had often been shown in small ways as well as large. Michael Fopp remembers him signing prints to raise funds for the Battle of Britain Museum at Bentalls department store in Kingston one Saturday morning. The queue stretched out of the shop and around the block. Bader looked up and saw a woman in a wheelchair waiting her turn in the queue. He at once walked up to her, asked what had put her in a wheelchair, told her she looked terrific, and led her to the front of the queue. The effect on her morale, said Fopp, was electrifying. A parallel story is told by Basil Hersov, whom Bader used to visit regularly in South Africa. 'We had a friend whose son had a lost a leg in the Angolan war. We invited him to dinner to meet Douglas. But the young man wouldn't come, because he said sitting at a dining table was difficult with

1

2

1 Patrick Lindsay (1928-1986), fine art auctioneer, racing car enthusiast and pilot: 'a life that was filled with adventure, danger and sporting activities'. For Carletto O'Donnell, 'Patrick was a giant of a character. His love for flying and cars, combined with his knowledge of the art market, resulted in his being a key founder of the classic car/aircraft auction market. Patrick's style of flying had a casual and relaxed effortlessness about it. This masked a lot of work and experience.' For a full account of his exploits, see his obituary in Chapter 6.

2 Brazil 1984. Back row left to right: Emi-Lu Astor, Angus Hamilton, Patsy King, Ossie King, John Bagge, Hugh Astor, Ian Macpherson. Front row left to right: Charles Chelsea, lady host, Patrick Lindsay, Brazilian host, Caryll Waterpark, Daniele Waterpark, Bruno Schroder, 2 Brazilian hosts.

an artificial leg. Douglas said, "Let me go and see him." When he got there, he said, "I don't know what you've got to worry about. You've only lost one leg. Look at me – I've lost two!"' Bader used his generous and energetic personality to fill such people with new courage and determination. It was a gift he had shown many times in the war, and it remained undimmed by time.

With Bader's passing a whole era seemed to slip away. It was unlikely that anyone would ever ask again of a prospective candidate 'Has he shot a German?', or declare that 'Women will be admitted over my dead body', or indeed dismiss the instructions of French Air Traffic Control with a brisk 'Bugger you!' He had many close friends in the Air Squadron, and is still remembered with enormous affection and admiration.

Patrick Lindsay was another much-loved character, whose brilliant career was cut short by his death at the age of 57. An auctioneer and director of Christie's, he was a keen vintage motor racer and pilot. His obituary in *The Times* speaks of 'a life that was filled with adventure, danger and sporting activities'. Tim Williams vividly remembers

an auction of historic aircraft at Strathallan in 1981, which Lindsay had set up in a marquee next to the airstrip. Prospective buyers examined the lots with a glass of fine champagne and 'the most delicious smoked salmon sandwiches'. Everything was perfect and conducive to the spending of large amounts of money. Only the auctioneer was absent. At one minute to two o'clock a Merlin engine was heard in the sky and a Spitfire came in to land next to the marquee. Out of it stepped Patrick Lindsay. He smoothed down his hair, walked up to the podium, and announced the start of the auction.

Patrick Lindsay died in 1986. He divided his collection of aeroplanes between three flying sons, two of whom (Ludovic and Valentine) became members of the Air Squadron in their turn. A lone flypast by his Spitfire, as his coffin was lowered into the grave, brought tears to the eyes of the many friends who attended his funeral. 'How he loved his flying,' wrote his wife Amabel to Simon Ames. 'It was so awful after his operation when they would not renew his flying licence. Every day that it was a fine day with a blue sky he would look up with nostalgic envy, and wish he was in the clouds.'

3

4

3–4 John Grandy leading the Army Helicopter Display Team, The Blue Eagles, past the Hermann Denkmal monument on their 1973 tour of Germany. The aircraft is the Agusta-Bell Sioux AH MK1, assembled under licence by Westland for the Army Air Corps in the late 1960s. The Sioux, which equipped light reconnaissance Army Air Corps Flights and Regimental Air Troops, was used by the Blue Eagles from their formation in 1968 until it was replaced by the Gazelle in the late 1970s. In 1973 the Blue Eagles undertook 75 public displays across the UK, France and Germany. 'By the end of the season all the pilots had a square backside, as the maximum cruising speed was about 65 knots.'

After the quiet years of 1977-83, the Squadron's programme of activities quickly picked up. As well as the visits to RAF stations, members were offered trips to Brazil, France, Germany, Texas and Russia, as well as the more domestic delights of Kenneth McAlpine's Lamberhurst Vineyard, the London Air Traffic Control Centre and British Aerospace.

There were also one or two curiosities that appeared briefly on Simon Ames's desk before being filed away. One was an invitation to the Cognac Air Rally in June 1981, where the winner was promised 'his own weight in cognac' as a prize. The other was a letter from Taittinger explaining that a projected trip to Reims in 1982 had to be scrapped because President Mitterrand had imposed a 30% Entertainment Tax on all such events, which would

put it beyond the company's budget. Luckily, this tax did not survive long, and the champagne houses were able to open their doors again by 1986.

Following trips to RAF Germany in 1982 and 1983, the Squadron began to show signs of bigger ambitions. Caryll Waterpark's plan for a tour of Brazil was a triumphant success (see Chapter 4), not only for the enjoyment of those who went on it, but also for showing that such things could be done. Thanks to Waterpark's business contacts in Brazil, and Simon Ames's influence in the airline industry, the trip cost very little – £450 all in, with hotels, food and transport laid on by the Brazilian Government and a surprise free upgrade to first class on British Caledonian Airways there and back. Thomas Noel wrote to Simon Ames on his

1 Thomas Noel (left) and Johnny Moss at the Wallop Challenge, 1993. Thomas Noel was introduced to flying by Eddie Liverpool, and obtained his pilot's licence at the age of 16. He joined the Air Squadron in 1983 and took part in the trips to Brazil, Germany, Russia and Jordan. On the last of these he made a film. He remembers his early years in the Air Squadron as a time of 'total comedy, a small group of friends having a wonderful time. It wasn't nearly as serious as it is now. The whole thing reminded me of *Dad's Army*, with me in the role of Pike.' Thomas has worked for many years in property and hospitality. He now owns and runs the Barnsdale Lodge Hotel on Rutland Water.

2 The visit to Bell Helicopters, Fort Worth, Texas, October 1989. Left to right: Adrian de Ferranti, Simon Berry, Eddie Liverpool, 3 representatives of Bell Helicopters, Johnny Greenall, Ginny Sutherland, Ian Sutherland. Of the machine in the background, a prototype of the Bell V-22 Osprey, Eddie Liverpool writes: 'This was the tilt rotor VTOL (Vertical Take Off & Landing) fixed wing aircraft which Bell were working on and which was the main reason for us going on the visit. We had hoped to fly in the prototype but there were technical difficulties. We were able to watch it in the "Hover" but sadly not making the transition to forward flight.'

return: 'The visit to Brazil was nothing short of a sensation, attributable to superb organisation and boundless Brazilian hospitality… I have enjoyed flights in the past – even long distance ones – but the BCal trip has set completely new standards. How will I ever travel second class again!'

In 1986, the Squadron were invited by their old friend Comte Frédéric Chandon de Noailles to stay at the Château de Saran near Epernay for a three-day champagne visit. This was an old formula, and it worked well. James Baring remembered a similar outing in 1971, and 'was confident that the hospitality and entertainment would exceed all expectations.' This turned out to be perfectly true. According to Eddie Liverpool (the only member ever to record one of these trips to Epernay) a delicious tea was waiting when they arrived, 'but it was not long before the teapots were replaced by Magnums of 1981 champagne, supplies of which appeared literally to be inexhaustible.' That night Frédéric and Camilla Chandon welcomed them for dinner at the Château, and the next morning at 7 they were floating in hot air balloons above the vineyards as the sun climbed into a dazzling blue sky. They flew 15 kilometres, and found 'as if by magic' a butler waiting to serve them champagne as they landed. After that it was 'back to the Château for breakfast', a tour of the Moët et Chandon cellars, a quick lunch, the Abbaye de Hautvillers, then dinner at the Trianon, where another Air Squadron salver was added to the Comte's collection. The following day, after a tour of the 18th century cellars at Ruinart, they

flew home. 'We were treated like royalty,' wrote Christopher D'Oyly in a letter to Simon Ames, adding (in case there should be any doubt) that they had 'consumed a quite remarkable amount of champagne.'

In the autumn of 1987 they visited Daimler-Benz in Stuttgart. The invitation had come from Graf von Waldendorff, who had been shooting at Stradsett the year before as a guest of Sir John Bagge. Two nights at the Hotel Graf Zeppelin and a number of high-octane dinners were offered by the automobile company, as well as a tour of the production plant and the chance to drive a Mercedes 380 on the test track at Untertürkheim. This included a near-aeronautical 2G experience when the car took a long curve on a vertical wall. On the last day, they were shown around the castle at Sigmaringen by its owner, Fürst von Hohenzollern, who turned out to be a keen pilot himself. Twelve members enjoyed this trip, and were thoroughly impressed with both the engineering and the hospitality.

Thomas Noel remembers one 'classic moment' on the tour of the Mercedes establishment, which was led by the President of Daimler-Benz.

Half way round, Bruno sidled up to the President and said, "What's in THAT room?"

"What room exactly, Herr Schroder?"

"That one there, the one which is locked, the one we have just walked by"

"We do not include that room in the tour."

"Why not?" said Bruno defiantly, smelling a very large rat.

There was an uncomfortable silence, after which the President moved rapidly from inventing the bicycle in 1917 to 1946, leaving a very pronounced gap. Bruno was like a bloodhound... "What is in that room? And what did you people do in the intervening years... You must have made something?"

Realising that Bruno was not going to give up, the President sighed wearily. "Oh very well. Open the door, Hans."

"Ja, my President.... " Click went the heels, and Hans opened the door.

"Turn on the lights, Hans."

"Ja, my President."

There before us was Hitler's Mercedes, Goering's, Goebbels' etc..... All in immaculate condition.

"Ah, I see," said Bruno, now looking more sheepish. Trying to change the subject, Bruno asked, "And what else did you make then?"

The President looked particularly worn. "9,500 Panzer Tanks, 4,000 V bombs, 3,500 armoured cars, 150,000...."

John Bagge interrupted, "Yes, that's all very well, Herr President, but my steering wheel doesnt work!"

Believe it or not his 25 year old brown S Class, which he had driven all the way from Norfolk, was whisked away and put through the factory. "Golly," said John, "where's it gone?"

Half an hour later, his old car re-appeared with sparkling new alloy wheels, new steering wheel, etc. John looked nonplussed. "I preferred it the way it was." "Very well," said the President. "Hans, take it back!"... And sure enough John's car came back reinstated, exactly as it was before!

On the way home Thomas and his brother-in-law Eddie Liverpool flew into a violent thunderstorm. When they landed at Southend they found a scene of devastation. It was October 18th 1987. The great hurricane had just passed through.

1988 brought trips to Old Sarum Airfield to see the Optica light observation aircraft, as well as Lotus Cars and Reymerston Hall in Norfolk where Wg Cdr Kenneth Wallis housed his remarkable collection (and factory) of autogyros. Since this was also the year of visits to HMS *Illustrious* and RAF Marham, one can see that the Air Squadron calendar had now recovered fully from the lassitude of the early Eighties.

In 1989 members donated a total of £6,500 towards the refurbishment of Dowding House in Moffat, a Sheltered Housing Project for the Royal Air Forces Association. The money was dedicated particularly towards a Guest Room where visiting family members and friends could stay overnight. The following year, some flying pictures were supplied by members to hang on the walls of this room, as well as a plaque recording the Air Squadron's generosity.

Also in 1989 came trips to Westland Helicopters in Yeovil and Bell Helicopters in Fort Worth. Five members flew commercial to Texas for a five-day visit that included 'Airsho 89' organised by the Confederate Air Force, the F-16 production line at General Dynamics, Carslake Air Force Base, and Texas Lil's Diamond A Ranch – which, despite its

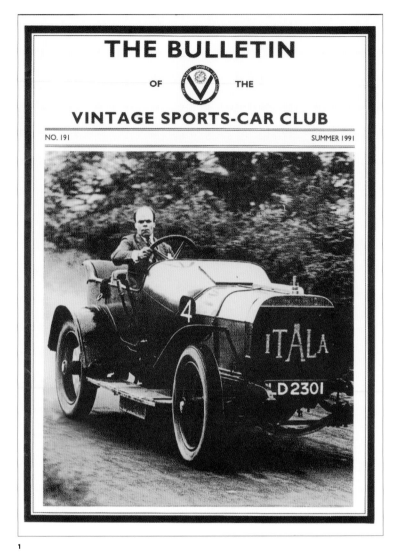

THE BULLETIN

OF THE

VINTAGE SPORTS-CAR CLUB

NO. 191   SUMMER 1991

1

1 By profession Sam Clutton was a surveyor and estate manager whose clients included the Crown and the Church. Privately he was a pilot, vintage car racer, organist, author and horologist. He wrote for the *Encyclopaedia Britannica* as well as the BBC on keyboard instruments, on which he was a leading authority. He owned and restored some magnificent clocks, but always restricted his collection to twelve pieces. He edited and updated the standard work on the history of watchmaking, Britten's *Old Clocks and Watches and their Makers*, and wrote several books on vintage cars. A fearless, positive and highly energetic man, he drove vintage sports cars at astonishing speeds and once impressed his friend Jack Williamson with a brilliantly unorthodox aerobatic manoeuvre in a Tiger Moth: 'He started into a loop and, near the top, slid backwards momentarily then rolled off twice and came back down the same leg. When he landed I complimented him on this manoeuvre which I supposed had been put on for the benefit of the spectators. But he explained that his briefcase in the cockpit under the cushion had floated past him and necessitated letting go of everything to catch it. This was most important because it contained a Breguet watch which belonged to Lord Harris and was to be passed on to me for attention. Having caught the briefcase he then couldn't remember where the ground was and had to take a couple of turns to locate it.'

improbable name, was a genuine working ranch.

One of the founders of the Air Squadron, Anthony Cayzer, died in 1990 at the age of 69. A quiet, reserved man, he complemented the dash and ebullience of Peter Vanneck and the charm of Hugh Astor with shrewd business acumen and consummate managerial skill. Obituaries appeared in *The Daily Telegraph, The Independent* and *The Times,* the last of these prompting a letter from Neville Barwick of the Missions to Seamen, for whom Cayzer ran the Finance and Investment Committees from 1974 to 1984: 'Chairmen fall broadly into one of two categories: one who accepts advice (without question and hoping it is sound), or one who listens to the advice and then takes as much trouble as is needed to master the problems so that he becomes the person truly "responsible". Tony Cayzer was a princely example of the latter.'

Hugh Astor wrote a heartfelt tribute, mentioning his warmth and generosity as a host, his striving for perfection in everything he did, and the loyalty he inspired in those who worked with him. 'During the War he served with the Royal Scots Greys and was mentioned in despatches, but in 1944 was demobilized suffering from ill health, from which he never fully recovered, although his spirit remained undaunted.'

1990 turned out to be a year of losses, with the deaths of John Bagge, Luke Annaly and Julian Savage. Of these Julian Savage had been a member for only a year. He lost his life at the age of 36, as the result of a flying accident in Kenya, where he had farmed and flown regularly for many years. Luke Annaly, known as 'Lukie', had served in the RAF

1944-48, and subsequently in 601 Squadron of the Royal Auxiliary Air Force, with Peter Vanneck and Desmond and Torquil Norman.

John Bagge was one of the Air Squadron's most assiduous attenders, with his own airstrip at Stradsett in Norfolk, which he cunningly laid out in a direct line with the runway at RAF Marham. John was the only member of the Squadron to be a Knight Commander of the Order of the Star of Honour of Ethiopia – a distinction he had earned for his part in liberating the country during the Second World War. He had learned to fly late in life with his son Jeremy, who had recently joined the Air Squadron himself.

Meanwhile, in the general flow of dynamism and fresh ideas, the Squadron began taking part in helicopter competitions. The first of these was Helimeet International, which took place as part of the Middle Wallop Air Show in May 1992. Forty teams took part in an event that included 'Slalom Poles, Rope and Bucket, Removing Doors etc, Navigation Exercise, Circuit Flying and Flight Planning'. Team members were Johnny Moss (Manager), Charles Pearson (Captain), Gilbert Greenall, Eddie Liverpool, Simon Glenarthur and Thomas Noel. The Air Squadron provided a trophy, which was won by a team from New Zealand. Although this was intended as a perpetual trophy, and there were plans to repeat the competition in 1994, this does not seem to have happened. Instead, a more limited contest was held in September 1993 under the name of the Wallop Challenge. Free fall parachuting, gliding,

● Henry Labouchere and Tim Williams with the 1930 de Haviland Puss Moth which has taken them around the world.

Jovial duo revisit old haunts

By BRETT QUINE

TWO British chaps on one hell of a jovial jaunt — from England to Australia in a 1930 single-engine plane — breezed into Wodonga yesterday.

And pilot Henry Labouchere (who left Australia in 1976) caused no small measure of mirth when he met some old friends at the one his past haunts, the Drage Air Museum.

"Its a bloody long way from Pom land," he said.

"I used to come up here and annoy the DCA (the Department of Civil Aviation) a bit — I shouldn't let them know I'm here, they're probably still after me.

"Jeeze we were a bunch of hooligans — or we were then."

Henry wasn't very keen about explaining his past antics on the strip.

Co-pilot, Tim Williams, was a little more composed after flying through France, Italy, Greece, Egypt, Pakistan, Singapore, and many other countries en route to Melbourne.

Tim reckons he has probably seen more of Australia than most of the natives since reaching Darwin in the de Haviland Puss Moth on Sunday.

He and Henry have flown over the country at heights ranging from 2500 m to 2 m — at times brushing against tree tops.

"It really is a mind-blowing experience," Tim said.

And he has a ready-reference guide for pilots of the northern hemisphere wanting to fly to Melbourne.

"Keep pointing south and you get there eventually."

Tim and Henry are tracing the route of the 1934 Great Air Race (which their plane was too old to enter) since October 20.

They touch down in Melbourne, the end of their journey, on Saturday to help celebrate Victoria's 150th birthday.

After staying in Melbourne for about two weeks Henry and Tim will head back to England on a somewhat faster and more comfortable plane.

Their Puss Moth will be shipped home.

1

1   The arrival of Henry Labouchere and Tim Williams in Wodonga is noted by the local press (1984).

balloning, fixed and rotary wing were all represented, with teams from each of the services plus the Air Squadron.

'The intention is for good fun rather than steely competition,' wrote the Director of the Army Air Corps, Major General Simon Lytle, and 'any team unable to field one or more disciplines will be encouraged to procure external assistance.' Eddie Liverpool led a team sponsored by Bruno Schroder. It included Ian Macfadyen (gliding), Johnny Moss and Thomas Noel (Gazelle helicopter), and the Red Devils (parachuting). Teddy Hall organised the ballooning, and the Squadron's guest balloonist, Crispin Williams, won this event, while the Navy won both the helicopter and fixed wing, the RAF the gliding, and the Red Devils the parachuting. Simon Ames, Robin D'Erlanger and Tony Haig-Thomas acted as judges, and were warmly thanked by the organisers for their 'dignified air of impartiality which was evident throughout and which attracted much favourable comment.' Twenty-five members and guests attended as spectators, on one of the warmest and sunniest weekends of the summer.

A set of embroidered badges was commissioned for the first of these competitions, to give Air Squadron members a professional team look. Badges and flying suits were then worn by Air Squadron pilots on their trip to Moscow and St Petersburg in August 1992. In style-conscious Russia, the new look was a great success. Flying suits quickly caught on, with a strong

2

3

2 The Wallop Challenge, 1993. Teams from the Air Squadron and each of the services competed in free fall parachuting, gliding, ballooning, fixed and rotary wing flying. The Air Squadron team included Eddie Liverpool (team captain, back row second from right) and Ian Macfadyen (gliding captain, back row far right). Ian's son Simon is standing at the far left. The Red Devils (front row) were borrowed by the Squadron for the parachuting event, which they won.

3 Russia 1992: arrival at Kubinka. From the left: Russian Base Commander, Michael Beetham, General Antoshkin, Caryll Waterpark.

recommendation from the Executive Committee that they should be the 'norm' for those arriving at events by air.

The visit to Russia in 1992 embodies the bold new spirit of the Air Squadron at this time. It brought vintage aircraft, challenging flying and unusual destinations together with diplomacy and cultural exchange in an exciting mix that had not been tried before. The trip itself, with its sense of discovery, its comedies of vodka and low-grade aviation fuel, is described in detail in Chapter 4. It is enough at this point in the story to note that it signalled the start of a new phase in the Air Squadron's development. Many members made it possible, but one was to prove its guiding spirit over the next decade: Caryll Waterpark.

Chapter 3   New Horizons   1994-2008

1

2

1　Fjord flying, Norway 2005.

2　Caryll Waterpark in Jordan, 1994.

3　Three Air Squadron Tiger Moths returning to England from Poland in 2006: G-ANRN (Jonathan Elwes), G-AGEG (Alex Norman), G-APMX (Ralph Hubbard).

3

New Horizons   1994-2008

For the first few years of the 1990s, the Air Squadron continued to build on its success, following a pattern developed in the previous decade. The programme was lively and varied, membership was steadily growing, and behind the scenes the Executive Committee and Simon Ames ran the show impeccably. Like any good team the Squadron had strength in depth, with active groups of members interested in different aspects of aviation, all bound together by a common spirit of patriotism, enjoyment of life, friendship and good works. A new energy and purpose had been evident from the first elections of Royal Air Force officers in the 1980s. Their leading light was now John Thomson, a passionately keen member of the Squadron who was heading inexorably for the highest rank.

In the early 1990s a new force came into play. Caryll Waterpark retired from business after the sale of CSE Aviation. He had bought into CSE (Channon Svejdar Erlanger) in 1955 for £10,000, and helped to build Oxford Airport into a thriving centre for private aviation. As Sales Director of CSE and later as Chief Executive Officer of CSE International, with European concessions for Bell, Piper, Lear, Embraer, Lycoming, King, Cessna and other leading manufacturers, he had developed a worldwide network of contacts and friendships among industrialists, financiers, political leaders, military chiefs, monarchs and diplomats – anyone who might conceivably wish to use a private aeroplane. When he sold an aircraft, he liked to deliver it in person. Long before the internet, he

pioneered the concept of the executive on the move: 'I ran CSE by telephone from Timbuktu,' is how he describes his operational style. From his logbooks and conversation unfurls a lifetime of flying adventures, in Africa, the Caribbean and South America, complete with sandstorms, Tarzan films, KGB colonels, rebellions and border wars. As if this were not exciting enough, he had a parallel career as a test-pilot, taking new foreign aircraft to the 'red line' limits for their UK Certificate of Airworthiness. When he retired in 1990 he began to apply his love of adventure, his global address-book and formidable powers of persuasion to extending the range and ambition of the Air Squadron.

'The turning point,' he later recalled, 'was when we stopped doing little trips to Europe and did huge trips to very difficult places to get to, with the complete support of HMG from every point of view.' Support was, of course, crucial – from his secretary for 35 years, Karen Rutson ('she was effectively managing director'), to King Hussein of Jordan. In organising visits to Russia (1992) and Jordan (1994), he was substantially helped by John Thomson, who, he says, 'as a serving officer in the Royal Air Force made huge efforts on behalf of the Air Squadron ... Where it was a requirement that we had the active support of the chiefs of staff of the place where we were going, John Thomson was able to provide it.'

The Waterpark vision was backed up with appropriate hardware. He put up owners of long-range pressurised aircraft for membership of the Squadron – notably John Scurr and Viktor and

1

2

1 Warsaw 2006: Robs Lamplough climbs out of his Spitfire cockpit after a difficult landing.

2 John Scurr (left) and Michael Graydon. John Scurr, a leading vascular surgeon, was one of the Air Squadron members who owned pressurised aircraft that could take several passengers to distant places. Michael Graydon joined the Air Squadron in 1995 during a highly distinguished career in the Royal Air Force. He was commissioned in 1959, flew Lightnings with 56 Sqn, commanded RAF Leuchars (1981-3) and RAF Stanley, Falkland Islands (1983-4), and was C-in-C Strike Command immediately after the 1990 Gulf War, with responsibility for the protection of the Kurdish minority in northern Iraq. He was appointed Chief of the Air Staff in 1992, serving until 1997. He was knighted in 1989, and became Chairman of the Air Squadron in 2005.

Lorraine Bondarenko – and, in 1995, persuaded Bruno Schroder to buy a Pilatus PCXII. This tactic brought in a passenger-carrying capacity that would make the long trips easier to achieve. At the same time a number of adventurous pilots with small or vintage aeroplanes joined the Air Squadron expeditions and soon became members: Tim Williams and Henry Labouchere (who had flown to Australia in a 1930 Puss Moth), Dru Montagu and Torquil Norman (both trans-Atlantic soloists), Jonathan Elwes and Nick Parkhouse (who had crossed Eastern Europe to Russia in Tiger Moths in 1989), David Hare (who flew around the world in his Piper Aztec), Terry Holloway (leader of the first RAF gliding expedition to the Andes, who had flown a Chilean Air Force Janus glider over Mount Aconcagua) and Bill Hall (who had

already piloted his Robin Aiglon to Sydney and Las Vegas, and would in 2002-3 fly it to Cape Town and back, twice). They added to a growing catalogue of 'men of steel' and 'stalwart aviators' (to use some favourite Waterpark appellations), whose confidence, experience and skill made the most ambitious plans attainable. The arrival of several 'women of steel' from 2002 (starting with Margaret Hare) contributed a bold new group of flyers to the Squadron's distinguished ranks, while quietly setting aside some outdated myths along the way.

In saluting the new, one should not, of course, ignore the old. The Air Squadron's traditional activities were thriving. Fly-ins to RAF, Army and Navy bases continued to stimulate and inform. John Thomson and Simon Bostock arranged inspiring visits to the Red Arrows in Cyprus

3

4

3 Bill Hall arrives at Darwin in 1985 after a 4-hour flight over the Timor Sea. With him is Emma McCune who later went on to work in Sudan for Street Kids International (SKI), opening more than 100 schools in southern Sudan and campaigning against the recruitment of child soldiers. She married the Sudanese guerrilla commander Riek Machar in 1991, but died in a car crash in Nairobi two years later. Bill Hall, son of Professor Teddy Hall, has accomplished many remarkable flights (including a solo trip around Africa in 2002). He was appointed the Air Squadron's Navigator in 2000.

4 Nick Parkhouse, surgeon and pilot, who joined the Air Squadron in 2004. Nick's ratings include PPL (A) (Night), French Mountain Pilot's Licence (Wheel and Ski), US Seaplane Pilot's Licence, PPL (H) (Night), PPL (B) and PPL/IR. He flew his Tiger Moth to Moscow in 1989 with Jonathan Elwes in the 'Glasmoth' expedition. He owns a Tiger Moth, a Tipsy Trainer, an R-22 and R-44, and shares in a DH Dove and Robinson Redwing. He won the Royal Aero Club Certificate of Merit in 1989 and the Geoffrey de Havilland Trophy in 1990. He is a Liveryman of GAPAN and Honorary Medical Adviser to the Historic Aircraft Association.

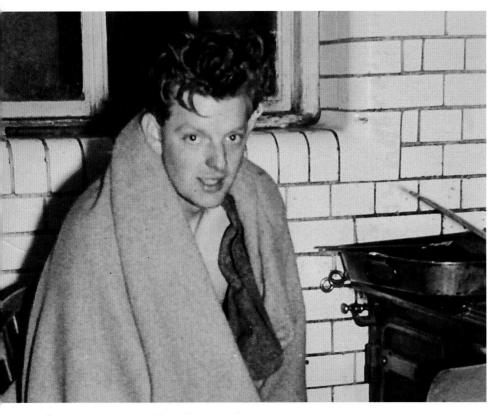

1

2

1 In 1952 Dru Montagu was forced by an engine failure to ditch his Sea Fury in the Channel off Lyme Regis, he was picked up by Air Sea Rescue, dried out and returned to his squadron at Culdrose. 'I was only 1500 feet up when the engine stopped. I tried to land on the golf course at Lyme Regis, because it's the only piece of flat ground in a bumpy area, but the wind blew me out to sea. They hauled the aircraft out by crane some time later and found a broken fuel pipe so I was exonerated. I was also very lucky.'

2 Inspired to fly by his father and uncle (both members of 601 Squadron), Dru Montagu served in the Fleet Air Arm in 1951-3 before moving to the USA and a career in oil exploration. For several years private flying was beyond his means, but in 1968 he took it up again, progressing from a Beechcraft Bonanza to a series of twin-engined Cessnas in which he crossed the Atlantic on annual visits home to England. In 1979 he flew a 337 from California, a 36-hour trip, and decided he needed something faster. A dealer friend in the US said, 'Take a look in the hangar, that's the airplane for you.' So he bought his first jet, a Cessna Citation 1, checking out in a week. He continued flying Citations all over North and South America, as well as the Caribbean where he has a second home, completing 34 solo flights across the Atlantic. In 2003, aged 72, he sold his last jet and learned to fly helicopters instead. In 2008, still flying his helicopter or his single-engined Maule practically every day, he embarked on a new adventure - gliding. 'I was inspired to fly as a young man,' he says, 'and it's still with me. If I don't fly for a few days I get itchy. I feel very happy in the air.'

3 Annette and Martin Gosling with their Robin DR 400 Regent in Norway 2005. Martin Gosling obtained his pilot's licence in 1979 at the Suffolk Flying Club and bought a Grumman AA5, then a Robin 160. Martin is also an active member of the Flying Farmers. He joined the Air Squadron in 2000.

3

and to Strike Command and RAF Odiham in 1994. Excursions to Cranwell, Brüggen, Kinloss, Yeovilton, Coltishall, Netheravon, Valley, Middle Wallop, Culdrose, Marham, Cottesmore, Leuchars and Coningsby followed – each visit adding a new perspective, new friendships and new understanding.

On each of these visits, Air Squadron members both give and gain enormous satisfaction from offering flights to service personnel who never have a chance to fly – cooks, waiters, administrators, cleaners, drivers – as well as the mechanics, armourers, engineers and technicians who put in the 15 hours of work that a fast jet needs for each hour it spends in the air. 'They are enormously appreciative,' says George Rolls, who regularly gives rides in his helicopter.

From time to time a few lucky members are offered a sortie in a front-line fighter. After a day of medical tests and fitting of G-suits, they are given an hour of cloud-scattering vertical climbs and effortless transits of the sound barrier. They return to earth transfigured, as if they have been consorting with the gods. James Astor flew in a Tornado F3 at RAF Leuchars. 'When I was chosen, I didn't sleep for two nights, I was so excited... Going supersonic was incredible. It was like being in a sports car but just being pushed back and back and back progressively more and more and more. I glanced down at the Mach meter and saw the needle swinging through, past every marker, and every marker is 100 miles an hour.' The best part of the flight was when the pilot said, 'You have control. Just do aerobatics, do whatever you like'. 'We were pulling up vertically through clouds and then dropping down and weaving, so you really got the sensation of speed, ducking and diving through the clouds. And the amazing thing, it is so quiet; you are in a pressurized cockpit and you have your helmet on so you just feel this rush of air over the canopy, there is no engine sound at all because you are leaving it behind.'

In 2005 Jonathan Elwes took the back seat in a Harrier T10 at RAF Cottesmore. Their sortie took them across Lincolnshire, Yorkshire and Cumbria, with simulated bombing runs as low as 100 feet. His pilot, Squadron Leader Rich Fewtrell, demonstrated a 50-knot landing, and transition from a take-off to a 50-knot hover. 'The *pièce de résistance*, however, was during our transit home. By deft use of the nozzle lever and vectored thrust, Rich decelerated from 420 knots to a mere 50 knots sitting on a blanket of white stratus. A brief 'hover' on cloud nine for a Harrier novice!'

In 2007 at RAF Coningsby Alex Howard had a ride in the new Eurofighter 'Typhoon'. 'I was warned by my pilot, Steve Formosa, that we were in what he considered to be an inferior aircraft, one of the Batch One aircraft, and that Bitching Betty, who was the computer that talks to you, was likely to come up with all sorts of spurious messages. And he was quite right; throughout the sortie she was telling us that we were running out of fuel and that we were about to run into mountains, which, given the fact that we were mostly over 35,000 feet, seemed unlikely in Norfolk.'

1

2

1 The Air Squadron visit to RAF Cranwell, 22-23 June 1995. This visit was made before the annual awards became a fixture at the College from 1996. Front row, left to right: Rory Cavendish, Caryll Waterpark, John Houlder, Simon Bostock, Simon Ames, Station Commander, Bluey Mavroleon, John Hogg, Michael Beetham, John Scurr. Middle, left to right: Adrian de Ferranti, John Grandy, Richard Everard, William Williams-Wynne, Edward Haig-Thomas, James Scurr, Gilbert Greenall, Roddy Blois, John Hoerner, David Corbett, Micky Astor. Back, left to right: guest, Alex Norman, 2 guests, Micky Suffolk, Robs Lamplough.

2 Lt Mark Thomson RN in a Sea Vixen FAW1 of 893 Squadron at full power about to be launched from the steam catapult, HMS *Victorious*, 1963.

3 David Corbett, who served in the 9th Queen's Royal Lancers (1954-60), learned to fly at Shobdon Airfield in Herefordshire in 1963; Shobdon has been owned by the Corbett family since 1964. David has owned various aircraft types since 1964, and in 2001 completed the build of his own Europa, which he has flown to most European countries.

4 Olaf Brun in a Tornado cockpit at RAF Leuchars in 2006. Olaf owns Great Massingham (ex-RAF) aerodrome in Norfolk, and flies three of his own aircraft from there.

5 James Astor at the entrance to a hard shelter, RAF Leuchars, 2006. The next day he was the lucky member chosen to take a guest flight in the Tornado F3.

6 Chinook helicopters at work, RAF Odiham, visited by the Air Squadron in 1994.

3

4

5

6

1 Terry Holloway flying Dr Helena Hamilton's Hornet Moth 'Horny' in 1997. Terry was custodian of this aeroplane from 1996 to 2002, when it made numerous appearances at Air Squadron outings, including flying cadets at RAF Cranwell. In the background is an identical de Havilland Hornet Moth, G-AELO, being flown by its present owner, Mark Miller. This aircraft was previously owned by Air Squadron member Simon Bostock. Terry Holloway served in the RAF for 34 years, retiring with the rank of Group Captain in 1995. A highly experienced glider pilot and instructor, he led the first RAF gliding expedition to Chile to fly over the Andes into Argentina in 1996. He is a Life Member of the Royal Air Force Gliding and Soaring Association. He has flown over 100 types of light aircraft in a flying career of 48 years and some 7000 hours. He is currently Group Support Executive at Marshall of Cambridge.

2 Alex Howard served as a pilot in the Fleet Air Arm before taking over the management of the estate at Colonsay, visited by the Air Squadron in 1973 and again in 2007. His father, Euan Strathcona, was one of the earliest members of the Squadron.

3 James Astor (left) and Nick Parkhouse explore the cramped interior of a Lancaster bomber, RAF Coningsby, October 2007.

2

1

3

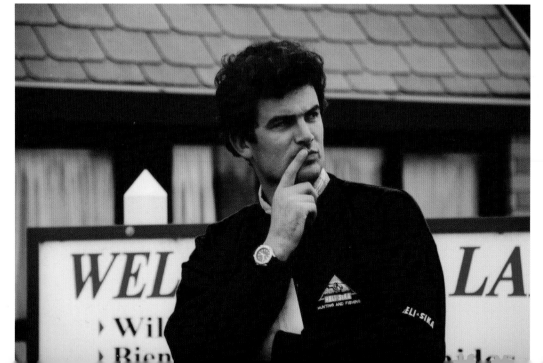

4

4 Charles Pearson's Agusta A109E Power, G-PWER. Charles is a company director and landowner who learned to fly in 1983 and joined the Air Squadron in 1985. His flying has been largely private, although he worked as a pilot for Hummingbird Helicopters in the Maldive Islands in 1989-90.

He too was taken aback by the relentless acceleration, and a pleasurable sense of disorientation: 'Once we had been detected by the other aircraft we were allowed to take two evasive actions to try and avoid contact. And that basically means pulling as hard as you can and doing something unusual. On our third run we rolled inverted and flew vertically down from 35,000 feet to 10,000 feet in as long as it has taken me to tell you about it... It was a surreal experience. For most of us who are earth-bound all our lives, and fly off to Majorca once in a while, to strap into an aeroplane like that and explore the third dimension in a way you couldn't really conceive, is extraordinary.' Yet most of all, recalling his own service in the Fleet Air Arm, he wanted to impart to his young pilot friends that their days of flying fast jets would be the most precious, the most exciting of their lives. 'It's an old buffer kind of thing to say, but I felt it very strongly.'

Apart from the RAF visits, the annual awards to cadets, the spring and winter dinners, and a varied programme of flying expeditions both short and long continued to keep members busy. In 1994 Terry Holloway and Ian Macfadyen organised a Gliding Day at RAF Bicester. 'It was the most wonderful flying day,' Terry recalls. 'A number of Air Squadron members flew solo in gliders for the first time and others were enormously generous with the loan of their own aeroplanes. Robs Lamplough sent me solo in his Chinese-built Yak, following "a very detailed five minute briefing". RAF Upper Heyford had only just closed with its

F111 bombers, and the Cold War was all but over. I was thrilled to be flying Robs's aeroplane over an active USAF Base with my bright red stars visible for all to see on the wings.'

That same year Robs Lamplough encouraged the Squadron to bring their vintage aeroplanes to the classic car races at Silverstone for an air and ground display. Simon Ames took on the role of Flying Display Director, and persuaded Denis Smallwood to climb a precarious ladder to a little wooden hut where he gave a brilliant commentary on the show. This event was such a hit that they went back every year until 1998. A second edition of the Wallop Challenge in 1995 also saw Squadron members competing with teams from the Army, Navy and Air Force in a variety of flying disciplines.

The awards took on a new solemnity with the creation of the Sir John Thomson Memorial Sword, first presented in 1995. This was the Squadron's response to Thomson's untimely death in July 1994. After the initial shock, his friends were determined to turn their loss to good: funds were raised, and a handsome sword was commissioned to be awarded each year to the country's best cadet. This sword, a glittering focus for the presentation ceremony, was installed at Cranwell in 2000, beneath a portrait of Thomson on the main stairs. It was to inspire the Swords of Honour given to the Air Forces of the United States, South Africa and Poland in later years.

In 1996 membership reached 100. This was also the year of the Air Squadron's 30th anniversary, celebrated at Le Touquet, where the first cross-

1 Colonel-General Nikolai Antoshkin of the Russian Air Force, the Air Squadron's special guest at its 30th anniversary party in Le Touquet, 1996.

2 Air Squadron members Prince Michael of Kent and Michael Graydon pose in front of Maxi Gainza's Yak 3 with young French men and women who were flown in Air Squadron vintage aircraft at the 40th anniversary party in Le Touquet, 2006.

3-4 Christopher Foyle ran a number of successful aviation businesses for many years before taking on the family bookshop on London's Charing Cross Road. He learned to glide at Dunstable in 1958 at the age of 15, moving on to powered aircraft in 1974. He has owned many different aircraft and flown all over Europe and much of the USA. In 1985 he acquired and flew the first Edgley OA7 Optica but after leasing to Hampshire Police it was destroyed in a crash. He has a particular fascination with the Russian manufacturer Antonov, and ran a fleet of their giant cargo aeroplanes as well as owning and flying an AN2 privately: this single-engined biplane (shown here) carries up to 14 people and needs only 100 yards of runway. Flying it, he says, is 'easy – a bit like driving a steam engine.'

5 Auster J5F, part owned by ex-Concorde Captain and Air Squadron member John Hutchinson.

4

5

channel dinner had been held in September 1966. An impeccably choreographed fly-in, masterminded by Simon Bostock and Martin Barraclough, led to a reception by the Mayor, signature of the *Livre d'Or*, and a dinner dance for 250 at the Hotel Westminster–an event made doubly memorable when the birthday cake, loaded with roman candles, caught fire.

Four helicopters and fifty fixed-wing aeroplanes, including eight vintage de Havillands, two Spitfires, a Grumman Avenger, a Mustang, two Antonovs, three Yaks and a Cessna Citation, landed at Le Touquet between 1015 and noon (average interval less than two minutes) on 21st September. The Barraclough-Bostock instructions to pilots were little short of a work of art, with every detail of aircraft speed, weather, routing, formations, approach, timings, communications, landing, parking, refuelling, immigration and emergency procedures minutely laid out. Pilots

were asked to 'set watches using the GPO talking clock (dial 123) minus one hour to give Zulu' and to pay strict attention to the buffer periods between groups of aircraft, which were included for minor inaccuracies in time keeping. 'The sight of so many varied and historic aircraft landing and parking on the airfield,' writes Martin Barraclough, 'impressed the older French citizens of Le Touquet who recalled that the town had seen nothing like it since World War II.'

There was a further display the next day when Philip Meeson landed a Rapide on the beach at low tide to commemorate the 60th anniversary of the last Imperial Airways service to Le Touquet. Five Squadron aircraft were then scheduled to take fifty underprivileged and disabled children on a pleasure flight from the sands, but 'anxious and uncomprehending officials' cancelled it. A grand final lunch was held at the Golf Club of Le Manoir, and departure that afternoon trimmed another few years off

1 John Houlder, who bought his first aeroplane in 1937, and was still flying more than 70 years later, always in his own special style. Terry Holloway remembers a typical incident: 'In 1999 we were visiting Tiree in Scotland, probably the most under-utilised large airfield in the world. Simon Bostock was acting as Air Traffic Controller and we were all briefed very carefully not to use or even taxi on the lazy runway on which a bright orange sea container was located, filled with emergency equipment for rescue helicopter operations. John Houlder took it upon himself to taxi along this runway and judged that he had sufficient space to taxi past the container. He hadn't, and there was a sickening crunch as his wing tip hit the container and the aircraft rotated through 90 degrees. John, unabashed, got out, looked at the damage, and said, "Oh dear". He immediately got out his penknife and started to cut up one of the traffic cones which had conveniently been put in place to stop people driving into the sea container. He cut both ends off, sliced it down the middle, wedged it over the offending flattened opening on the leading edge of the wing and said "There we are, has anyone got any tape"? As it happened, I had a roll of metal "speed tape" and the traffic cone was firmly "glued" to the leading edge of the wing. "Well John," I said, "that will safely get you back to Elstree." "Oh no," said John, "I am going up to the Shetland Islands from here, then I am having a week in Ireland – it's got a bit more flying to do before I get back to Elstree." And so it was, and John was entirely responsible for modifying a traffic cone into a leading edge of an aircraft wing – and highly successful it was!'

2 Philip Meeson's DH 89A Rapide was built in 1944 and entered service with the RAF before being sold to BEA. Initially used on the Highland and Islands services it was named 'Sir Kier Hardie'. The aircraft finished its days with BEA operating the Scilly Isles services where it was renamed 'Lord Baden Powell'. This was the last Rapide to be operated by BEA. The aircraft has been overhauled and returned to her original livery and is now called 'Jemma Meeson', after Philip's daughter.

1

the life of the Air Traffic Controller as dozens of aircraft requested permission to leave at once. Eventually the tarmac was cleared without mishap.

The Guests of Honour were Philippe Cotrel (Mayor of Le Touquet), Prince Faisal and Princess Alia of Jordan, and the Squadron's old friend Colonel-General Nikolai Antoshkin, Commander-in-Chief of the Combat Air Forces of the Russian Federation, who, thanks to the generosity of Bruno Schroder, was flown first class from Moscow with an interpreter and minder to play a full and enthusiastic part in the celebrations. On the last day, Micky Suffolk offered to fly him over to his home in Wiltshire for dinner. Antoshkin readily agreed, and a second minder was dispatched from the London Embassy to meet them. They were escorted to the cellars after dinner and shared a bottle of Russian Kümmel, its label bearing the coat of arms of Tsar Nicholas II and the date 1912. The proceedings became much less formal after that, and even the minder began to relax. The only tricky moment came the next day at Gatwick Airport, when Micky Suffolk had to explain to Customs and Immigration how a Russian Air Force General came to be leaving the country without having officially entered it.

In 1997 came the great trip to Pakistan, which is agreed by those who took part to have been 'the best ever'. The enormous challenge was matched by extraordinary rewards. Even for people who are regularly privileged to enjoy spectacular visions of the earth's beauty, this was something exceptional. Magnificently vast and wild, the valleys of the Karakoram and the Hindu Kush are unforgettably engraved on the memories of all who flew there. Even John Houlder, who takes everything in his stride, allowed himself a moment of lyricism. 'Difficult flying? Not particularly. Either you know how to fly or you don't. If you do, the world is your oyster.'

Questions about the future size, activities and constitution of the Air Squadron began to be raised

in the late 1990s. There was a time of intense self-scrutiny as the Committee put together a petition for the grant of the title 'Royal'. After much careful redrafting this was submitted by Robin Braybrooke. The reply from Robert Fellowes, dated 2 July 1996, was as follows: 'I am afraid that Her Majesty's Ministers have advised The Queen that it does not at present qualify for the title "Royal" in such a way as to enable Ministers to give positive advice to The Queen. Ministers have said, however, that recent events and initiatives over the last ten years lead them to believe that the Squadron might meet the criteria at some time in the future. By these recent events and activities they mean those such as the sponsored activities for the Air Squadron Trophy and the Sir John Thomson Memorial Sword. I suggest that you and I should keep in touch about the activities undertaken by the Squadron in the next two or three years so that, should the right moment arise, a further application can be made which can be passed to Ministers.'

Peter Vanneck, who knew Palace procedures well, thought this was a standard rebuff, designed to filter out the half-hearted. He was in favour of endowing more flying scholarships and applying again in two years' time. For one reason or another his advice was not followed, and the matter has lain there ever since.

One positive result of the application was that it stimulated Hugh Astor to write an account of the early days of the Air Squadron. From this it is clear that Anthony Cayzer originated the idea – a detail that would certainly have been forgotten, and has only come to light as a result of researches for the present book.

By 1997, most of the very early members had died or ceased to play an active role. Peter Vanneck and Hugh Astor themselves died within two months of each other in the summer of 1999 – both saluted with multiple obituaries in the newspapers and remembered with love and admiration by all who knew them. Of the nine founding members, only John Houlder and Caryll Waterpark were still flying and actively involved.

Shortly before the Winter Dinner of 1999, Caryll Waterpark circulated a letter to members asking them to consider the future. 'From an aviating Drinking Club to the pre-eminent international Flying Squadron in thirty-five years is not bad going,' he remarked; but there was a 'down side'. 'The Air Squadron arguably reached its peak in Pakistan and now faces crises of identity and direction'. He pressed the case for younger members, more pressurised aircraft, more serving RAF officers, a new Executive Committee, new rules of election, and, for the first time, a formally appointed Chairman. Most of these suggestions were readily accepted, including his recommendation for Chairman: Christopher Sharples, 'who meets all the qualifications (young, good looking, slim of waist, a member of the Royal Yacht Squadron, but above all a passionate aviator of both helicopters and fixed wing).' He might have added 'a first class manager, who listens to others, thinks strategically and stays calm in a crisis'.

1 Viktor Bondarenko's parents were musicians in the Red Army who defected to the West in 1947. In 1965 Viktor started his own business in Germany, which eventually became the main transport contractor for NATO in Europe. He owes his success, he claims, to flying. 'An aeroplane was my first investment. The competition thought I was doomed to fail, but I was forced to work and be successful to pay for the aeroplane.' His English wife Lorraine shares the duties as Captain of their Challenger jet. When they met in 1972, she was teaching English to businessmen in Munich - an occupation of which she says, 'I much prefer the job of co-pilot.'

2 Susie Whitcombe, who joined the Air Squadron in 2007, pictured on the wing root of her Yak 50.

3 Catherine Day with Gilbert Greenall in Norway 2005. This trip to Scandinavia was Catherine's introduction to the Air Squadron and she was invited to join in 2006. Catherine got her PPL in 1994 at home in Northern Ireland and continues to fly whenever possible, whether piloting the Civil Service aircraft for travel to Europe on Government business, or paragliding in the Alps. In 2008, she moved to Kabul to work for the Foreign Office and joined the Flying Club of Afghanistan in the hope that, before the end of her posting, the club will be able to get a plane and operate it. She says that there is nothing like the perspective that flying gives people, which is badly needed today: "pilots understand something extra. It has to do with liberty and being above everything. It makes them look further and wider than other people, and it gives them a gentle twinkle at the back of the eye".

4

4 Polly Vacher with her Piper Dakota, which she has flown solo around the world twice, as well as to every listed airfield in Britain, in aid of Flying Scholarships for the Disabled, a charity founded in memory of Douglas Bader. Polly learnt to fly at the age of 50, having worked as a music teacher all her life. An extract from her book *Wings Around the World* can be found in Chapter 6.

These abilities were to prove crucial in the coming years, particularly in the months before the South African adventure in 2003. Christopher remained Chairman until 2005, when he handed over to Michael Graydon.

The organisation had always kept a low public profile, carefully managed by Simon Ames, who knew the good and bad sides of the press from long professional experience. In 1999, Bill Hall created the Air Squadron website (www.airsquadron. org). This was a significant new move. 'We decided to have it,' he says, 'because it gave us a corporate image. It helped when we wanted people to take us seriously. We were also trying to move people to email to reduce paperwork for the secretary.'

As the first official Air Squadron publication, the website has become a repository of information and pictures, both for members' and public consultation. When Phil Lever died in a gliding crash in July 2000, his diary of the millennium

tour of the USA was published on the website as a tribute. Reports by Sandrine Filippi of the trip to Pakistan, and Bill Hall and Christopher Sharples of South Africa, have provided an informal history of the Squadron's more spectacular recent activities.

In the summer of 2002, a survey was conducted to decide if ladies should be admitted as members. The decision was triggered by a conversation between Christopher Sharples and a pilot at Netheravon in 2001. 'She asked me how many lady members we had. I felt I had been placed on the spot. So I put it forward, not at a dinner where one good speech against it could kick it into touch, but in a letter to all the members. I had a lot of responses, and they were well-reasoned, not fuelled by post-prandial drinks.' Although objections were expected from some traditionalists, the idea was wholeheartedly accepted by a large majority. Typically robust was Adrian Swire's response: 'Whilst we would all need to listen carefully if there was a very strong minority against, I myself would welcome membership being open to ladies. What I would not favour would be some sort of half-way house, e.g. "Associate membership" for ladies. All or nothing.'

The first lady member was Dr Margaret Spittle, a consultant oncologist of worldwide repute. As the wife of David Hare, she had already taken part in many of the Squadron's flying trips, and had always felt welcome. It was, she said, a 'perfectly natural transition'. When she heard that Winter Dinners could no longer take place at White's, she offered not to attend. This gracious offer was declined by the Squadron, and a nostalgic farewell

1

1 Ireland, June 2008. The Squadron aircraft lined up in front of Castletown House, Co. Kilkenny, the home of George and Wendy Magan. The temporary landing strip is visible beyond the line of aircraft.

2 Montenegro, 2008. Michael Graydon exchanges gifts on board the training ship *Jadran* with the Montenegrin Chief of Staff, watched by senior naval officers.

3 To commemorate the 150th anniversary of the Charge of the Light Brigade, a group of Air Squadron members (Bill Hall, Maxi Gainza and Jonathan Elwes) flew to the Crimea where they were greeted as 'intrepid British Aviators' by the local media. With the colours of Lord Cardigan's 11th Hussars and the 4th Light Dragoons hitched to the Tiger Moth's wing struts, Jonathan flew low level down the 'Valley of Death'.

2

3

was said to the roast grouse, billiard tables and scarlet-walled dining room of White's.

After Margaret Spittle came Mic Mac Moss (daughter of Johnny, and a frequent participant in Squadron outings), Catherine Day (a high-powered young civil servant), Lorraine Bondarenko (co-captain of a Challenger jet with her husband Viktor), Susie Whitcombe (an artist as well as an accomplished pilot) and Polly Vacher, who has flown twice solo around the world and in the summer of 2007 landed at every British airfield in the Jeppesen's guide. Polly Vacher's record-breaking endeavours have all been carried out for the charity founded in memory of Douglas Bader, Flying Scholarships for the Disabled. The names of her many sponsors are written on the wings of her orange and black Piper Dakota aircraft, and she has recounted her extraordinary adventures in her book *Wings Around the World*.

In 1998 Christopher Sharples organised a visit to the Royal Yacht Squadron at Cowes, followed by a joint expedition with the RYS to the Western Isles of Scotland in June 1999. This turned out to be Peter Vanneck's final Squadron outing. Torquil Norman flew him to the Isle of Skye in his Dragonfly. 'The weather was lousy on the way home,' he recalls, 'and Peter said he couldn't have enjoyed the flight more! I felt very lucky to have had a week with him so near the end of his life.'

There followed trips to Southern Spain and Morocco (1999), the USA (2000), Venice and Arnhem (2001), Epernay and Cognac (2002), the Isle of Man (2002 and 2005), South Africa (2003),

St Omer (2004), Norway and Sardinia (2005), Le Touquet (for a 40th anniversary party even more spectacular than the 30th), and Poland (2006), Scotland and Italy (2007), and Ireland and the Balkans (2008). As the trips became more ambitious, the secretariat was enhanced with the appointment of Karen Rutson as Administrative Assistant and Maureen Evans as book-keeper and accountant. Individual members also contributed as Trip Managers, responsible for planning itineraries, ground arrangements and finances. The ethos of well managed events with disciplined flying continued as strongly as ever.

The 40th anniversary at Le Touquet was a particularly memorable gathering; it was also an 80th birthday celebration for Caryll Waterpark. He was given a model of a Lake Amphibian aircraft and an enormous birthday cake with a girl inside. The Royal Air Force produced two Jaguars for the occasion, which stood among Squadron aeroplanes old and new on the airfield for all to admire. On Charles de Gaulle Day Michael Graydon took the salute at a commemoration service in the War Cemetery. It was, by general agreement, a superb show, brilliantly organised by Terry Holloway.

Among so many successful events there was only one that failed, yet even that was turned to advantage by a characteristic gesture of boldness. After much research and reconnaissance a sortie to the Crimea in 2004 was cancelled in the face of last-minute bureaucratic difficulties about the distribution of avgas in Ukraine. Refusing to be defeated, however, a hardy trio of members (Jonathan Elwes, Maxi Gainza and Bill Hall) set off the following year to retrace the Charge of the Light Brigade with a Tiger Moth trailing regimental banners through the sky, along the famous 'Valley of Death'. In an article for *East-West* magazine (2006), Maxi wrote, 'The Light Brigade took seven-and-a-half minutes to reach the guns and silence them, where it took us only one. A minute well worth the 4,500 miles, the 40 sectors and the 64 flying hours it took Jonathan and his Tiger to reach this far and return home.'

The Air Squadron's trips to the USA and South Africa were, like the tour of Pakistan, bold and exhilarating adventures, all three described in detail in the next chapter. Less ambitious, yet perhaps more historically fascinating, were the pilgrimages to Arnhem and St Omer. Arnhem was preceded by a visit to the Parachute Regiment at Netheravon, where members were trained in the art of falling safely from the sky by the Red Devils, in preparation for the annual commemorative drop over Holland from a Douglas DC3. James Scurr remembers the Arnhem jump as 'extremely moving. It was scary even when we did it, and an amazing learning experience actually to be there – much more powerful than just reading about it.' Martin Barraclough vividly describes both the training and the final jump in his book *Fifty Years Have Flown*. On the evening of 21st September 2001, the Squadron were guests of the Parachute Regiment at their Arnhem Dinner, where Winston Churchill presented General Sir Mike Jackson

with the Air Squadron Poignard. The next day at Soesterberg airfield, they were amazed to find several veterans of the 1944 battle dressed in orange overalls preparing to jump with them. Once inside their Dakota, they sat in tense, crowded rows on the floor, 'facing aft, the large double doors removed from the gaping rectangular hole in the side of the fuselage through which we would exit.' The engines started 'with a characteristic whine of the starter motor, a cough and a cloud of oil smoke', and they rumbled along the runway, gathering speed. As they left the ground, 'it was impossible not to think of all those thousands of young men fifty-seven years earlier who must have sat, more desperately encumbered than us, in row upon row of DC3s lining up and taking off for Arnhem.' The jump safely accomplished, there were battlefield tours, receptions, dinner. The next morning a service of remembrance was held in Oosterbeek cemetery, when '1,750 Dutch children – one for each soldier lying there – laid a bunch of flowers on every grave.'

A ceremony equally moving attended the unveiling of the British Air Services Memorial at St Omer on 11 September 2004. Many Air Squadron members had contributed to the £60,000 cost of the monument, 'in memory of members of the British Air Services and air forces from every part of the British Empire who served on the Western Front during the First World War 1914-1918'. St Omer had been the headquarters of the Royal Flying Corps in France, and over 50 of its squadrons had operated from there during

1

the course of the war. Standards of nine RAF Squadrons (including 16 Squadron, which was formed at St Omer) were paraded at the ceremony, which began with a flypast by a single Spitfire, followed by paired Jaguars and Mirages of the RAF and the French Air Force.

There were three visits to Italy in the years 2001-7. The first, to Venice for the 2001 Regata Storica, was organised by Tim Williams, who rows, builds and restores Venetian boats when he is not flying vintage aeroplanes. The Regata Storica is the city's biggest rowing event, with

crews in traditional costume racing to a finishing line on the Grand Canal. Tim took his fellow members to watch the action from an antique Venetian barge. He also arranged dinner in Palazzo Donà, a private dwelling whose décor includes lanterns from the Venetian flagship at the Battle of Lepanto in 1571, which was commanded by a member of the Donà family. The flight to Venice was marked by vicious thunderstorms over the Apennines, which will not readily be forgotten by those who were attempting to avoid them. Egidio Gavazzi was

2

3

1 Ralph Hubbard, jeweller and pilot, goes wing-walking. The Boeing Stearman is flown by fellow Air Squadron member Vic Norman, who keeps six of these biplanes at Rendcombe in Gloucestershire. Vic obtained his PPL at age 17 and studied aeronautical engineering in London. He met Patrick Lindsay racing vintage cars, bought a biplane and became a keen aerobatic pilot, performing professionally at air displays. He saw an opening for a British wing-walking act and in 1987 bought and modified the Stearmans, which now do 80-100 displays per season.

2 Torquil Norman in his 1936 de Havilland DH90 Dragonfly. This aircraft, one of only two left in the world, was bought as a wreck in South Africa in 1979 by Tony Haig-Thomas and Martin Barraclough, and rebuilt in England. Sold in 1982, it went to the USA. In 1992 Torquil found it as a wreck again in St. Louis, Missouri and returned it to the UK for rebuilding. Henry Labouchere and he then flew the aircraft to the US in 1995 and back to the UK in 1996 via the Greenland ice cap and Iceland.

3 Martin Barraclough's route to Venice in August 2001.

flying a fabric-covered aircraft and wondering how much of it (or its pilot) would be left if he encountered hail. Martin Barraclough, in a group of ancient aeroplanes from England, took a long southern detour in the face of 'jagged lightning and impenetrable walls of rain and black cloud'. After passing Florence they searched for a way through the Apennines, but 'valley after valley seemed to end, not in clear air, but a dark forbidding confluence of mountain and cloud.' Finally Torquil Norman in his Dragonfly saw a letterbox of light, and they followed him through it to the north.

In 2005, the Squadron was invited by Viktor and Lorraine Bondarenko for a two-day party at their villa in Sardinia. The invitation was simply for 'a pizza', which struck one guest as a rather odd pretext for a thousand-mile flight – until the wood-fired bread oven, staffed by a pair of excellent Sardinian chefs, began turning out 'the most unbelievably delicious pizzas you have ever tasted'. Yachts, friends, and the turquoise sea in bright summer weather did the rest.

By 2007, the Italian trips were becoming extremely popular. Seventy-five members and guests flew to Siena in September that year for a programme that included the first Air Squadron wedding – Roddy Blois and Celeste Goschen sharing their nuptials in the packed chapel at Il Borro with the entire touring party. With the wise words of the Vicar of Tuscany ringing in their ears, the guests spilled out into the tiny medieval square, toasted the happy couple with champagne, and strolled down to lunch at the Osteria. For some members, Il Borro is a place full of memories. A rambling hilltop village, linked to a great house and vineyards by a long stone bridge, it is now owned by Ferruccio Ferragamo, son of the celebrated Hollywood shoe-maker and head of a great Italian design firm. In former days the estate belonged to Duke Amedeo d'Aosta, who rented a house for many years to Egidio Gavazzi, and used to welcome Desmond and Torquil Norman, Tim Williams, Henry Labouchere and the King of Romania to its crumbling splendour every summer. Looking around the Ferragamo winery, with its

1

1 Roddy Blois in his Cessna 172F built in 1967 and recently re-engined with a 180hp engine to give dramatic STOL performance. Roddy has represented the UK in all World Championships in Precision Flying since 1987.

2 Celeste Goschen on the day of her wedding with Roddy Blois, Il Borro, Tuscany, on 10th September 2007.

stainless steel fermenting tanks, its amphitheatre for fashion shows, smart secretaries, cool modern offices and immaculately restored brickwork, Henry remarked, 'This chap must have spent zillions doing it up. I can hardly believe it's the same place.'

The next day there was a choice of visits: the Italian Air Force Museum at Vigna di Valle near Rome, or the Frescobaldi vineyard at Castelgiocondo. Both parties returned to Siena convinced that they had made the better choice. Martin Gosling had other things on his mind. He was about to take off from Celsetta near Rome when his engine started rattling strangely and he had to abandon the flight. Bill Hall got the distress call when he reached Siena and flew straight back to pick him and his passengers up. Two days later, after flying

north to Milan and borrowing the Como Aero Club's float planes for some scenic local flights, the visitors were entertained to lunch by Bianca and Gerolamo Gavazzi, brother of Egidio, on their island in the middle of Lake Bosisio. A keen pilot and environmentalist like his brother, Gerolamo had created a wildlife sanctuary on the island. He had spent years campaigning to clean up the waters and shores of the lake, ridding it of industrial and agricultural pollution, water-skiing and other intrusions. True to the family's lineage as silk-makers, no trace of his political struggles was evident in the suave and relaxed host that greeted the party as they stepped off the boat, showed them around the delightful little house, and welcomed them to a magnificent lunch in the shaded gardens behind.

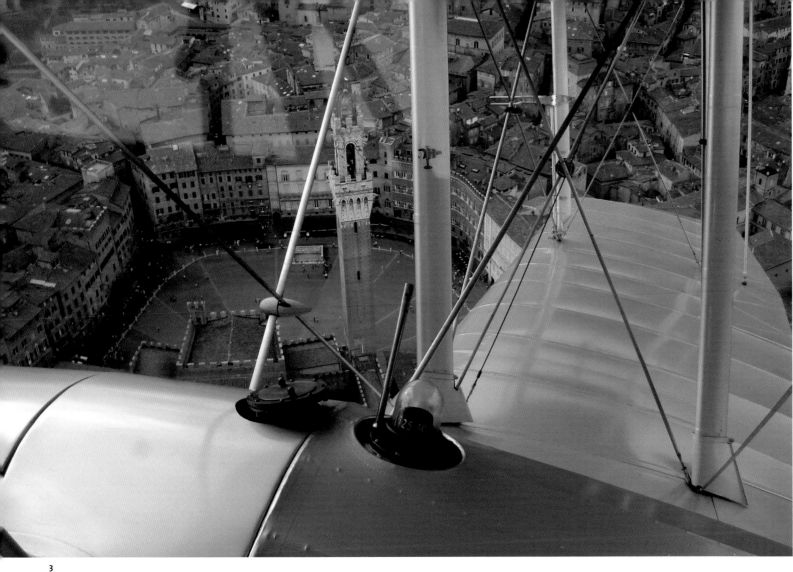

3 Siena's 14th century Campo and the Torre del Mangia photographed from Torquil Norman's DH Dragon, September 2007.

4 Tim Clark (left) and Jonathan Elwes at Siena airport, September 2007. Tim Clark, a lawyer in the City of London, learned to fly at Denham in 1995 and bought a Beech Baron which he uses regularly for visits to Italy. On his first trip with the Air Squadron, to RAF Brüggen in May 2000, he was asked to give a lift to four senior RAF officers. 'I thought this has got to be good... I landed heavily, but they were very nice about it.'

The following day was spent on Lake Como, with a steamer ride to the house and gardens of Villa Balbianello, home of the pipe-smoking explorer and mountaineer Guido Monzino, who bequeathed the place to the F.A.I., the Italian equivalent of the National Trust. The views across the lake to the mountains of Switzerland proved irresistible to Susie Whitcombe, who set up her easel on a terrace and began sketching the scene in oils. As the party sailed back to Cernobbio through golden afternoon light, they heard that Paolo, a third flying Gavazzi brother, was performing an impressive aerobatic display over a different steamer on the lake, which he had mistaken for the Air Squadron's vessel. His show was described to an appreciative and amused group by mobile

1   Italy 2007. In an RV8 over Tuscany, Marcus de Ferranti (front) and Julian Stinton (rear). Marcus spent 10 years in the RAF as a Jaguar and Harrier fighter ground attack and reconnaissance pilot. He is currently a Hawk pilot on contract to the Royal Navy training Naval Air Defences. Julian Stinton flew Phantoms and the Tornado F3 in the air defence role, was a tactics instructor on Hawks, and went on to run squadrons and stations with a staff exchange tour in Washington. He had operational roles in both Gulf Wars and in 2007 was appointed Air Commodore in charge of the Air Warfare Centre.

2   Tim Williams on the Air Squadron trip to Italy which he organised with Egidio Gavazzi in 2007. Tim gained his PPL in 1970 and bought a Jackaroo, G-APAM, in pieces in 1974, which he rebuilt and flew, then converted back to a Tiger Moth in 1987. He bought a 1930 Puss Moth, G-AAZP, in 1981, which he rebuilt, then flew to Australia in 1984 with Henry Labouchere. In recent years he has raised over £100,000 for SSAFA closely aided by Valentine Lindsay, Robs Lamplough and Marcus de Ferranti.

telephone. That night at dinner in the Villa d'Este, a new Air Squadron headscarf was launched (design by Maxi Gainza, silk by Ferragamo), and the Gavazzi brothers were presented with gifts from a grateful Air Squadron, enchanted by their delightful stay. Notable among the gifts were four bottles of Bruno Schroder's 'flying whisky' from Islay.

The vintage aircraft group (Torquil Norman, Henry Labouchere, Casey Norman, Tim Williams and Martin Barraclough) flew home the next morning in pellucid weather, their transit over the Alps captured in a series of glittering images by the 'paparazzo' Barraclough.

Despite the obvious success of the trip, Egidio Gavazzi, who had organised it all with Tim Williams, confessed that he found the experience 'nightmarish': there were so many choices to make, so many hotel rooms to book, so many things to go wrong. 'Thank heavens for Tim, who does these things magnificently.' In fact there had been a certain amount of unintended comedy, with

buses sent to the wrong places or leaving at the wrong times, but the general opinion was it had all worked superbly.

The Italian press noted the Squadron's presence in an article entitled 'Carriages of the Sky' (*Carozze del Cielo*) by Gianemilio Mazzolini for *Style* magazine: 'Where is the gentleman driver in his tweed jacket who is not happy going for a run in an open Jaguar in the rain? Transfer this concept to the sky and one has a gentleman pilot.'

In 2005 the Squadron flew to Scandinavia on a trip organised by Suzanne Maltzahn, whose family entertained the visitors lavishly in Denmark. Much of the flying was below the cloudbase of 500 feet, but with excellent visibility. Going on to Norway, the weather deteriorated. Alex Norman, who flew with Michael Graydon in John Scurr's Cessna 172, remembers 'fighting our way up fjords, trying to read the GPS, and telling Mike "It'll be a left turn around this mountain and a right turn around the next one, and don't go below 200 feet because

3

4

3 Susie Whitcombe sketches Lake Como and the Swiss mountains during the Air Squadron visit in 2007.

4 Lake Como, September 2007. Paula White (left) and Luisa Miguens Bemberg model the new Air Squadron *foulard* designed by Maxi Gainza and manufactured by Ferragamo.

there appears to be an outcrop in the middle of the fjord." It was fairly bracing stuff. And I have to say that within about four and a half minutes it became apparent why Mike is an Air Chief Marshal and I'm not. He's a brilliant pilot and a complete fanatic. Whereas my tendency is to drift along and look out of the window, much as I used to when I was a tank commander in the army, forever getting lost, Mike always has an eye on the instrument panel, tweaking or adjusting the mixture or the heading. In eight days of flying I only twice saw him look up and say, "Well, Alex, this is rather good, isn't it?"'

The really 'bracing stuff' happened to Christopher Sharples and Johnny Moss, whose engine failed over the sea as they approached the coast of Norway – a nightmare for pilots and their passengers, as Gaynor Llewellyn vividly remembers:

BANG! Clunk! Rattle! Rattle!
The engine had suddenly decided it was giving up the ghost.

'Pan Pan Pan… N656JM…Cessna 182 partial engine failure en route Odense/Oslo- IFR –Flight level seven zero (7,000ft) unable to maintain altitude, losing 400 ft per minute,' Johnny alerts Oslo Approach. Christopher is at the controls and looking directly ahead. He lifts the nose tenderly as his instinct tells him that this will slow our speed but also our descent. The sea looks cold and choppy, but still some way below. Our descent eases to 200 ft a minute, but we have 30 miles of icy water to cross and our speed is down by a third. The engine is signalling its death throes.

'Gayns have you the Epirb (Emergency Personal Indicating Radio Beacon) in your hand? Do you know how it works?'

'Yes,' I reply while quickly reading directions: 'Pull down yellow sliding tab, pull out red clip'. Easy. At least they will know where we are when we hit the water.

'Gayns, roll up some coats and place them between us.'
From the rear luggage compartment, I wrestle

1

1 Italy 2007. John Hutchinson and Tim Williams go ashore after a flight in one of the Como Aero Club's float planes.

3 Italy 2007. Tim Williams flying home in his Puss Moth through the Alps.

2 Egidio Gavazzi in his Yak 9. One of four flying brothers from an old silk-making family in Monza, Egidio is a vintage warplane enthusiast and the founder of Italy's leading wildlife photography magazine, *Airone*.

2

3

to extract the coats that can be used as cushions to protect the two pilots when we impact the water. I notice the small hatch door in the rear. An alternative exit for me if Christopher or Johnny blocks my route out of the front side door.

Oslo Approach: 'Please change your frequency. A helicopter will be with you shortly. A lifeboat has been sent to intercept your course. Divert course 15 degrees west to Torpe. All other aircraft are being advised. Let us know when you sight land. We have an alternative landing site available.'

Silence except for the awful sound of metal grinding against metal from the engine. Johnny is flicking back and forth through the manual on his knee; now and again he lifts his head to view the dials – not so easy as they are vibrating like a pneumatic drill – or to remove his headset a fraction to listen to the engine. Christopher seems motionless with a steady hand on the controls. The Cessna is almost in a glide as it continues to struggle forwards with the propeller turning inconsequentially and sounding more dead-beat every minute.

By now I am sitting on the bare metal seat with the cushion in front of me for impact protection. The helicopter has arrived and is tailing us at a short distance. There is still no sign of land and the sea seems closer than before. But the Air Sea Rescue helicopter is now flying alongside. I can see the pilot giving a wave. That cheers me up.

Thank goodness Johnny insisted we wore immersion suits. Not the most flattering or comfortable with their tight necks, floppy feet and

1 The Air Squadron in Norway, 2005. Left to right: the local guide, Christopher Sharples, Suzanne Maltzahn, David Hare, Bruno Schroder, Margaret Hare, Bill Hall, Gilbert Greenall, Annette Gosling, Catherine Day, Terry Holloway, Martin Gosling, Gaynor Llewellyn.

2 Serious business, flying... Gaynor Llewellyn enjoys the elegance of a survival suit, while Johnny Moss is not at all amused. In fact they were to come perilously close to ditching in the sea off Oslo when their engine failed in mid-flight.

3 Cousins Alex Norman (left) and Casey Norman at RFC Rendcombe with G-AGEG, a DH82 Tiger Moth, built in 1940. Alex is the son of Desmond Norman, the aircraft designer, who was one of the earliest members of the Air Squadron. After Sandhurst and the Army, Alex became Defence Correspondent of *The Spectator*, and has since written a series of books about the Dalai Lamas of Tibet. While continuing to fly and write he has recently completed a degree in Philosophy and Theology at Oxford. Casey, son of Torquil Norman, flew a Cessna 182 from Gloucestershire to Sydney with David Ponte in 1996. He now runs Genie Toys plc in Cheltenham.

1

stiff canvas; hot too, so we only have underwear underneath, but essential. To think we nearly didn't bother. We laughed so much as we struggled into them. We're not laughing now.

My mind begins to wander forwards to what may happen. If we survive we'll need a mobile. As Christopher's has all the contact numbers I choose his and slip it silently down my front inside my suit. All zipped up we wait. An outward calmness of concentration envelops us.

'Land!'

We can see a good sized runway some 9 miles in front of us. We are now at 2000 ft, travelling at 80 knots. The engine is still banging away and the oil temperature is rising and the pressure dropping. But we might just make it.

We are making so much noise that the fire brigade, who are on alert and alongside the runway, have already heard us. We continue to edge along the east side of the airfield continuing our slow descent. I realise the engine could stop at any time. It seems like ages but then comes the comforting contact with the runway. As we throttle back the windscreen is immediately enveloped in black oil and then the engine stops. We are

met by the fire brigade. Relief all round. (I learn later that there is only a 30% chance of surviving a ditching in the sea…)

A few of the party flew to Spitzbergen on midsummer's day, which Catherine Day recalls as an extraordinary, at times terrifying, experience. She was co-pilot in Gilbert Greenall's Cessna 182, which was starting to sound ragged after 500 miles over the sea from Norway. They decided to approach the airport over the land, 'not a brilliant idea' as their GPS gave no information north of 70 degrees, and they found themselves flying in cloud with no idea of the height of the land below. Things got worse when the wings started icing up and they had to descend. 'We were lucky not to hit a mountain. You take strange decisions after five hours in the air.'

When they came out of the cloud they saw 'a vast landscape in a magic orange-yellow light that seemed to come from all over the sky. There were no trees at all. I've never seen anything like it.' They spent two nights in Longyearbyen, which felt 'like an outback town, with reindeer in the streets and blonde girls carrying huge Mausers in case of polar bears,' then joined the main party for the return flight south.

2

3

In 2006, the Squadron visited Poland, with the aim of paying tribute to the Polish Air Force for their part in the Battle of Britain. Jonathan Elwes organised the trip, having visited the country several times and flown across in his Tiger Moth in 1989 (a journey described in his book *Glasmoth*).

The Air Squadron's tour began with a symbolic gesture: Robs Lamplough would fly his Spitfire over Warsaw accompanied by two Polish Air Force MiG 29s. On subsequent days, there would be a wreath-laying ceremony at the Polish Air Force memorial, the presentation of a Sword of Friendship to Lt-General Stanislaw Targosz, Commander of the Polish Air Force, visits to the aviation academy and museum at Deblin, flights with 13 Squadron (transport) and tours of the monuments and salt mines of Krakow, including a visit to Auschwitz.

On the first day, 5th September, the fly-in by the Spitfire and two escorting MiGs ran into formidable difficulties. The weather was wet and violently windy. Robs Lamplough's GPS went down after he took off from Berlin, forcing him to navigate with map, stopwatch and compass. Then

the Spitfire's propeller sprang a leak and sprayed the canopy in a thick brown slick of oil. Robs tried opening the canopy, was splashed in the face with oil and quickly shut it again. He then flew the aircraft by looking through a side quarter pane. Of the two MiG pilots, only one spoke English, and his radio failed just as the three planes met outside Warsaw. On the ground, Maxi Gainza stood under an umbrella, running a substitute radio service between Robs, the MiGs and the control tower on his mobile phone. Yet the three aircraft appeared over the airfield exactly on time, and the Spitfire made a perfect landing.

Ceremonies followed, flights with the Polish Air Force (fast, low level, and brilliantly executed), and many a glass of vodka. If Pakistan bears the palm for the most exciting long trip, Poland seems to be the favourite among the shorter ones. Like all the Air Squadron's sorties there were moving moments, there were difficult moments, and there were moments of comedy. Alex Norman, flying his uncle Torquil's Tiger Moth, found himself butting into a ferocious headwind between Deblin and Warsaw with a broken radio and low supplies of

1

2

1, 3 The mountains of Spitzbergen, which presented an unexpected hazard when the GPS was found not to cover territory so far north.

2 The approach to Svalbard, Spitzbergen, 800 NM north of Norway's North Cape. .

3

fuel. He decided to turn back rather than risk a forced landing, and had to work his way round an air display at Deblin before landing. He was immediately invited to dinner in the officers' mess by a General of the Polish Air Force. 'Before dinner we had several vodka toasts – first to Polish-British Friendship, then the Friendship of the Air, then the Friendship of the Polish Air Force and the Air Squadron, then the Friendship of the Royal Air Force and the Polish Air Force, then the Ladies of the Air Squadron, and then All the Ladies of the World! The room was full of high-ranking officers, all celebrating a successful inspection. I promised the General a flight in the Tiger Moth the next morning at nine, but luckily it rained until noon. I couldn't have walked in a straight line to my bedroom door at that time of the morning, never mind flown the Tiger Moth.'

Aftewards, Martin Barraclough and Jonathan Elwes assembled a handsome photographic record of the trip. This was subsequently printed and bound. A copy was despatched to Poland, where it was placed in the Chamber of Honour of the Air Force Headquarters in Warsaw. The Commander of the Polish Air Force, Lt-General Andrzej Blasik, in a letter of thanks to Jonathan Elwes, wrote of the 'very close and great relationship between the Air Squadron and Polish Air Force.' With touching grace he added, 'We would like to stay with this friendship forever.'

Chapter 4 Intercontinental

K2, the world's second highest mountain
(28,251 ft) - final destination of the Air Squadron
mission to Pakistan in 1997.

Intercontinental

The Air Squadron's proudest flying achievement is, by common consent, the five overseas trips that took place between 1994 and 2003, to Jordan, Tanzania, Pakistan, the USA and South Africa. Bold in conception, meticulous in planning, all involved a large group of light aircraft flying to distant places over wild and inhospitable parts of the earth.

Although many pilots make such journeys, the distinctive style of the Air Squadron is to combine adventure with diplomacy. In their bags they carry a dinner jacket as well as a survival suit.

The appeal of these journeys lies in the challenge – physical and mental. Mark Thomson, whose youth was spent landing fast jets on aircraft carriers at night (one of the most lethal forms of aviation yet devised), enjoyed flying across the North Atlantic in a very small aeroplane because it took him 'off the map', into untried areas of experience. Gilbert Greenall sees the long journeys as a way of 'sharpening focus', living in the moment, refusing to 'discount the present for the future'. Others speak of adventure, discovery, risk, new friendships, Zen-like states of awareness, and mental purification: flying clears the mind like nothing else.

The pioneer of these trips was Caryll Waterpark, himself an aviator of limitless appetite. He had dreamed for years of shaking his fellow members out of their comfortable routine of social jaunts around Europe. As the new millennium approached – a time of bold resolutions, grand gestures and once-in-a-lifetime celebrations – he must have felt the golden moment had come.

These epics did not spring fully formed from his brain. There were several prototypes. Experiments were made, details were adjusted, until the mix of group and solo, planned and improvised, good works and adventure, was just right. A brief survey of these prototypes will form a useful prelude to the main story.

2

1

2

BRAZIL (1984)

In 1974 the Piper Aircraft Corporation began using the Brazilian state manufacturer Embraer to build their Navajos and Senecas under licence. When Piper offered these to CSE Aviation for sale in Europe, Caryll Waterpark flew to Brazil to look at the factories. He saw Embraer's own first production aircraft, the Bandeirante, and was at once impressed. 'It was a lovely plane, beautifully designed, natural to fly, safe and very strong.' He bought one on the spot. It was not long before he was selling the Bandeirante, and its successor the Xingu, in very large numbers. (Piper, he recalls, were 'furious'.)

In 1984 he was attempting to persuade the Royal Air Force to buy Embraer's latest creation, the T-27 Tucano trainer. This was a long and tricky campaign, with a fellow Air Squadron member, Desmond Norman, contending for the same contract with the Britten-Norman Firecracker. Caryll Waterpark sensed an opportunity for some behind-the-scenes PR work. 'I went to Colonel Ozires Silva [the Chairman of Embraer] and said, "Look, if you can arrange a VIP visit by this funny little organization that I belong to, it will probably be of benefit." At the same time I approached Britain's ambassador to Brazil. He was very keen. I knew then that every door would be opened.'

So it proved. On April 7th the Air Squadron group (consisting of Caryll and and Daniele Waterpark, Hugh and Emi-Lu Astor, Bruno Schroder, Angus Hamilton, Charles Chelsea, David Constable Maxwell, Patrick Lindsay,

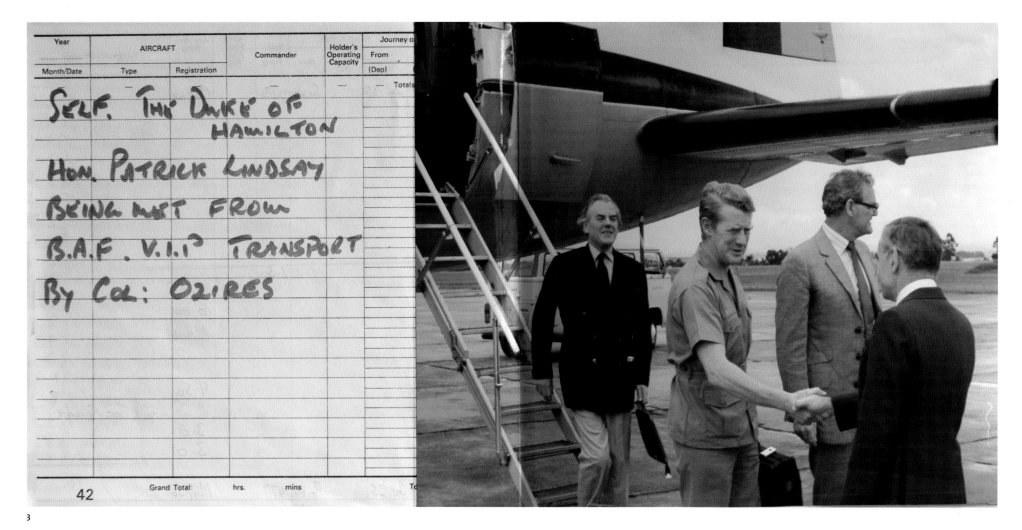

Year	AIRCRAFT		Commander	Holder's Operating Capacity	Journey o_
Month/Date	Type	Registration			From (Dep)
	—	—	—	—	Totals

SELF. THE DUKE OF
 HAMILTON

HON. PATRICK LINDSAY

BEING MET FROM

B.A.F. V.I.P TRANSPORT

BY COL: OZIRES

42   Grand Total: hrs.   mins   To_

3

1 Gilbert Greenall with his Cessna 182. Gilbert is a doctor who specialises in disaster relief for the United Nations. He also farms in Herefordshire and Somerset. An active Squadron member, he has taken part in trips to Russia, Pakistan, USA, South Africa, Norway and Poland.

2 Mark Thomson in Italy, 2007. Mark Thomson is an ex-Fleet Air Arm pilot, and an energetic Committee member.

3 Brazil 1984, from Caryll Waterpark's logbook. The Chairman of Embraer, Colonel Ozires, greeting Angus Hamilton, Patrick Lindsay (on steps) and Caryll Waterpark.

David Checketts, Ossie and Patsy King, Thomas Noel, Ian Macpherson and John Bagge) flew with British Caledonian Airways from London to Rio de Janeiro. They spent a day in Rio, then flew to São Jose dos Campos for a tour of Embraer and a chance to fly the Tucano. Angus Hamilton was curious to try the new aircraft, and climbed in with Embraer's pilot. After about twenty minutes of flight, they went into 'an aerobatic sequence involving several flick manoeuvres (entered below 110 knots) and several zero-G manoeuvres'. They suddenly lost all throttle response. The Brazilian pilot took over, lowered the undercarriage and made an emergency landing in a paddy field. As the wheels ploughed into the soft earth, the nose undercarriage broke and the aircraft somersaulted forward. They had

a tense few minutes in the cockpit, suspended head down in live ejection seats, until locals came and dug them out.

Meanwhile a presidential banquet had started. Thomas Noel remembers the scene vividly:

'A corporal came rushing across the tarmac looking very nervous. He whispered into the President's ear something we couldn't hear. The President put both hands on the table and drew himself slowly up to the normal "I am going to make a very serious speech" pose. He said in very poor English, "Your Royal Excellencies! Honourable Air Squadron! I am sorry to announce, there has been an unfortunate ACCIDENT! Excellency Royal Duke Hamilton has crashed our beloved prototype! Not his fault, our pilot is an imbecile. He will be dealt with accordingly."

1

1   Angus Hamilton on his airstrip at
Archerfield, east of Edinburgh. The Hamiltons
are a strong aviation family. Angus was in the
RAF and later a test pilot. His father was one of
the first to fly over Mount Everest in the 1920s
when he was in the RAF.

2   Colonel-General Nikolai Antoshkin,
Commander-in-Chief of the Combat Air Forces
of the Russian Federation, who welcomed the
Air Squadron to Moscow in 1992.

'Meanwhile the Brazilian pilot had been taken to hospital. When he heard this, Hugh Astor, who had a very slow grand English accent, stood up and said, "Gosh, Mr President, how simply ghastly! Poor chap. Can we visit him in hospital, perhaps with some gift, or grapes or something?"

'The Brazilian Joint Chiefs of Staff looked puzzled by this remark. At this point Angus came stumbling across the tarmac looking as if he had just done the whole of the Battle of Britain single-handed. With blood pouring from his forehead he mumbled, "Anyone got a drink?"

'"Oh lord," said Patrick Lindsay. "Here we go."'

When he had recovered Angus Hamilton wrote a brief report on the incident and no more was said – until a few weeks later, when Caryll Waterpark met Prince Philip, who remarked, 'There are less than two dozen Dukes in the United Kingdom and I hear you have been trying to kill one of them!'

The following day they went on to Brasilia, where the British Ambassador, John Ure, hosted an official dinner. He said afterwards that he had never before managed to bring together so many Brazilian Government Ministers for a social occasion.

The party next boarded the President's Vickers Viscount for a flight to the Air Force Academy at Pirassununga (São Paulo), where they were able to admire, among other things, a reliquary containing the heart of the aviation pioneer Alberto Santos-Dumont. After a display by the Air Force aerobatic team, the *Esquadrilha de Fumaça* or Smoke Squadron, they flew back to Rio, where a farewell party marked the end of an exhilarating week. Whether or not the Air Squadron's visit played a part in the British Government's decision to buy the Tucano, it certainly provided an amusing outing. It was to be a model, in several ways, for more ambitious sorties to come.

2

RUSSIA (1992)

In August 1992, using contacts between John Thomson (then C-in-C Strike Command) and senior officers in Russia, a visit was engineered to Moscow and St Petersburg. This was to include visits to Russian Air Force bases and low flights over territory that had been hidden from western eyes for the past 75 years. Although old enemies were now officially friends, the Russians still insisted on placing their own military navigators on board the visitors' planes. Caryll Waterpark, riding in Micky Suffolk's Piper Aztec with Michael Beetham, had equipped himself with British 'bombing maps' of Russia which were, he says, 'remarkably accurate'. After stopping in Vilnius to pick up their Russian navigator, they flew

on towards Moscow, following his instructions politely. It was not long before the navigator noticed that they had no need of his help. He looked piqued for a moment or two, then threw his map over his shoulder.

Their host in Moscow was Colonel-General Nikolai Antoshkin, a hero of the Chernobyl disaster of 1986. Antoshkin had led a team that dropped thousands of tons of sand by helicopter onto the burning nuclear reactor. Their action had stopped the fire, but all his fellow aircrew had subsequently died from radiation poisoning. Antoshkin himself needed regular blood transfusions to stay alive.

A brass band played as the Air Squadron landed in Moscow, and the Russian genius for high spirits quickly took hold. The hospitality was spectacular. Even the Minister of Defence, Pavel Grachev, allowed his enthusiasm to get the better of him. He was inspecting the Squadron's aeroplanes when he noticed that Robs Lamplough's P-51 Mustang had a jump seat in the back. He at once invited himself in for a ride. His two KGB minders, standing on the wings, thought this a very poor idea; it looked too much like a kidnap attempt. The Minister told Lamplough to ignore them and start the engine, which he did, blowing one of the minders off the wing as he opened up. The other dutifully held on, braving scorched trousers from the exhaust, until Grachev leaned out and punched him. As he fell to the ground, Robs moved off, but decided, in view of the low cloud, driving rain and angry KGB officers,

1

2

that a flight was too risky. He took the Minister for a fast taxi round the airfield instead, making him 'a very happy man'.

The friendliness of the Russians amazed everyone. Michael Beetham recalls: 'I really knew nothing of the Russians until then. We had held official meetings in Berlin in 1976: all very formal and polite. They gave us a case of vodka, we gave them a case of whisky. I remember asking one of them on that occasion where he went on holiday; you could see the shutters come down at once. It was impossible to hold a personal conversation. This time it was completely different. They were marvellous hosts, charming, with a good sense of humour, and very open. I wondered, *How on earth did we ever think of fighting this lot?*'

Visits to Air Force bases, and discussions with the personnel, revealed that the Russians were in quite serious difficulties: they had trouble recruiting and retaining staff, maintenance programmes had lapsed (peeling paint and deflated tyres were much in evidence), and, thanks to the break-up of the Soviet Union, their nuclear bombers were all stuck in the Ukraine. Not mentioned, but soon discovered, was the poor quality of Russian aviation gasoline, which was to cause spluttering engines and anxious moments over the coming days.

Yet the trip as a whole was a tremendous success. Bill Hall remembers skimming along the Moscow-St Petersburg railway line at 100 feet, which no Englishman could have done for the past 50 years or more. Gilbert Greenall

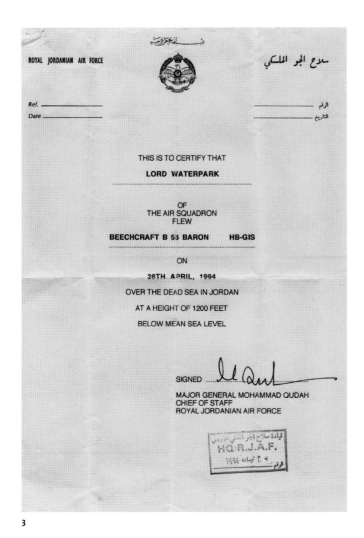

ROYAL JORDANIAN AIR FORCE

سلاح الجو الملكي

Ref. _____
Date _____

الرقم
التاريخ

THIS IS TO CERTIFY THAT

LORD WATERPARK

OF
THE AIR SQUADRON
FLEW

BEECHCRAFT B 53 BARON   HB-GIS

ON

28TH APRIL, 1994

OVER THE DEAD SEA IN JORDAN

AT A HEIGHT OF 1200 FEET

BELOW MEAN SEA LEVEL

SIGNED ....

MAJOR GENERAL MOHAMMAD QUDAH
CHIEF OF STAFF
ROYAL JORDANIAN AIR FORCE

3

1 General Antoshkin's friend from the Bolshoi opera, Vera, who sang at the Metropol Hotel and on several bus trips for the Air Squadron visitors to Moscow.

2 Susanna Parry, Thomas Noel's guest on the trip to Jordan in 1994, gets airborne with the Red Arrows in Cyprus.

3 Flying below sea level: Caryll Waterpark's certificate from the Royal Jordanian Air Force testifies to an unusual feat.

was profoundly struck by the Russian style of drinking: 'They start in the traditional way with lavish toasts, and then drink till they're in a heap. Completely inert, every time!' Many others affectionately recall General Antoshkin's friend Vera, an operatic lady of great allure, singing Russian ballads at the farewell dinner in Moscow's Metropol Hotel.

Beyond the social and personal pleasures of the trip, however, there was a growing sense of the Air Squadron's potential for diplomacy. With aviation as a common interest, international friendships were being formed in the most surprising places. Such friendships lay beyond the reach of professional diplomats, yet helped them in their work. It was a good feeling. Members reflected on this with satisfaction, and hoped to build on it in years to come.

CYPRUS AND JORDAN (1994)

In the spring of 1994, at the invitation of King Hussein and the Royal Jordanian Air Force, the Air Squadron visited Amman. On the way, they called in at RAF Akrotiri, where the Red Arrows were rehearsing for the new season. Both invitations came through members serving in the RAF: John Thomson (who had shared a room as a cadet at Cranwell with the future Chief of the Jordanian Air Staff, Mohammed Qudah), and Simon Bostock, Commandant of the Central Flying School, who was also in charge of the Red Arrows.

Most members flew to Cyprus in their own aircraft, Robs Lamplough cutting a particular

dash in his vintage Mustang. Martin and Zaza Barraclough travelled by commercial airline, accompanied like film stars by 50 pieces of Air Squadron baggage.

In Cyprus, the visitors stood on the cliffs near Akrotiri and watched the Red Arrows display over the sea. They inspected the engineering works, hobnobbed with the pilots, and wangled rides for their girlfriends in the sleek red-liveried Hawks.

After two days in Cyprus, they flew to Jordan, on an off-airways route across Israel and the Dead Sea which only Henry Kissinger and the Secretary-General of the United Nations had been allowed to take in the last 45 years. Caryll Waterpark, who was flying with John Thomson in a Beech Baron, remembers with amusement that an El Al pilot, hearing a babble of English voices on the Israeli military radio frequency, asked what on earth was going on. He was told by controllers 'to mind his own business and get off the frequency.'

As they crossed the Dead Sea, they saw the winking lights of Jordanian anti-aircraft installations tracking them from the shore. This was rare, quasi-illicit stuff, a piece of Waterpark magic. He had, of course, cleared it at the highest level, negotiating with two governments who did not speak to each other. Permission had cost him several trips to the Jordanian and Israeli embassies in London – a piece of shuttle diplomacy which he recalled later as 'great fun'. All the pilots were presented with a certificate recording the remarkable fact that they had flown over the Dead Sea at a height of '1200 feet below sea-level'.

1

2

In Amman King Hussein was ill, and unable to welcome the Squadron personally. His place was taken by his brother, Crown Prince Hassan. Visits to Crusader Forts, Petra, the Royal Jordanian Air Force College, and two nights under canvas in Wadi Rumm (used frequently as a rest camp in 1917-18 by Lawrence of Arabia, who described it as 'my personal resort') completed a memorable adventure.

TANZANIA (1995)

The following year, the Squadron were off again, this time for a safari in Tanzania. Their route took them to Bastia, Corfu, Iraklion, Luxor, Jeddah, Djibouti, Mandara, Malindi, Dar es Salaam, Zanzibar and Mafia Island, with an optional extension to the Seychelles. On the way south they stopped for two days' sightseeing at Luxor, and

were impressed in an appalled way by a refuelling scam at the airport that involved pumping large amounts of metered air into the tanks. Once this had been stopped, officials informed them that a handling agent was needed – a very expensive one as it happened. They refused this unnecessary service and, adopting a formation recommended by John Houlder, began walking towards the office: 'Form a line abreast and they can't pick us off,' said John. 'If we go in crocodile fashion they will get the weak one at the back who will start giving in and that will affect everybody.' Having crushed the bureaucrats, they visited the Valley of the Kings and the temples of ancient Thebes. They returned 48 hours later to find soldiers guarding the aircraft, sitting in the shade of the wings and smoking. As Jeremy Bagge observed, 'It was very lucky the aeroplanes didn't blow up.'

3

In Jeddah, Bruno Schroder made a big decision. He had until then travelled entirely in hired aeroplanes, some of dubious quality. His current machine was more dubious than most, with an engine that constantly leaked oil. Caryll Waterpark said, 'Come on Bruno, it's time you bought yourself a decent aeroplane. Leave this pile of junk here.' He did. By the end of the year he had ordered his Pilatus PCXII.

The Squadron's next stop was Djibouti, adjacent to a war zone. The danger of a missile attack meant flying in as high as possible, then spiralling down tightly to land. John Scurr was not taking any chances with his Citation. He filled the airbrakes with milk bottle tops as a form of improvised 'chaff' against radar. 'Luckily,' he said, 'we did not have to deploy them.'

Flying in Tanzania posed problems of a different kind. 'As you are aware,' wrote Caryll Waterpark in his preparatory notes, 'foreign registered aircraft are in fact banned from making internal flights in Tanzania. I enclose the Authority from the Director of Civil Aviation to the Air Squadron.' He then signed off, 'God willing, I will meet you all for tea and cucumber sandwiches in the Selous Game Reserve on 17th September'.

One of the most remarkable photographs of the trip features John Scurr's Citation taking off at Ras Kutani in Tanzania. The aircraft is poised a few feet above the dirt runway, clouds of dust swirling up behind. The image is startling and surreal – a piece of gleaming white technology suspended for a moment above an ancient landscape. There was danger here too, as the strip was covered in loose stones; if any of these had been sucked into an engine on take-off, serious damage would have followed.

The Citation had already done one dirt-strip landing and take-off, at Mbuyuni, where trees were felled and the strip specially extended for the jet to use. 'My greatest fear,' says John Scurr, 'was that a wild animal would wander across the runway while I was trying to land. In fact a giraffe's bones later proved very useful as chocks for the wheels.' As soon as they touched down, a crowd of curious locals appeared, amazed that an aeroplane could fly without propellers.

1

2

3

1 The Air Squadron party in front of John Scurr's Cessna Citation, Ras Kutani, Tanzania 1995. The locals who gathered were astonished that an aeroplane could fly without propellers.

2 Charles Dobie, Tanzania, 1995.

3 Jeremy Bagge, already showing a taste for speed as a schoolboy.

They stayed at Mbuyuni, where Squadron member Charles Dobie runs a camp on the Rufiji River. Martin Barraclough recalls a day spent 'in alarmingly close company with hippos and crocodiles' before they flew on to the more arid country of Ruaha Game Reserve in western Tanzania. Finally they enjoyed a couple of days on the beach at Ras Kutani, then turned for home.

Passengers on the Citation, however, were offered a special treat – a two-day trip to the Seychelles. Here Ian Macfadyen witnessed another example of the Waterpark style. After landing on the first island, they were refused permission to fly on to the next. An airport official explained that they did not have the required permissions, which would take at least 48 hours to obtain. Waterpark asked for a telephone. He wanted to speak to the President. The official said he did not think it very likely that the President would speak to him. Waterpark replied that it was extremely likely: 'I taught him to fly.' The official, now less sure of himself, asked for their passports and disappeared into his office. He came back a short while later. 'Permission granted,' he said.

Not all officials were so troublesome. At Mandara on the Kenya-Ethiopia border, a police sergeant named Letila brewed coffee while the aeroplanes were refuelled, dealt briskly with all the official forms and made everyone feel thoroughly at home. On the return trip he greeted them as old friends. All agreed that he was a most splendid man. A few weeks after returning to England, Jeremy Bagge received a sad letter. There had been floods in Kenya, Sergeant Letila's house had been washed down the river and his

1 Dr John Taylor in his TBM 700 2C. The son of a pilot and gliding instructor, John went solo in a glider at age 16 in 1953, taking his PPL in 1969 and making his first Atlantic crossing in a Piper Aztec in 1975. He has since owned and flown several light twins, an Islander, two Cessna Citations, and a Stemme power glider which in 2007 he flew at 26,600 feet. With 389 patents registered at the European Patent Office, including the thermostatic controls and cordless power supply in today's electric kettles, John has devoted his retirement to philanthropic work in education. His most spectacular creation is the 'chronophage' (time-eater) clock which he designed and built for Corpus Christi College Cambridge, where it was inaugurated by Professor Stephen Hawking in September 2008.

2 (opposite) John Hogg's aircraft looking lonely among the Himalayas, 1997.

farm had been destroyed. 'He asked me if I could help re-establish him. So I sent him a cheque for £100 and he was so pleased. He rebuilt the house and bought some cattle. Then something else happened, and I sent him a cheque for £75. I thought of the law of diminishing returns. Then he wrote again and he got a cheque for £50. And I said that was going to be it… Some months later his wife had a child, and he was so delighted with what I had done that he christened his son Jeremy Bagge Letila. So now I am just waiting for him to ring me up and ask me to educate him at Eton. Or, as Sarah said, "Just hang on, in a couple of generations this Jeremy Bagge Letila will probably become President of Kenya and poor old Alfred, our eldest son, is going to have a lot of answering to do…" '

PAKISTAN (1997)

The idea of flying to Pakistan for the 50th anniversary of independence was Ian Macfadyen's. He had visited the country on official business and thought it would make a good destination for the Air Squadron. He made an outline plan, discussed it with Caryll Waterpark, and sent it to his friend Muhammed Abbas Khattak, Chief of the Air Staff in Pakistan. Khattak asked a promising young Wing Commander, Asim Suleiman, to look into the feasibility of the plan.

Asim was one of Pakistan's top fighter pilots. He took the proposal home and gave it some careful thought. Here was a group of British pilots planning to fly light aircraft with a variety of performance characteristics into the Hindu Kush and the Karakorams, some of the world's highest mountain terrain. A wrong turn would lead either to exitless gorges or hostile international borders. Any mistakes or technical failures would very likely be fatal. There were practical complications too. Jet fuel and avgas would have to be carried to remote airfields. Military regulations stated that no propeller-driven aircraft with less than four engines were permitted to fly these mountain routes. There would be food, ground transport,

1　Born in 1958, Asim Suleiman graduated from the Pakistan Air Force (PAF) Academy Risalpur in 1978 and went on to do Fighter Conversion and Operation Conversion Courses. He flew all types of fighter aircraft on the PAF inventory. He is a proficient fighter pilot and has served as an Instructor in Operational Conversion Units and the coveted Combat Commander's School. He commanded a Fighter Squadron and a Fighter Base of the PAF. Asim was selected to serve on the Chief of Air Staffs staff as ADC, APSO and PSO. He was Air Attaché in the Pakistan High Commission at New Delhi for 4 years. He is also a Director General Air Intelligence. Air Vice Marshal Asim Suleiman was elected a member of the Air Squadron as a consequence of his extraordinary contribution to the success of the expedition to Pakistan in 1997.

accommodation and entertainment to be laid on for 50 people. As if this were not enough, they wanted a ride on the Khyber Railway.

Asim is a man of disarming simplicity. He was intrigued by the plan. He called Caryll Waterpark, and asked if they could meet. Caryll said, 'I'll be there in forty-eight hours.' They met in Islamabad, and at once drafted a detailed schedule for the trip.

Six weeks later, everything was fixed. Asim sent a 'very elaborate' book detailing all the arrangements to London.

There was just one final hurdle: official clearance. Asim recalls, 'I had to brief the Chief of Operations on the subject. He was a very busy person. I made one or two attempts and he was not available. When he became available, the Air Squadron had already arrived in Dubai. The next day they were supposed to come to Quetta, and I was to fly there to meet them. So I said, "Sir, could you give me some time so that I can brief you on the Air Squadron visit?"

'He said, "OK, I don't have much time, you will

have to do it in fifteen minutes."

'I said, "Sir, it would take an hour plus, maybe two hours."

'And he said, "No, I don't have that kind of time, so you have to do it very quickly."

'So I briefed him – I just ran through the programme in five or ten minutes.

'But now he said, "Who is going to do that?"

'I said, "Sir, I am going to do that."

'"Is everything in place?"

'"Yes, sir."

'"How did you do this? How could you get a train on your own? How are we going to position the fuel in the northern areas? We don't operate these fuels from there! This is a logistical issue. It needs a lot of logistics. How have you managed it?"

'I told him that luckily the fuel in those areas was supplied by the Pakistan army and one of my uncles was actually the one who was looking after the army fuel in those days. He had gone out of his way to help me, and put fuel in those places.

3

2 David Mauleverer, a BOAC/British Airways pilot for almost 35 years, who flew Boeing 707s, then as a Training and Check Captain on Super VC10s and Boeing 747s worldwide. He is a Past Master of the Guild of Air Pilots and Air Navigators, a Fellow of the Royal Aeronautical Society and a Fellow of the Royal Institute of Navigation.

3 Robert Camrass with his wife Zoe (right) and Isla (Lady) Abinger, Lake Como 2007.

'But now there was another issue: we had to have fuel inspection teams so that the purity of the fuel could be checked. Had we done all this?

'I said that we had. But he could not conceive that a Wing Commander with such short service could have thought of all the intricacies. And when he got to know the kind of people that were going to come, he said, "Man, you are in for trouble! I don't think you on your own can manage this... Can you stop them?"

'"No, sir. We can't stop them because they are already on their way."

'"How will you manage it?"

'"I think, sir, that things are in place."

'"I don't think you have the capacity to manage all this."

'I could not say anything, because the proof would come when the Squadron arrived. I said, "You will have to trust me – you will have to trust the Air Force system."

'He said, "Well, I trust that system but I don't know how you have managed to use that system. Who has counter-checked it?"

'I said that I had counter-checked it. I gave him answers to all his questions – how I had confirmed and got reassurances from the people who were supposed to be receiving us.

'At last he said, "Luck be with you! But if anything goes wrong it is your responsibility. You are taking the responsibility now, because you say you have put everything in place. "

'That was the way it happened. I stuck my neck out for the visit. He seemed to have been convinced because otherwise the visit wouldn't have gone through. It was a brave decision on the part of the Squadron to fly, and on the part of the Pakistan Air Force to permit it, because at the end of the day the flak would have come to the Air Force and nobody else. People would have said, "How come you had people there who knew that this was a dangerous option and yet you permitted it to happen?"'

Now there was the small matter of getting there: 5,000 miles across Europe, the Mediterranean, Egypt, Saudi Arabia, the Indian Ocean and Baluchistan. For the less experienced flyers this was a daunting prospect. One such was Robert Camrass, not yet a Squadron member, although a qualified pilot with a robust little aeroplane. H e had just sold his textile business, and was looking forward to a long relaxing yachting holiday in the Mediterranean with his wife Zoe. Then one day they met Caryll Waterpark, who made a sudden, alarming proposition: 'Come flying to Pakistan!'

They took a few days to think about it. It was tempting but risky, and full of unknowns. After much discussion, they decided to say no. But this was not the answer Caryll Waterpark had in mind. 'This is the trip of a lifetime!' he said. 'You have got to come!'

Robert objected. 'I don't have an instrument rating. I've never done a trip like this before. I'd like to do it in my own time...'

'That's no problem. I'll find you an instrument-rated pilot.'

Two days later Caryll rang back. 'I've got David

1   John Hogg, a stalwart of the Air Squadron for many years, refuelling in Tanzania 1995. John Hogg flew regularly from Rochester Airport near his home at Brenchley in Kent, and took part in all the long Air Squadron trips. Jeremy Bagge, who flew with him to Pakistan, described him as 'the ideal travelling companion: well-informed, interesting to talk to, always good-humoured and patient.' Many members of the Squadron enjoyed his shooting invitations to Glenormiston, his Scottish estate near Peebles, where he was a most genial host. After John's death in a flying accident in 2003, his wife Sally generously endowed the Geoffrey de Havilland Flying Foundation in his memory.

Mauleverer, British Airways Training Captain for 747s. Would that be good enough?'

They could hardly say no.

The journey from London to Quetta was, recalls Robert, 'hard work' – up at six each morning, then eight hours flying, with a short stop for fuel, lunch and arguments with officials on the way. The last leg, from Dubai to Quetta, was particularly tense. With anything stronger than a five-knot headwind his aircraft would run out of fuel; the only alternate was a rather lonely military base in Baluchistan. But the weather stayed calm and they arrived in Quetta with a good few litres left in the tanks.

A glance at a map of Asia will show that the direct route from Dubai to Quetta crosses southeastern Iran. This was forbidden airspace to British pilots. They would be expected to fly east across the Gulf of Oman and the Arabian Sea before turning north over the coast of Pakistan. Jeremy Bagge, flying with John Hogg in a Cessna 182, wondered if a little informal diplomacy might be applied.

'I said to John, "Look, why don't we ring up Teheran, and say we're just a small contingent, guests of the Pakistan Air Force – might it be possible just to nip across the corner, because we're very harmless individuals?"'

No-one thought this likely to work, but he decided to give it a try.

'Tehran said, "Ah, English! We haven't heard any English for years! How are you?"

'I said, "We're just a little flying club here, and we're going on to Pakistan, but it's a hell of a long way round in a single-engined aircraft." So the chap said, "No trouble at all, we'll give you clearance," and we flew across the corner.'

Quetta is an old frontier town, high in the mountains of Baluchistan, with a fighter station, army base, and vast military training area. It is also the home of the Army Staff College, set up by Lord Kitchener in 1905. The visitors were welcomed by Air Commodore Sehti of the Pakistan Air Force, and immediately interviewed by local press and TV. Then there was tea, served on the lawn of the Officers Mess. Sandrine Filippi, a French photo-journalist and niece of Caryll Waterpark, noted the

2 Christopher Sharples (left) and James Gibson Fleming arrive in Quetta, Pakistan, 23 September 1997.

3 The local press in Quetta welcomes the Air Squadron, September 1997.

dreamlike feeling of relief after hours of flying, the soft grass and fresh mountain air, and the wives of the Pakistani officers, 'gentle and smiling in their rustling saris'.

The next day (24 September) they were shown around the Army Museum and Staff College – including the bungalow where General Montgomery had stayed when he was stationed at Quetta in the 1930s. They visited a carpet factory, a bazaar, and a military training and recreation centre in the hills. David Mauleverer remembers

Royal Squadron warmly received in Quetta

By Our Staff Reporter

QUETTA: Royal Squadron of the United Kingdom arrived on Tuesday on the first leg of their tour to Pakistan at the special invitation of the Chief Of Air Staff, Abbas Khatak in connection with 50 years celebrations of Pakistan.

The members of Squadron, a private flying club of the professional and private were received at the PAF base Samungli by the Air Commodore, Arshad Sethi and other officers of PAF.

Welcoming the members of the Royal Squadron at a reception held in their honour, Mr Sethi said that the air expedition of the Royal Squadron in Pakistan would go a long way in further cementing ties of PAF with the club, adding that the climate was favourable in Quetta for small aircraft to land.

He hoped that members of the club will have a comfortable stay in Pakistan and added that it would over come challenges of flying air crafts in Skardo and Shengrilla where small flights could hardly be undertaken given the unfavourable climatic conditions obtaining there.

Speaking on the occasion, the Air Marshall, Mr. Nian Macfadyen hailed the PAF for according what he called "marvelous" welcome.

He informed that today's PAF Samungli Air Base was once Royal Airforce station in 1930 during British domination and added that he had also visited Pakistan before. He said that his team members were proud to be here in Pakistan/Balochistan.

He hoped that they would be enjoying very much their stay in the country and would leave for England on October 5.

The team will be having two days stay in Quetta and visit Quetta Staff College, Hana Resort and a local carpet weaving industry.

Other members of Squadron were also present on the occasion.

with particular pleasure a notice by the hotel swimming pool saying 'Please no Kalashnikovs, guns, or knives.'

Before dinner that evening, the Squadron met their guide and organizer, Wing Commander Suleiman, who laid out the rules for flying in the days to come. 'I had divided the aircraft into three categories, so all the aircraft with compatible speeds should be flying together. In fact I told Lord Waterpark when he came, "You call yourselves an Air Squadron but you have never flown like a Squadron, and I will make your people fly like a Squadron."' A Pakistan Air Force navigator was assigned to each group, with Asim on John Scurr's Citation out in front 'to clear the area and the weather'.

Jeremy Bagge admired Asim's efforts to organise them, but thought, 'Poor man, he hasn't got a hope in hell of controlling us all'.

Setting off the next morning, they discovered that 'flying like a Squadron' was easier said than done. They were required to fly line astern, each aircraft in the group keeping an agreed distance behind the one in front. Robert Camrass recalls that 'most of us hadn't done any formation flying before. There was Robin Rotherwick in his very lightweight aeroplane, leading his group because he was the fastest. There was quite a lot of turbulence over the desert and he kept going up and down. And because everybody was following him they got into a sort of wave. But then they would get out of phase and one was going down while another was going up – it was an absolute shambles!'

There was also John Houlder, who, according to

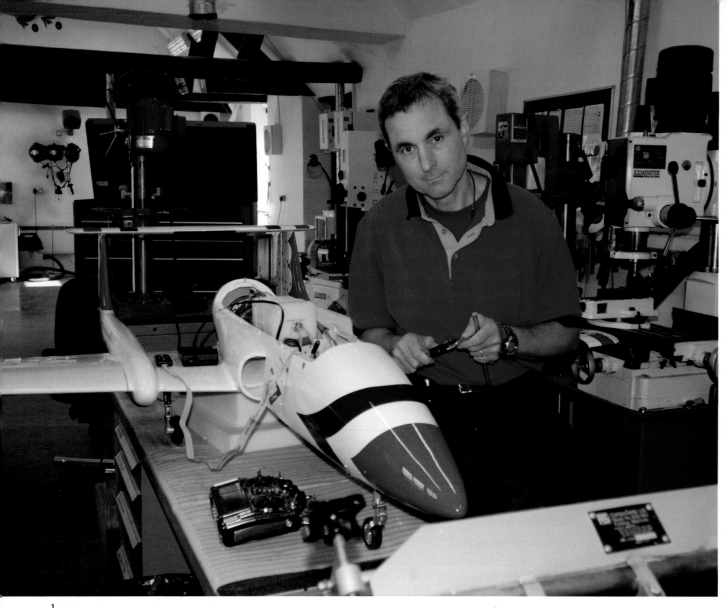

1 Robin Rotherwick constructing a jet-powered model in his workshop at Cornbury Park. Robin built his first full-sized aircraft (Shadow Streak) in 1990. Next came a Glasair IIRG in which he flew to the Himalayas with the Air Squadron Pakistan expedition. This was followed by a home-built Sky Arrow. In 2003 he started building a Glasair III which he first flew five years later.

2 Inside the train to the Khyber Pass, September 1997.

3 The railway from Peshawar to the Khyber Pass, built by British engineers between 1905 and 1925.

Camrass, 'would go along at a low level in order to look at the sheep and the cows and the villages, and then suddenly he would rise up into his group, and that would cause mayhem.'

Ian Macfadyen found the spectacle embarrassing. He had in fact initiated the wave pattern. Flying in Robin Rotherwick's quick little Glasair, which had overheating problems as well as a tendency to run away from the group, he suggested they lose speed by raising the nose of the aircraft. This would allow them to keep in formation without constantly changing the power.

Ian Macfadyen's diary also records that John

Houlder's erratic flight path was not entirely the result of agricultural curiosity:

'Just after takeoff John Houlder (No 2 in our group) called "Lost Leader"; he subsequently spotted the leader (low down as we had agreed a 100kt climb) and plunged earthwards to meet him – at idle rpm! At about 100 feet he recovered above the local high ground. Halfway up the climb, John Houlder again had problems – overheating cylinders – and flew off out of the formation. We did not join up again until 45 minutes later.'

Practice soon led to improvement, however. 'After some difficult flying,' Ian Macfadyen noted, 'things began to settle down, and we arrived in Peshawar in good order.'

26th September, a Friday, was devoted to shopping, swimming, and the Peshawar Golf Club, where a couple of 'internationals' were played between the visitors and their hosts. Ian Sutherland and Eddie Liverpool took on Air Marshal Sahib Saeed and Air Vice Marshal Riazuddin Shaik (AOC Northern Air Command), while Margaret Hare and Sally Macfadyen challenged two Group Captains. The result – 2-0 to the home teams – suggest that the Pakistan Air Force take their golf even more seriously than their British counterparts.

The next day, the party travelled on the Khyber Railway. This extraordinary feat of British engineering, begun in 1905 and completed in 1925, sends the train up the steep slope to the Khyber Pass by a series of zigzags. There are 34 tunnels

2, 3

2

1 The airfield at Chitral, Pakistan, 1997. Pakistani troops guarded and refuelled the Air Squadron aircraft in this remote mountain location.

2 Winston Churchill at the Khyber Pass, 27 September 1997. His grandfather had served here on the North-West Frontier in 1897, in a campaign that was to be the subject of his first book - *The Story of the Malakand Field Force.*

and 92 bridges and cuttings along the 27-mile line. Outside Peshawar, it cuts across the runway at the international airport, making the train driver one of the few in his profession to be subject to Air Traffic Control.

With armed guards along the track, music, dancing, and splendidly uniformed railway staff, the Air Squadron rode in style to the top – re-living the grandeur of the Raj in the train's pale-green interior and wiping soot off their faces at the end of each tunnel. Ian Macfadyen, a steam train enthusiast, rode on the driver's footplate all the way.

As they approached the Khyber Pass, they saw Pashtun children waving at them vigorously. It was only when Robin Rotherwick's watch-glass was smashed that they realized what was going on: the waving hands were actually twirling slingshots.

Up at the pass, the party enjoyed a remarkable view. It is described by Michael Palin in his book *Himalaya*:

Below the walls of the fort that guards the Khyber Pass there is a viewing platform on which rows of chairs are set out, facing Afghanistan, like circle seats at the theatre. They convey an air of expectation, of something about to happen, of a curtain about to rise on great events.

Casts of thousands have at one time or another filled the plains below, as greedy armies, seeking the great prize of India, gathered at this narrow western gateway. Darius I, King of Persia, led his soldiers through the Pass nearly 500 years before the birth of Christ. He was followed, nearly two centuries later, by Alexander the Great. Six hundred years ago I would have seen Tamburlaine's army, down from Samarkand, toiling up the hill towards me, and 400 years after that, the lone, exhausted figure of Army Surgeon Brydon bringing news of the annihilation of 17,000 of his colleagues who had set out to conquer Afghanistan for the British.

For the Air Squadron visitors, a Pakistani army

1

1 Children in the Kalash Valley, near Chitral, where the inhabitants are believed to be descended from the armies of Alexander the Great.

2 John Houlder and Ian Sutherland in Pakistan, 1997.

officer analysed the terrain with the help of a model in a sand-box. Sandrine Filippi described 'helmeted soldiers with their guns positioned towards this vast mountain saddle, a gigantic empty space where a narrow road winds through a kind of silent Tartar desert, only inhabited by memories of past invasions.' Winston Churchill recalled that his grandfather had served here on the North-West Frontier in 1897. The campaign had been the subject of his first book, *The Story of the Malakand Field Force*, written when he was twenty-two.

After lunch and sword-dancing on the close-clipped lawns of the Khyber Rifles Officers' Mess, they returned to the train, and zigzagged down to Peshawar for dinner at the house of Air Vice Marshal Shaik – 'another wonderful evening of the most generous hospitality.'

On 28th September the mountain flying began:

first over the Lowari Pass (10,230 ft) to Chitral in the Hindu Kush – a flight of about 80 minutes – and then on, a couple of days later, to Skardu at the foot of the Karakoram Range. They were blessed with perfect weather. At Chitral they were invited to open the brand new Hindukush Heights Hotel. Its owner, Prince Siraj Ul-Mulk, amazed everyone by unveiling a stone plaque carved with all the names of the Air Squadron visitors. The view from the hotel's camphor-wood balconies was superb: Sandrine Filippi spoke of 'fields of wheat, rice and sunflowers set in a mosaic of emerald, tourmaline and absinthe... the air so pure and light it seems to tinkle like a sonata.'

After a lunch of lamb curry, rice and spinach, apricot and apple compote, they watched a polo match between Chitral 'A' and the Chitral Scouts: '6 a side with no rules, 2 chukkas of 25 minutes each way and only one pony each,' as Ian Macfadyen noted. The play was 'ferociously competitive' and highly entertaining. Dinner that night was with the Chitral Scouts, hosted by Major General Habib of the Frontier Corps. 'Another magical evening of music and dancing on the lawn of the former British Officers Mess (with old regimental diaries on display dating back to the 1930s). More gifts – Chitral hats for the men and lovely embroidered waistcoats for the women.'

The next day (29th September) they drove up to the Kalash Valley where, it is said, descendants of Alexander the Great's army still live, worshipping pagan gods. Local girls danced, in long black woollen dresses ornamented with cowrie shells

2

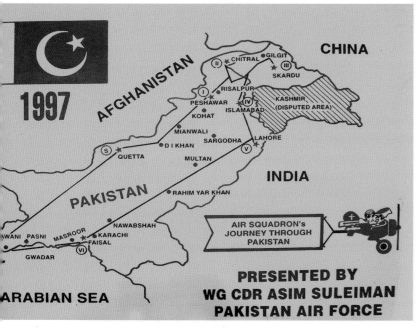

1997

AIR SQUADRON's JOURNEY THROUGH PAKISTAN

PRESENTED BY
WG CDR ASIM SULEIMAN
PAKISTAN AIR FORCE

and embroidered in blazing colours. After a picnic lunch by the river, they returned to Chitral, where they were welcomed by a parade of pupils at Sayurj, a charitable boarding school founded by a retired Indian Army Major, G D Langlands. Langlands was a revered figure in Chitral, still running the school at the age of eighty.

On 1st October, they were up early for the flight to Skardu – three hours through clear blue skies over majestic mountain scenery. No sooner had they landed than they were greeted with an invitation to view K2 and surrounding peaks from a Pakistan Air Force C-130. Caryll Waterpark remembers the scene vividly: 'They were still washing blood out of the aircraft as we boarded – it had been used the night before for transporting casualties from the war in Kashmir.'

'An amazing flight,' wrote Sandrine Filippi. 'These wild wastes of petrified snow, where enormous grey and white glaciers flow into the vertical explosion of the mountain masses, leave us dumbfounded.'

Meanwhile the Pakistan Army were working quietly and efficiently behind the scenes, making everything run smoothly. At Skardu James Gibson Fleming recalls a conversation with a soldier who was helping to refuel his aeroplane. He asked the young man how long he had been stationed up there. The soldier said, 'I'm not stationed here. I came up by lorry from our base at Shikala.'

'How far away is that?'

'22 hours' drive.'

Fuel of a different kind was in short supply.

A few bottles of wine had entered the country on board the larger aeroplanes, but these had long since gone. Micky Suffolk telephoned Room Service at one hotel and asked if there was any chance of some whisky.

'I am afraid not, sir,' said the waiter. 'That is quite impossible. It is only permitted if you are an alcoholic.'

'As it happens,' said Suffolk, 'I am an alcoholic! And so are all my friends! Would you please send up a bottle at once?'

The following day a second polo match was played, on a long, narrow ground at least 400 years old. (The sport, which originated in Persia some 2000 years ago, was played in India long before it was taken up by the English in the 19th century.) The winners were presented with an Air Squadron Shield procured in Islamabad by Captain Peter Jackson RN, the British Defence Attaché, whose help had been crucial to the trip in many ways.

That night they heard gunfire from Kashmir, a reminder of the continuing dispute between India and Pakistan, still unresolved 50 years after the end of British rule. (An understanding of this dispute, and of Pakistan's position in it, was all that the Air Squadron's hosts asked them to take home with them. Ian Macfadyen recalls that 'Kashmir did inevitably come up and their case was made to us in conversation, but it never embarrassed any of us.')

Sandrine Filippi confessed that for a moment she mistook the distant sound of exploding shells for fireworks, 'such is the serenity of this imposing

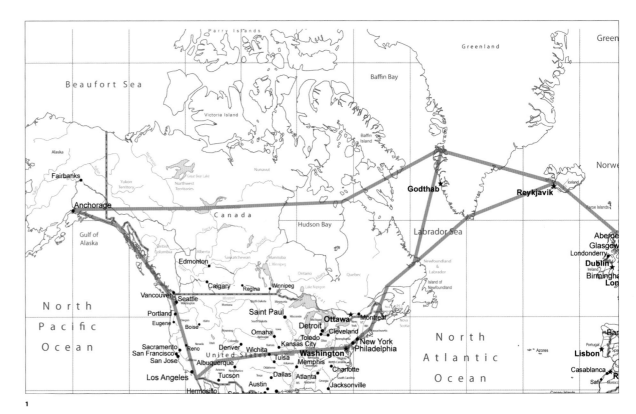

1

mountainous solitude.'

On Friday 3rd October, they left for the capital, just ahead of the first heavy snowfall of autumn. Another night at Skardu, and their aeroplanes would have been trapped for the next six months.

Back in London at the winter dinner Caryll Waterpark presented each of the participants with a set of Pakistan Air Force fighter wings. It had been the most exciting of trips. 'The country was hugely challenging, and the conditions we faced were fearsome.' Another member, quoted in the Air Squadron News, described it as 'the most magnificent, memorable flying expedition that I have ever been on.' For Robert Camrass, brought along initially by sheer force of Waterpark enthusiasm, 'There was an enormous adrenalin run. You could almost feel it across the air between the aeroplanes. Nobody's ever done it before, and it's unlikely that anyone will ever do it again, so even ten years later you still get a rush of excitement when you think about it. It was a unique trip.'

Asim Suleiman, looking back on the visit,

and the grilling he had received from the Chief of Operations, reflected, 'Now that I am in his position, I would say the same to a younger officer. But when you are young you can do a lot, and you leave a lot to optimism. I won't say luck; optimism. Believe me, God was so kind that, except for one odd day when there was some problem with the visibility, I think we went bang on with our timings. Everything was flawless. Actually it was – as they say in cricket – a copybook shot.'

USA 2000

For the millennium trip to North America, Bill Hall, Caryll Waterpark and Michael Graydon devised a programme that combined ceremonial grandeur, tours of military installations, and plenty of exciting flying – 13,000 miles of it. Behind it all lay an enormous effort of organization and research, which included discussions with the US Air Force and Navy, the US Congress, the Royal Air Force and Royal Navy, and the staff of the British Embassy in Washington. A file about an inch thick was

1 A map of the Air Squadron's route to the USA and Alaska in June 2000. There were only three fixed points on this itinerary: Washington DC, Nellis Air Force Base (Nevada), and San Diego. Members followed their own routes, particularly when storms scattered them widely on the westward journey from Washington.

2 Phil Lever at Nellis Air Force Base, June 2000. Phil died in a gliding accident in Spain shortly afterwards.

3 Left to right: Terry Holloway, David Hare, Margaret Hare, Michael Marshall at Cambridge Airport, June 2000. The aircraft is the Hares' Piper Aztec, G-TAPE, which has flown with the Air Squadron to Pakistan, South Africa and the USA.

3

issued to participants, with contacts, biographies, information about places to visit, procedures, schedules, hotels, dress codes, and instructions on how to deal with the press.

Despite the paperwork there was an unusual freedom of organization about the trip. Members were at liberty to take any route they chose around three fixed points:

- Andrews Air Force Base, Washington DC (17-19 June)
- Nellis Air Force Base, Las Vegas (22 June).
- San Diego, California (24-26 June).

Most members flew across the North Atlantic during the week 7th-14th June, via Wick, Keflavik, Narsarsuaq, Goose Bay, Sept Isles, Boston and finally Andrews Air Force Base just outside Washington, DC – a distance of 3541 nautical miles from London. After leaving Washington, they reached San Diego by various routes, one or two following their intended path, most scattered by a line of ferocious thunderstorms to airfields across Kansas, Missouri and Oklahoma. From San Diego they turned north to Canada and Alaska, where float planes and salmon-fishing awaited. They returned to Britain in separate groups. Some stayed on for extra fishing and social visits in Canada, but all were safely home by 11th July.

Throughout the trip, Christopher Sharples (recently elected the Squadron's first Chairman) recorded sequences for a documentary film, as he had in Pakistan. He also sent regular bulletins home by email, reporting the progress of the various contingents.

There is another record of the trip: an email diary by Philip Lever, a young guest pilot flying his Cessna 182 with Johnny Moss on board. Philip was about to become a member of the Air Squadron, but died in a gliding accident less than a month after his return from the USA. His diary, which was posted on the Air Squadron website in his memory, captures all the excitement and tension of a great flying adventure. For a sense of what it was actually like to be on the trip, it could hardly be bettered.

The crossing of the Atlantic in a Cessna 182

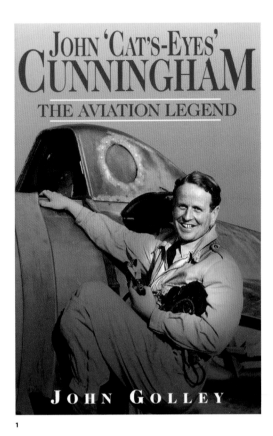

JOHN 'CAT'S-EYES' CUNNINGHAM
THE AVIATION LEGEND

JOHN GOLLEY

1

was a great deal longer (around 30 hours) as well as more exciting than in a Boeing 747. Phil Lever describes his first sight of Greenland: 'After an hour or so we could see Greenland from about 150 miles away. As we approached, the cloud layer below cleared and the stuff above thinned out. "Awe inspiring" does not describe the sight of 50 miles of pack ice, a few lone icebergs, the mountains and the icepack stretching out into infinity across the world's biggest island. We reached the coast on the south-east corner and overflew one of our diversion fields called Kulusuk, a cold war relic of an airstrip on a little island surrounded by ice. We then donned oxygen cannulas and climbed up to 12,000 feet for the cruise across the ice cap.

'The ice cap is a flattish featureless expanse of ice that starts about 20 miles inland and stretches right across the country at heights of up to 9,300 feet. Apparently it is all ice, down to near sea-level. We set off into the most amazing scene of bright blue skies and white ground and .... nothing else. It was breathtaking. Somewhere near the middle we saw an abandoned ice station that used to be a radar station and a few reindeer, visible on the white background from 60-70 miles! We had lunch along the way, consisting of sandwiches made up at breakfast time. Johnny Moss at this stage was wearing a cap, headset, spectacles, sunglasses and oxygen cannula on his head whilst eating a sandwich and also wearing an enormous orange immersion suit.'

Having reached the United States, the first

major rendezvous was at Andrews, where the US Air Force had prepared a splendid welcome. 'Our route,' wrote Phil Lever, 'took us down the coast over the Hamptons and on straight over the top of JFK Airport in New York. In better weather the views would have been fantastic. The controllers were obviously curious as to the stream of "British Blips" on their screens – every time we were handed off, someone was asked what all of these Limeys were doing! As we approached the Washington area, the group became more tightly packed as the quicker planes caught up to the snails and the fun began. The Washington Approach controllers obviously knew the plan and the last 45 minutes was a very busy period as we were vectored for sequencing and sent in all directions across the sky to put us in order. The controllers did a fantastic job of organising our gaggle and the "big arrival" worked like a dream.'

First to arrive was Torquil Norman's Leopard Moth, with John Cunningham as Guest of Honour on board. Torquil had flown the aircraft from England in the summer of 1999, left the aeroplane in the USA over the winter, and taken it flying again the following spring in preparation for the Air Squadron's visit. He remembers the morning of 17 June vividly:

'John and I went out in a taxi to where the aeroplane was sitting in a shed in a little field outside Washington. Of course I was scared stiff that the bloody thing wouldn't start and then John Cunningham would never get to Andrews Air Force Base... Anyway it started like a bird, and we

2

2 Torquil Norman in his DH Leopard Moth, G-ACOJ, which he flew solo across the Atlantic in 1999 and then used to bring John Cunningham to Andrews Air Force Base, Washington DC, in June 2000. Torquil's account of his transatlantic adventure can be found in Chapter 6.

flew up and down the Potomac for about twenty minutes to burn off some time and at exactly 12 o'clock we were over the end of the runway at Andrews. We landed and we were the first plane to taxi in, and I think all these American Air Force Generals who were lined up to welcome us were rather amazed because I got out and then there was John in a rumpled brown linen suit.'

The following day they visited the National Air & Space Museum with a special tour of the Paul E. Garber Preservation, Restoration, and Storage Facility arranged by Michael Fopp, who is Director of the RAF Museum in Hendon.

On 19th June a party of over a hundred gathered for dinner at the Mayflower Hotel, where Michael Graydon gave a speech thanking Senator Ted Stevens, General Joe Ralston (Supreme Allied Commander Europe (NATO)) and General Mike Ryan (USAF) for their help and encouragement. He went on to pay tribute to all the American servicemen who had fought in the two World Wars, and recalled the many campaigns in which

1

British and US forces had served side by side. 'Thank you,' he said, 'for decades of support and friendship through the 20th century. Thank you for the rebuilding of Europe – the Marshall plan, that brilliant and imaginative scheme to restore that shattered Continent. For your leadership throughout the cold war period, that extraordinary period of confrontation with the Soviet Union. And now, having won the Cold War, the challenge of leading the West in the complex world of today.'

He presented scrolls signed by the Duke of Edinburgh for Senator Ted Stevens and General Mike Ryan, making them honorary members of the Air Squadron. He then came to the climax of the evening: the gift of a millennium sword, to be awarded annually to the most worthy air cadet under training. 'This sword is dedicated to the United States Air Force, in appreciation of a century of Anglo-American Friendship and co-operation in the cause of peace.'

At this point the room darkened. A single spotlight lit a curtained space. It was, says Caryll Waterpark, 'a magical moment. The hush, the darkness, that single light, then the curtains slowly opened and there stood the Pipe Major of the Scots Guards in his splendid uniform – an enormous man – playing the bagpipes as the sword was carried in. The drama of it was incredible.'

From Washington, the party split up and headed for Nevada, each taking their own route. Bruno Schroder and David Mauleverer found themselves in Springfield, Missouri, 'eating sandwiches and chips at 40 degrees in the shade', before meeting a line of spectacular thunderstorms that were to complicate everybody's plans. Bruno took his Pilatus up to 29,000 feet to avoid the storms and went on to the Grand Canyon.

Christopher Sharples and James Gibson Fleming in their single-engine Cessna managed to weave through between two sections of the front, but John Scurr's Citation, with Michael Graydon on board, was struck by lightning as they climbed out of Kansas City en route to Colorado Springs. 'It was a bit like hitting a brick wall. There was an enormous thud, and the aeroplane lit up for a second. Then everything was very quiet. The next thing was Air Traffic Control asking, "Are you still there?" Our transponder had been knocked out, which meant our blip on the radar screen had disappeared.'

Thanks to a spare transponder, John Scurr was able to fly on, but Phil Lever and Johnny Moss, heading for Hutchinson, Kansas, were stopped in their tracks. 'A hundred miles of sky lighting up like a scene from Dante's *Inferno* told the tale in very plain language. We didn't have enough fuel to press on further south and west so we turned back for 40 miles to Tulsa. The airport is in the city itself and being vectored in to the runway we couldn't clearly make it out. The ATC guys dipped and brightened the runway lights which lit it up like the proverbial Christmas tree. A very welcome sight indeed. We landed at 2200 local time after 9 hours in the air feeling pretty frazzled and extremely glad to be back on the ground.'

Ian and Sally Macfadyen, flying with John Hogg, also had their adventures that day. 'As we got nearer our destination, we could see an enormous wall on the radar – bright red – clearly a huge storm going through. It was quite clear we weren't going to go into Kansas City because it was underneath all that. So we diverted to a tiny airfield somewhere in the middle of Missouri – Sedalia. The storm you could see was coming in.

'There was virtually nobody there at that time of night except for a rather simple chap, who was the dogsbody of the club, I suppose. We said we'd like to stay somewhere, and he said, 'Yes.' Then we said, 'Could you possibly take us into town?' and he said, 'Yes.' So we waited around a bit, and then the storm hit us. And it was spectacular – incredible skies, lightning, heavy rain, everything. The hangar next to us, where this chap was working, was struck by lightning, and disappeared into the night, blacked out completely. We thought, is he all right? We had to go over and see, and got drenched in the process. He was all right as it turned out, and eventually he got us into his car to take us into the town.

'We set off in the most appalling weather, and it was dark, the car was stuck in second gear, with this simple chap taking us along, and we were going along in the middle of the highway, where enormous 40-ton lorries were roaring past at us at 50 miles per hour. We were doing 25 or so in the middle lane – we wanted to turn right somewhere – and it was absolutely terrifying.

'We got into the middle of town eventually, and I said "Stop!" because I could see a police station. It took about four times to tell him: "Would you please stop? We want to get out."

'"But I'm taking you to –"

'"No thank you very much, we want to get out. We've had quite enough of this!"

'It was,' concludes Ian, 'very kind of him to help.'

While these adventures were going on, Michael and Rosemary Fopp were stuck at Andrews Air Force Base replacing the alternator

1

on Robin Rotherwick's homebuilt Glasair. Three days of cramped and sweaty work eventually put the aircraft into working order again and they were able to leave for a fast dash across the US to San Diego. Meanwhile the owner of the Glasair, Robin Rotherwick, had jetted back to London for the Queen Mother's 100th birthday (and his own wedding) before returning to join the rest of the

group in California.

Meeting again in Las Vegas, the Squadron were given a tour of the US fighter training facilities at Nellis Air Force Base, including an enormous collection of captured Warsaw Pact hardware. Christopher Sharples had an outing in an F16, which he described with relish in his email of the day:

'Out to the ramp and up the ladder into the

1　Michael Fopp, Director General of the Royal Air Force Museums, built this Lancair 320 himself over a period of eight years. Michael's wife Rosemary also flies the aircraft, which they keep at Cranfield and use frequently for European travel. In 2000 they flew Robin Rotherwick's home-built Glasair across the USA. Only two other of these high performance Lancair 320s were built in the UK; this one has been nicknamed "The Silver Streak" because of its high speed

2　Christopher Sharples after his flight in a USAF F16 at nearly twice the speed of sound.

2

cockpit, not that easy a task in itself as the seat is a snug fit to say the least. Harry Schmidt (previously a national football player) was the pilot in command and after extensive pre flight checks both on the ramp and at the hold before take off, we were hurtling down the runway at a rather more impressive speed than is achieved by the Cessna 182.

'Next minute we are upside down, next pulling loads of G in a tight turn and next climbing up to 50,000 feet that we reached in probably a couple of minutes. You can definitely see the curvature of the earth at that height and I am just beginning to enjoy the view when Harry says, "Let's see how fast this thing goes," and promptly points the nose almost vertically downwards. That's when we reached over 1,000

mph, well over the speed of sound, which was fine until we pulled 7G (seven times normal gravity) on recovering from the dive towards the desert of Nevada. The pressure suit helped a lot but the G forces are still intense and take some getting used to.

'Then it was a succession of aerobatics such as the Immelman, Cuban 8, Split S and Barrel Roll. "You have the jet," said Harry as he handed over control. Surprisingly, the F16 is really easy to fly and after a couple of minutes straight and level – which helped dispel the queasiness brought on by the aerobatics – Harry suggested I try the Loop. Not a problem as it turned out with all that power to play with.

'After a few more aerobatics it was time for the low level stuff: following the contours of

1

the mountain ranges of Nevada just a couple of hundred feet above ground level, launching a surprise attack on an imaginary enemy (known as a 'Pop up' attack) and then a high G break-off to escape retaliation.

'By the time we returned to the base, we had clocked up an hour of intense flying and had pulled plenty of those Gs. Definitely feeling somewhat battered, and also rather queasy, I had nevertheless just enjoyed an amazing flying experience.'

On 26th June they were in San Diego, where the Air Squadron hosted a reception for the US Navy at the Aerospace Museum. Michael Graydon again welcomed the guests, and Mark Thomson presented a silver model of Douglas Bader's Spitfire. The following day they were shown around the 85,000-ton aircraft carrier *Constellation*, which had been commissioned in 1961 and served in the Vietnam and Gulf Wars. A group photograph was taken on the flight deck, together with more playful shots of Air Squadron pilots in various martial and contemplative poses. All were struck by the

enormous scale of the carrier, which would be decommissioned in 2003 after 42 years of service, 30 different captains, and 395,710 deck landings.

Now that the official visits were over, the party moved north towards Alaska, through California, Oregon and Washington State, then up 'the Trench' – a 500 mile valley through the Canadian Rockies. 'I would quite like to see some bears,' wrote Phil Lever. He was not disappointed. One of the team filmed a bear waiting at a salmon leap in a fast flowing river. Suddenly a fish came flying through the air, and was snatched in mid-flight by the bear's open jaws.

As they travelled north they saw enormous tracts of empty land. 'Every time you think you reach the middle of nowhere, fly on a while, you'll be closer to the middle again… The Canadian we talked to yesterday said that there are 50 airplane wrecks within 50 miles of here, testament to the climate, geography and over-eagerness of pilots to get to their destination.'

A large party gathered in Alaska to cruise along

1 The USS *Constellation* which the Air Squadron visited in San Diego in June 2000.

2 The GPS display on Bruno Schroder's Pilatus PCXII as they flew over the North Pole, July 2000.

the ice-bound coast, fly seaplanes, catch salmon and grill them, fresh from the water, on wood fires. No official functions, no dinner jackets or speeches, just a group of friends enjoying the open air.

Yet now the journey home beckoned – across more empty territory… Bruno Schroder decided to fly over the North Pole, something he had long dreamed of. He invited John Rahm, a Swiss pilot who used to work for Pilatus, to be his co-pilot. John persuaded Suzanne Maltzahn to come along by saying, 'Suzanne, you will never do a trip like this again.' Their route was Yellowknife (North West Territories) to Resolute and Alert,

then over the North Pole to Spitzbergen – 5½ hours in total from Alert. Bruno proudly photographed his GPS when they were over the Pole. Landing at Spitzbergen, he sent Caryll Waterpark a card from the northernmost post office in the world.

Meanwhile Bill Hall, Robin Rotherwick, Gilbert Greenall and Mic Mac Moss flew back in a group with Phil Lever and Johnny Moss. On 2nd July, at Iqaluit in the Canadian Northern Territories, Phil wrote, 'We flew for 1200 miles today and landed at one little hamlet. That was it. No habitation and no change of scenery to speak

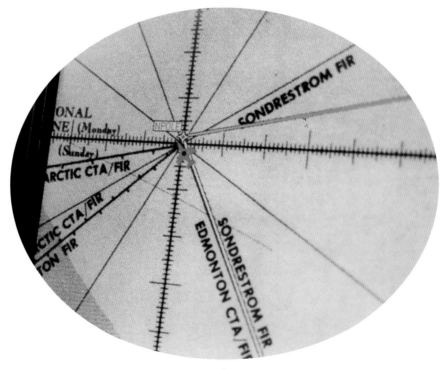

2

1939 60th Anniversary 1999

Cape Record Flight

5th - 9th February 1939

Alex Henshaw, flying his Percival Mew Gull G-AEXF, prepared by Jack Cross, landed at Wingfield Aerodrome on this site on February 6th 1939 during his historic London – Cape Town – London flight, which broke all associated records existing at that time.

Elapsed Flight Times

Gravesend to Wingfield   -   39 hours 23 minutes
Wingfield to Gravesend   -   39 hours 36 minutes

This plaque was unveiled by Victor Smith on November 26th 1999 to commemorate the 60th anniversary of this flight and the unbroken solo record which it set.

ULTRASIGNS

1 The plaque in Cape Town commemorating Alex Henshaw's record-breaking flight from Gravesend in 1939.

2 Jacket design by Michael Turner of the night take-off from Gao for Alex Henshaw's book *The Flight of the Mew Gull*.

of. The wilderness leaves one cold and small and rather lost. The aeroplane and GPS know the route. Man on his own would be swallowed up by this place.'

They flew back across Greenland and Iceland, with some menacing weather and plenty of sitting around waiting for it to break. At Keflavik they were joined by John Scurr's Citation. 'New faces for dinner,' Phil wrote, then added, 'I am as tired as I have ever been. The strain of flying across so much nothing is putting me off my sleep. Flying isn't the walk in the park I once thought.'

Three days later, he and Johnny Moss were back at Old Sarum. They had been away for 29 days, travelled 12,500 miles, and spent 102 hours in the air,

Looking back on the trip, Johnny Moss valued it most for the friendship that had blossomed with his young co-pilot: 'I didn't really know Philip at all when we set off, but as we crossed the Atlantic, pottering across between Wick and Keflavik, we just started talking. I think it is something about sitting side by side, and maybe it's because you are not face to face, you can talk about a far wider range of subjects than you do if you are sitting watching the facial expressions. There is something very intimate about being in a small aeroplane, on your own, isolated above this grey and rather unforgiving-looking sea, and any inhibitions drop away. You are, I think, very relaxed, and it builds a tremendous bond. He told me all about his life, which was a fascinating story of what had happened to him, good bits and bad bits and how he had ended

up where he was, doing what he was doing with the farm. I told him all about my life, the Army and so forth. So we really had a fantastically close relationship, which we built on every day we flew together. We also developed a feeling of mutual trust. I had a lot more flying hours under my belt than he did, particularly with all my military helicopter flying; he had something in the order of two or three hundred hours, if that. But he was a very good pilot, very competent, extremely diligent about everything he did. For the relative inexperience that he had, he was extremely knowledgeable, and we had fun working it out together.'

SOUTH AFRICA (2003)
Prelude – overtones of war

The flight to Cape Town in March 2003 was to be the Air Squadron's most bold and ambitious trip yet – 16,500 miles there and back, with a wealth of hazards, both man-made and natural, along the way. Yet the goal was a tempting one: to commemorate, in the centenary year of powered aviation, Alex Henshaw's record-breaking 1939 flight from London to Cape Town and back; to do it in light aircraft; and, having got there, to make a tour of South Africa, a fascinating prospect in its own right.

There was a diplomatic mission too. After its emergence from *apartheid*, South Africa had still to find a new way forward in the world. It seemed

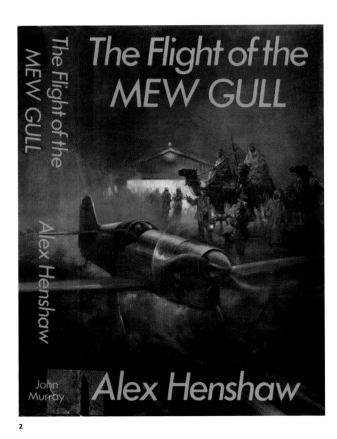

2

a good time to make a gesture of friendship – possibly an award to the Air Force cadets, of the kind that had already proved so successful at home and in the USA. Enquiries with the President's office made it clear that this would be well received.

James Gibson Fleming and Bill Hall started planning the trip. Caryll Waterpark, who had been flying in Africa for more than fifty years, was their special adviser. In early 2002, reconnaissance visits were made. James Gibson Fleming checked safari routes and accommodation, and then Bill Hall – to everyone's surprise – flew the whole route solo, down the west coast of Africa and back up the east coast, because he 'wanted to show it could be done'. (His highly entertaining account of this flight can be found among the members' writings in Chapter 6.)

By May 2002 a programme was ready. A Sword of Honour (commissioned from Wilkinson Sword) would be presented to the South African Air Force in Pretoria, there would be a banquet with the Vice President, an airborne safari through Namibia and Botswana, visits to the Victoria Falls and battlefields of the Zulu wars, and, to vary the pace, some relaxing nights at game lodges and farms.

Now there were bookings to confirm, deposits to pay, decisions to be made. There was also the tricky question of which route to take. Caryll Waterpark laid out the choices:
– Over the Sahara and down the west coast (the shortest)
– The central spine, i.e. the old Imperial Airways route, down the Nile, Khartoum, Entebbe, Ndola,

Victoria Falls, Johannesburg, Cape Town (the most spectacular)
– Or the east coast route: Djibouti, Mombasa, Dar es Salaam, Beira, Maputo (Lourenço Marques), Durban, Cape Town (the longest).

He added some useful advice:
I have done it many, many times and it is enjoyable flying, provided you take all the right precautions. Whatever happens you are going to have to cross the Inter-Tropical Convergence Zone (ITZ) both outbound and return. The criteria being "get up early, fly in the mornings, and if the ITZ is very active land and wait until the weather has improved. NEVER fly at night."

I do strongly suggest that you get Alex Henshaw's book about his record-breaking flight to Cape Town and back because African weather conditions have not changed in sixty years and the Gulf of Benin is described as 'the armpit of Africa' for good reason.

As the members weighed up the pros and cons of the three routes, a new series of considerations began to impinge. The world political situation was deteriorating. After ten years of steadily mounting global optimism, with the collapse of communism and *apartheid*, the growth of free speech and liberalised trade through the internet, and all the hopes that gathered around the new millennium, the terrorist attacks in America on 11th September 2001 came as a horrifying shock. New fractures replaced the divisions of the Cold War. In response to al-Qaeda's *jihad* against the USA and its allies, President Bush declared a War on Terror. In November 2001 American and British forces invaded Afghanistan. There was talk of a war in Iraq as well.

Caryll Waterpark now decided that the Air Squadron should change its plans. He wrote to the Committee on 20th September 2002:

I am getting more and more disturbed by the proposed Air Squadron flight to South Africa in March 2003. Never has the Air Squadron on previous international flights undertaken them with the political implications of the trip so unfavourable as the present situation over Iraq.

1. All of North Africa from the west coast to the east coast is Moslem, with the inherent risk of kidnapping, bombing and political instability in the countries to be landed at and crossed.

2. The cost of getting insurance for the Air Squadron aircraft covering these countries, such as Egypt, the Sudan, Djibouti, Morocco, Algeria, Mauritania etc is liable to be prohibitive, if indeed obtainable at all.

3. I believe, with millions dying in sub Sahara Africa from starvation and countries which we have to fly to or over ruled by vicious dictators, that the Air Squadron flights will attract large publicity, ALL of which will be unfavourable.

Instead of flying their own planes across Africa, he advised taking scheduled flights to Cape Town and using hired aircraft to carry out their programme of presentations, visits and tours.

Bill Hall disagreed. He wrote to the Committee on 22nd September:

Caryll's letter makes several useful points and will obviously have to be distributed. It is a potentially dangerous trip and everyone needs their noses rubbed in the fact. That being said one

can think up all sorts of potential risks (kidnap, bombs, chemical attacks etc) which are impossible to dispute, but if one continues down that route nothing ever gets done. Flying down Africa in light aircraft was never "sensible". One war more or less does not change that.

As for insurance, the premium for his flight round Africa earlier in the year was £500. 'This was when everyone was very unsure about Afghanistan.'

Christopher Sharples, as Chairman, wrote to express his surprise at Caryll Waterpark's change of heart, while James Gibson Fleming declared that whatever anyone else decided, he intended to go.

The difference of opinion now escalated. Like the tropical thunderstorms of the ITCZ, it formed a potentially fatal obstacle to the expedition.

On one side stood Caryll Waterpark, unshakeably convinced that the trip had become too risky; on the other, James Gibson Fleming and Bill Hall, who had invested much time and effort in organising it, and were determined to see it through. Although Caryll Waterpark was a lone voice, he carried immense authority. Several members decided to pull out. The Committee acknowledged the validity of the arguments on both sides, but insisted that individual members must make up their own minds.

This compromise did not satisfy Caryll Waterpark, who now expressed his views with even greater force. In a letter to all members dated 1st October, he wrote:

I would like to cast back in history to the decision

for the Air Squadron to fly to South Africa in 03. It was taken directly after USA 2000 and the options were China or South Africa. The world is a very different place after September 11 and has certainly got even more dangerous since Bush's winds of change speech to the United Nations and the virtual certainty of war in Iraq in the coming months.

Bill Hall set off on his truly epic trip, undertaken by a master pilot of immense experience in long distance travel all over the world. His report on the voyage makes wonderful reading and is in itself a classic of understatement and sangfroid, which actually, I think, should have been published. But read between the lines.

At Bamako a near haboob is blowing, which causes an Air France Boeing to overshoot and depart off Lord knows where... Weather delays caused by thunderstorm activity... Flight plans not received or misunderstood... At Lome more weather delays and flight clearance problems... At Pointe-Noire no avgas, fills aircraft with mogas. That's all right for Bill's aircraft but what about the high compression ratio Continental engines in other aircraft... In his next flight even Bill admits to a few tense hours as he progresses through CB and lightning, at night, as his gyro instruments fail... Arrives, at night, at a major international airport which is documented as open 24 hours but is in fact closed... Another airport is opened for him... He sleeps in the aircraft... but at last he is in South Africa, the weather is marvellous and he is back in civilisation once again. Phew!

The return trip up the east coast is undertaken

with no further problems, other than no avgas in Djibouti. A flight of quite extraordinary courage and fortitude but for any less experienced flyer could have gone badly wrong.

Let's look back at today and whether the same route could be flown. The answer is "no".

The last few days the Ivory Coast has been declared a war zone. Bill Hall would have been flying through this zone on his way from Bamako to Lome. The Times reports Nigerian fighter jets standing by to shoot down any unidentified aircraft. Three years ago when Bruno and I were flying back from Cape Town we wanted to route the west coast and Timbuktu. We were unable to do so as there were 12 countries in central and north west Africa which refused to give us clearance and rebels were rampaging about the airport in Timbuktu.

The Imperial route is still the safest from a purely flying point of view but currently there is intermittent supply of aviation gasoline in Kenya and also in Tanzania. When I telephoned three days ago there was no avgas in Lokichoggio or at the alternate, Lodwar. This of course could change and tomorrow fuel may be back in plentiful supply. Charles Dobie, who was over in London last week, is selling his Baron and buying a turbine because of the increasing difficulty of avgas supplies. However, if you fly around in Africa all of the above is par for the course.

Whilst we are talking about flying in Africa, let me just tell you a little bit about my own experiences.

I have had a bullet through the tail of the aircraft in Luxor. Arrested and released in Zambia for no flight clearance. Refused onward clearance to Libreville

from Lagos control with inflight instructions to return to Abidjan. Arrived in Sierra Leone at night after a 12 hour flight from Recife, Brazil, to find Sierra Leone airport closed and no fuel left to fly to any viable alternate. Had my aircraft impounded by Russians in Fort Lamy Chad, when I unintentionally landed in the middle of a covert re-supply operation by the Russians for that poisonous little dictator of Ethiopia, who has now been given sanctuary by Mugabe, much like Idi Amin still lives in Jeddah.

Flew into a sand storm between Wadi Halfa and Khartoum which glazed the windscreen and blocked the filters, all which had to be changed in Khartoum.

And talking of sand storms, I was flying a 30-passenger airliner, the EMB 130, from Rio to UK and had to land in Sal, Cape Verde Islands. The diversion was Dakar, 300 nm or so out into the Atlantic. On that particular day there was an enormous sand storm covering the whole of the western desert. The President of Mauritania, in his Falcon 20, was killed when his aircraft ran out of fuel looking for a place to land.

The visibility in Sal was 2000m or less in sand from the desert!

Was kept under house arrest in Tananarivo, Madagascar, for 3 days, even though I had flown President Rene of the Seychelles into a conference of African Heads of State. On another occasion was asked by General Khama, son of Seretse Khama, to fly some of his army up to the Kaprivi Strip, which, at that time, was also a war zone with intense fighting going on between Zambia, Selous scouts (Smith's lot) and rebels (Mugabe's lot) and Botswana.

I dropped off the General's re-supply of soldiers and flew back the wounded and medical staff, but left the corpses behind – they had been out in the bush for three days.

Shall I go on? There are many more such experiences.

The almost certainty of an Iraq war gives a completely different complexion to a flight that, even at the best of times, was going to be the most demanding of any flight yet to be undertaken by the Air Squadron.

The other side of the coin is, you can have hours of extremely enjoyable flying, over spectacular countryside, without any weather problems, clearance problems, fuel problems, with lots of cheerful African faces who can be extremely friendly and full of charm.

In your letter you say that you are going to get someone to write a more balanced report of flying in Africa. Looking back over these pages, I think I have just written it.

This was enough for Martin Barraclough. He had done plenty of flying as a young man in East Africa, and knew he could cope with the hazards. But 'in the light of Caryll's two letters, I believe that the committee now has no option but to cancel that part of the Air Squadron tour of South Africa that involves flying out from, and back to, the UK in members' own aircraft, and make it absolutely clear that, as a committee, we now consider it too dangerous.' As an alternative, perhaps flippantly, he suggested a tour to Bermuda – 'no such political problems – only a lot of water!'

Bill Hall was goaded into a sharp reply.

As far as I can see the bottom line is that Caryll (and I) are still here in spite of all the incidents.

The incidents are, in a way, what makes it interesting – to fly a light aircraft round Africa (or to fly a light aircraft at all!) is to take life on and one has to have the confidence that one can cope with what man and nature throws at you.

One also has to realise that there is the possibility that you may get dealt bad cards and get a situation that you cannot deal with. The secret is, of course, to try and minimise this possibility but it is always there.

This trip was never going to be a perambulation looking at the animals and staying in grand hotels.

For what it's worth I've just talked to Overflight, they have aircraft operating in West Africa without problems, they just avoid Ivory Coast this week.

The route is still open.

Opinions, doubts and questions continued to be aired, creating an atmosphere of uncertainty. John Houlder announced that he was going ahead; Terry Holloway said he was inclined to cancel but wanted firm guidance from the Committee. Christopher Sharples was in a difficult position. If the Committee ignored the warnings and something went wrong on the trip, they could be held liable. On the other hand, none of the Committee believed that a war with Iraq had any real bearing on the matter. A special meeting of all interested members was suggested, but Bill Hall thought this would favour the doubters. Instead, Christopher Sharples invited members to send in their written opinions for a special meeting of the Committee on 31st October. Caryll Waterpark took this opportunity to repeat his warnings about fuel shortages, local wars and natural hazards, adding a new risk, 'political fallout':

The danger is, with one and a half million Africans starving, particularly in Malawi but also Zimbabwe and parts of Mozambique, and a further two million at risk in areas of the southern Sahara, that if an African newspaper gets hold of the Air Squadron flight to Cape Town and treats it with ridicule as a bunch of rich white men flying to Cape Town in their private aeroplanes, AT A TIME WHEN THE WHOLE WORLD IS IN TURMOIL, are we doing the right thing and could it rebound to our discredit? …

If an incident were to occur, can you imagine the reaction of the world press – "who are these people and what on earth are they doing?" The resultant publicity could well be terminal for the Air Squadron as a whole.

He added, for good measure, a private comment from a Foreign Office acquaintance: "you must need your marbles examined".

Bill Hall again reacted with a few well-chosen words. 'There are thousands of aircraft flying round Africa. Very few have bullet holes in them.'

As for political fallout and ridicule, he asked, 'Why should the world press (apart perhaps from *Pilot* magazine) even notice us? On past trips we have not got beyond the local press in Quetta and San Diego.'

John Scurr, a keen participant in earlier Squadron trips, was not reassured. 'Having adopted Caryll Waterpark as my aviation mentor, I propose

I am interested to learn that the Air Squadron is planning to celebrate the centenary of powered flight in 2003 with a goodwill flight to South Africa. That sounds simple enough, but I have been down that route, in a BAe 146 of what was then The Queen's Flight, and I think all the participants will find it quite a challenge.

I have no doubt at all that the Air Squadron members will be received with great hospitality in South Africa and I am sure they will make many new friends.

I am delighted to have this opportunity to offer my very best wishes for a successful and enjoyable enterprise.

1

1 A letter of encouragement for the trip to South Africa from the Honorary Air Commodore.

to accept his advice ... Clearly I am concerned about the safety aspects of this trip and would not wish to endanger either myself, passengers or plane. My greatest concern is what this might do to the Air Squadron as a whole. It would be a great pity if this did prove to be a terminal event.'

On 31st October, the day of the Committee meeting, James Gibson Fleming made a robust statement of his own intentions:
I am personally prepared to take the risks for a number of reasons:

- I am already planning to minimize the risks of mechanical failure and fuel problems by making sure I have the range and have thoroughly worked on my aircraft

- I intend to carry excellent satellite navigation, communication and weather information gathering equipment

- Our routing (as a result of long range) minimizes the number of stop offs in dodgy places

- Bill is arranging clearances and fuel drops

- The challenge of this trip is what the Air Squadron is all about for me. Very little worthwhile is achieved without the acceptance and then management of risk

- I rather naively think we do have a modest diplomatic role to play and I know that there are all sorts of people who have heard of this trip who will be surprised and ruefully unimpressed if they hear we are pulling out due to the first whiff of an Iraq war.
That evening the Committee held its meeting. They decided the trip would go ahead.

Three months later the situation changed again. In January 2003, the USA, Britain and a handful of other states signalled their intention to invade Iraq despite opposition from the United Nations. On 30 January Nelson Mandela made a speech in Johannesburg castigating George Bush and Tony Blair for undermining the authority of the UN. 'What I am condemning is that one power, with a president who has no foresight, who cannot think properly, is now wanting to plunge the world into a holocaust.'

On 2 February 2003, less than five weeks before the scheduled departure, Caryll Waterpark tried one last appeal to his fellow members. Following Mandela's 'extraordinary vitriolic' speech, he wrote that he would consider it 'deeply repugnant if the Air Squadron were to make an official visit to South Africa at the present time'. He added that with British forces already en route for Iraq, such a visit would be 'frivolous, unpatriotic and immoral'.

This letter caused more consternation, and further defections. In response to this new crisis, Christopher Sharples organised a conference call, with the participation of fourteen key members. By the end of the call, he said, one of three decisions needed to be taken:-

1. To cancel the trip

2. To postpone until 2004

3. To continue as planned but with possible amendments to the programme.

He then gave a summary of the situation, including developments in the last 48 hours. These included consultations with senior

1

1   Robin Rotherwick piloting his home-built Glasair over the Western Sahara.

military figures, who said they were 'relaxed' about the trip and could see no moral issue at stake. He asked members in turn for their views. Over the next twenty minutes a few doubts were raised, but the consensus was clear: 'Postponement is not the preferred option. The trip will proceed'.

London to Cape Town
As with the USA, Christopher Sharples recorded the journey on film and kept up an email news service so that friends and relations at home could follow the Squadron's progress. These emails were thrilling to receive at the time; re-reading them now, one relives all the drama of this extraordinary adventure. What follows is based very largely, but not exclusively, on those emails. Quotations, unless otherwise attributed, are all from that source.

The journey began, for most of the Air Squadron, with a flight on 6th March to Jerez in southern Spain. The next day they flew on to

Lanzarote – a sea crossing of 700 miles, which meant wearing bulky orange survival suits, with life rafts at the ready, in case of engine failure over the Atlantic, still cold at that time of year.

'The sea crossing was uneventful,' wrote Sharples. 'Tomorrow is the real start of the adventure with a 1200 mile flight, much of it across the Western Sahara stopping at Nouakchott in Mauritania and then Bamako in Mali. It is going to be hot.'

Saturday 8th March
'It certainly was hot today. Most have arrived in Bamako, Mali, whilst some have stayed behind at Nouakchott in Mauritania. Several flew for over 8 hours across the featureless desert, with no sign of habitation at all, and out of range for radio contact for much of the time. The temperature on arrival at Bamako was 40° (104°F) but very dry. Arriving aircraft were greeted with friendly faces and demands for Air Squadron T Shirts, caps and stickers.'

'Mali is certainly one of the poorest countries

and the journey into the town from the airport was a real eye-opener.'

Returning to Bamako airport early in the morning, they found that fuel was in short supply. 'We tried all sorts of inducements: Air Squadron caps were very popular, then T shirts, then badges, then all three and still the fuel was nowhere to be seen. The problem proved to be that whenever a passenger jet arrived, the fuel company rushed over to refuel the airliner and our meagre requirements were quickly forgotten. And the passenger jets kept on coming. Eventually, we learnt that in addition they had been transferring our fuel from drums into a lorry by hand which is why it had been taking so long.'

At midday (40° again) they were on their way, 'climbing painfully slowly with the engines struggling in the intense heat in meagre visibility due to the ever present dust up to 11,000 feet.' Bruno Schoder and Adrian Ferranti, with their passengers Suzanne Maltzahn and Carl Castell-Castell, took a diversion to Timbuktu, the fabled trading city in the Mali desert, while the rest continued to the coast of Togo at Lome.

After 4 or 5 hours in the air, the main group left the Sahara behind and entered the more humid atmosphere of tropical West Africa. The 'Stormscope' instrument, which a few of the aircraft were carrying, now began to give warning of thunderstorms ahead. 'Before long we were plunging into a black cloud delivering turbulent air and torrential rain.' This was the first taste of the ITCZ, and it was not pleasant. As Bill Hall explained,

'there are clouds up there that if you go into them will spit you out in bits.'

Gilbert Greenall and Mic Mac Moss were approaching Lome in their Cessna 182, when radio contact with them was suddenly lost. 'After 20 minutes, and some time after they were due to land, concern was mounting for their safety.'

Mic Mac Moss describes what happened: *There we were flying in a single engine Cessna heading for the most notorious thunderstorm belt in Africa, otherwise known as the Inter Tropical Convergence Zone. I recalled being taught 'don't go anywhere near a thunderstorm'. Big ones can rip the wings off a light aircraft and they are generally very bad news. It was my turn as pilot in command and Gilbert Greenall was in the right hand seat.*

The weather was definitely changing. We'd flown for hours across the featureless, dusty, dry, hot desert of the Western Sahara passing south west of Timbuktu. This unfriendly territory had already been the scene of one scare when Johnny (Gilbert's brother) had a fuel problem and had had to divert to a remote desert outpost in Burkino Faso to have it fixed.

The humidity was increasing fast as we approached the coast and the border with Ghana. We had been warned that this could be the most dangerous part of the trip. 'Thunderstorms ahead' came the warning over the radio from John Steel, whose aircraft was equipped with a Stormscope.

We managed to establish radio contact with our destination at Lome, despite much static interference. They told us to call when closer.

The visibility was deteriorating fast. The dust-

1　Mic Mac Moss in South Africa, 2003

2　Fuel was often unavailabe in parts of Africa except by special arrangement. Drums of avgas had to be shipped in and hand-pumped into the aircraft - a slow process.

laden air of the Sahara was now getting mixed with loads of moisture from the high humidity and it was becoming darker and more sinister by the minute. Although we knew thunderstorms were ahead, we wouldn't be able to see them in the enveloping gloom. Soon we were in complete IMC (in cloud) and being bounced around so much I was worried my head would hit the roof. The Cessna had a mind of its own and one minute was sinking like a stone and the next going up like a rocket, lifted by some invisible force. I was having trouble maintaining control. Torrential rain and lightning flashes were making us feel distinctly nervous.

Then it happened: a blinding flash coupled with a deafening bang. The lights went out. But not just the lights, we had lost all electrical power, which was everything that mattered except for some basic vacuum powered instruments. The engine kept going thanks to the magnetos but we had no radios, navigation instruments or GPS, which meant we would soon be very unsure of our position. There is high ground in the area so we had no way of knowing whether it was safe to descend.

Gilbert crawled into the back to retrieve the portable GPS but in the turbulence everything had been thrown around and he couldn't locate it. Shouting above the din of the rain and engine (the intercom had packed up) he suggested we head south to the coast where we could descend safely over the sea and get out of the cloud.

All this took a while and we knew that by now Lome control and our group would be worried, whilst we were left to battle the elements in a hostile world of our own with no way of contacting anyone.

We gave ourselves a big margin to make sure we were well out to sea before going lower. Finally we broke out of the cloud and were able to work out the direction to Lome.

We still had to get the wheels down and I didn't fancy using the hand pump which was slow and laborious. Gilbert suggested we try recycling the power again to see if it would come on. It did, briefly, but just enough to lower the wheels before the electrical power gave up altogether. But now, thank goodness, we could see Lome runway in the distance.

My landing was far from perfect; my legs were like jelly. We taxied to the aeroclub with a strong smell of sulphuric acid coming from the cowling. The battery was nearly on fire. We were greeted by relieved faces as we were well overdue and they feared the worst.

We were lucky. I agree it is a very good idea to steer clear of thunderstorms.

Gilbert Greenall recalls, 'I remember seeing all the instrumentation disappearing. We are so reliant these days on these lovely gadgets; when they go you are just looking at a blank piece of plastic... I asked Micmac Moss to maintain the heading and the height and we'll just think about what's gone wrong and what we've lost and what we're going to need. I used a paper map to calculate distance and time to the coast, where it would be safe to descend and approach Lome from the sea. It was a fairly simple procedure of just going through first principles. Just don't do anything untoward and quietly work it out. But I was worried for a moment.'

On Monday 10th March, they were stuck

2

all day in Lome: 'Thunderstorms block further progress. The Air Squadron played it safe today and the most adventurous activity proved to be a taxi ride to the aero club and back again to the hotel (which given the traffic conditions is quite a risky undertaking). An early start to the airport proved fruitful when a lorry load of fuel in drums arrived and the next couple of hours were spent hand-pumping it into the aircraft.' The plan was to leave at 10, but it was clear that Gilbert Greenall's Cessna needed work. Also, satellite pictures showed thunderstorms moving across their intended route during the afternoon. They decided to stay another night.

At 6.15 the next morning they set off on the 450-mile journey across the sea to Principe and Sao Tome, off the coast of Equatorial Guinea. These islands had been an independent republic since 1975, after some 500 years of Portuguese rule. The economy, once based on sugar, coffee and cocoa, now relied on tourism and the recent discovery of oil. The population, noted Sharples, 'live a simple lifestyle unaffected by a fast-paced 21st century. Tourists are rare but it is completely safe, unlike its neighbours on the mainland coast to the east.'

As they approached Principe they saw its elevated runway surrounded by palm trees and dense vegetation. On the ground they were met by a large and curious crowd. The arrival of so many small aeroplanes was a unique event, and there was barely room for them all to park. Customs and entrance formalities were brief, and the pilots

and their crews were soon heading for their hotel, where a day's rest was planned. 'Some of us felt we needed it.'

Wednesday 12th March. 'Nobody is complaining at spending a day on this isolated little island just north of the equator. Some have gone big game fishing (Tim Williams, James Gibson Fleming, Carl Castell-Castell, Adrian de Ferranti, Bill Hall, John Steel), others exploring the small town and the flora and fauna (Gilbert Greenall, Johnny Greenall), and some just loll around by the pool or the beach in the high humidity and heat (Robin Rotherwick, Mic Mac). Christopher Sharples wrote emails and Bruno Schroder conducted a board meeting by satellite phone. For the rest, it is the first day since leaving the UK when there is no need for an early start; no need to think about filing flight plans or checking clearances for the next destination; no hassle from officials... no worries about weather forecasts and thunderstorms; no need to spend a couple of hours checking over and refuelling all the aircraft, in fact no need to do anything at all.'

At 7.15 the next morning (13th March) they set off to the neighbouring island of Sao Tome, where fuel had been specially shipped in for their flight to Luanda. The fuel had come in by night to prevent vapour problems in the heat of the day. It was in drums, so once again it had to be pumped by hand – 'a sweaty business in this climate.'

The route from Sao Tome lay southeast across the sea and parallel to the coasts of Gabon, Congo, Zaire and Angola – a trip of 750 miles that would take the

1

smaller aircraft around 6 hours – with lifejackets, life rafts and shark repellent at the ready.

The Foreign Office, Christopher Sharples reported, was not encouraging about Luanda. Its website warned of 'widespread criminal violence, including muggings, car jacking and armed hold-ups that can occur in any area and at any time... Despite a ceasefire in April 2002, over a third of the population is displaced, there are high levels of poverty exclusion, widespread disease, a shattered infrastructure and millions of mines and items of unexploded ordinance around the countryside... Angola is not a sensible destination for leisure travel. Which is why we don't intend to do much more, apart from a dinner with the Defence Attaché, than go from the airport to our hotel and back again.'

Landing at the airport in the first place was no simple matter, however. With no radar, the overworked traffic controller had trouble keeping track of the arriving and departing aircraft. His technique with the approaching Air Squadron flight of seven aeroplanes was to ignore them. 'We came

closer and closer and still most had no approval to start the landing procedures. Bruno Schroder and Adrian Ferranti found themselves circling at 3000 feet above the runway and were still having no luck with air traffic. Finally, in exasperation, they announced that they were going to make a landing and proceeded to approach the runway still asking for permission. At the very last minute authority was granted and they landed without incident.'

The rest of the night stop in Luanda went smoothly enough and dinner with the British Defence Attaché, Adrian Gilbert, 'provided an interesting insight to the life of expats living in Angola. So rich is the country in natural resources that some are optimistic the economy may recover from the ravages of the war.'

From Luanda on 14th March, David and Margaret Hare, John Hogg and John Houlder flew to Botswana, while the others headed for the deserts of Namibia. They planned to meet again in Cape Town on 21st March.

Namibia, Christopher noted, 'is bigger than

1 Namibia's Skeleton Coast, 2003.

2 Jagged rock formations in Nambia. Whilst much of the coast is endless stretches of sand dunes, other areas are forbidding, with no place for a forced landing.

3 A desert landscape in Namibia.

2

3

the UK and France combined, with a population of less than 2 million, which is not surprising given the harsh terrain that makes up most of the country. The Namib and Kalahari deserts are both awesome in their ruggedness and yet spectacular to fly over. Sand dunes stretch as far as the eye can see but are occasionally interspersed with contorted rock formations and sometimes a river flowing through deep canyons from Angola or the mountains to the east.'

On their first day they flew along the Skeleton Coast. James Gibson Fleming, who had temporarily taken over the email diary, wrote that the coast was 'so named because of the whale bones and the carcasses of ships that have foundered on its treacherous shores; it stretches along the whole western side of Namibia. Strong currents and shifting unmarked shoals have trapped many a vessel over the years and even if the mariners were able to make it through the pounding surf and struggle ashore, the chances of surviving in the arid sands of the adjoining desert were, until radio communications, nonexistent.'

Atmospheric conditions were interesting too, with cold sea air meeting warm desert air to form bands of coastal mist that extend up to 30 miles inland, bringing moisture to plants and animals, as well as creating a hazard for aviators. Luckily, the mists had a habit of clearing by 10 am.

With vast inhospitable distances between camps, flying seemed a good way to explore the country. The remotest camp, Serra Cafema, was supplied once a month by lorry from Windhoek, 1200 miles away.

In this strange new environment they were pleased to find that 'flying in and out of the different camps requires skills that most of the Air Squadron pilots have acquired through operating in short field landing strips on farms in the UK.' Yet there was danger too. With fully laden aircraft, and engine efficiency reduced by heat and altitude, as well as soft sandy surfaces on the airstrips, take-off distances were enormously increased.

Bruno Schroder remembers a close shave. 'We took off from the last airport in Namibia and I had Adrian Ferranti in the right hand seat. He's a full pilot so I like to let him fly it. The standard thing is that you pull up the flaps from 30 degrees to 15, which I did. Suddenly the plane wouldn't fly any more, so I yelled at him, "I'll take control". We thundered off across the veldt at 150-200 feet, going like smoke. I put up the gear to stop the drag, and eventually we got well over 100 knots. I then pulled up the rest of the flaps. It taught us all that you have to be very careful. It was a very long runway, and I thought it was fine, but I should not have pulled up the first 30 degrees of flaps, which I would have done in England or America or anywhere else. In those hot and high conditions it needed every bit of flap you could get.'

Not all Air Squadron members had flown to South Africa in their own aeroplanes. Some had flown commercial to Cape Town or Johan-

Pilot (87) recreates epic flight over Africa

Pensioners John Houlder and Lady Isla Abinger in the cockpit of his 1959 Aero Commander 680. PICTURE: ROGAN WARD

Own Correspondent

It's been a long and happy retirement for 87-year-old English pensioner John Houlder and his 77-year-old friend, Lady Isla Abinger.

But their favourite activity is a far cry from a gentle stroll on the beach, a crossword puzzle or afternoon quiz programmes.

Over the past fortnight the two have re-created a 15 000km record-breaking journey from the United Kingdom to Africa in a 1959 Aero Commander 680 light aircraft.

The two flew through destinations including Spain, Lanzarote,

Togo, Angola and Namibia, before reaching Stellenbosch airfield on Saturday for the air show.

The journey was part of a re-creation of pilot Alex Henshaw's return journey from the UK to Cape Town in 1939. The original flight took four days, and still stands as the fastest journey on this route by a single pilot in a light aircraft. Henshaw is still living in England and is aged 90.

Houlder is the owner of Elstree Aerodrome near London, and is one of the oldest people in Britain to hold a pilot's licence. He and Abinger have been firm friends for many years, and loved embracing

the challenge despite their ages.

"John and I have flown a lot around the countryside in England, and it was the (Africa) trip we both wanted to take part in very much," Abinger explained.

Asked how he felt on reaching Cape Town, Houlder played down the magnitude of the journey: "'Here we are', I thought. I knew we would get here. I don't know Henshaw personally, but I have always been fascinated by his journey."

The two fly home in the coming days. They were accompanied on their trip by eight aircraft, part of The Air Squadron, a UK flying club.

1 A press interview with John Houlder following his remarkable achievement in flying his Aero Commander from London to Cape Town at the age of 87.

2 Approaching Cape Town, March 2003.

nesburg and hired light aircraft for local touring. Mark Thomson and Maxi Gainza, for example, flew around the Okavango Delta in a Cessna. Skimming low over this natural wetland, with its dazzling wealth of wildlife and vast untouched spaces, was an experience which Mark Thomson describes as witnessing 'the breathtaking God's magic of the terrain'. At night there were close encounters with the African bush. After tying down their aeroplane at the end of one day, their guide asked if they had piled branches from a thorn bush around the wheels.

'What for?' they asked.

'So the hyenas don't eat your tyres.'

'Surely thorns won't stop them,' said Mark.

'They will if you pee on them.'

And so the bold pilots unzipped, and their tyres survived the night.

The different groups flew south to Cape Town. Landing at Ysterplaat at the foot of Table Mountain, they were greeted by an official delegation. It was Friday 21st March, and they were 6,500 miles from home.

Almost at once the weather changed, from continuous sunshine to rain and high winds. It stayed changed for several days.

On Monday 24th March a fly-in picnic was scheduled at Cape Agulhas, the southernmost point of Africa. In view of the rain – and forecasts for lots more of it – many members decided to drive. Some hardy souls, however, were determined to brave the sky.

'The wind was building with strong gusts and occasional heavy showers. The rain became more persistent and the cloud became lower and lower. Table Mountain disappeared in the gloom completely. The lobster lunch at Cape Agulhas was looking a bit doubtful.

'Gilbert Greenall and Mic Mac Moss were

1

2

1 Flying round Cape Agulhas, the most southern tip of Africa, in a severe storm, March 2003.

2 Margaret Hare, John Hogg and David Hare with their Piper Aztec at Dundee airstrip after visiting the battlefield of Rorke's Drift.

3 Harold Bloch and his wife Jean, who helped to organise Air Squadron activities in South Africa.

attempting to have their electrical problems sorted out once and for all and were going to catch up with us later at Plettenberg Bay. A mechanic turned up who took bits of the aircraft to pieces and then announced that he was going home. Whether this was to get hold of some spare parts or because he had just had enough, nobody was quite sure. So it was a rather disconsolate Gilbert, not helped by a bout of food poisoning, that was left sitting in the hangar as we waited outside for the clearance to start engines.'

'Permission finally came through for us all to start engines and taxi to the holding position before take off. The weather had brightened a little and things were looking up apart from the fact that we were now running two and half hours late.

'In no time we were lifting off into some nasty turbulence coming off the Table Mountain. Our track took us along the coast past the various headlands with ominous names such as Danger Point. No wonder the Cape of Good Hope is also called the Cape of Storms. The gale force headwind reduced our progress by a third and created monster breakers rolling in from the ocean that crashed in a mosaic of white foam on the rocks below as we skirted the southern tip of Africa. The idea of having to ditch due to engine failure was not inviting as the cold current from the Antarctic meant that survival time would only be in minutes.

'The break in the weather did not last. Torrential rain and a lowering cloud base meant for a bumpy ride along this treacherous coast. Keeping over the sea to avoid high ground inland, we proceeded mostly eastwards towards Cape Agulhas. Air traffic

3

was expecting us and gave us guidance over the radio for positioning for a landing at the military base at Overburg, near Agulhas. A heavy rainsquall had moved over the airfield and we were flying completely blind in thick cloud.

'Following precisely the instructions from the traffic controller, we positioned ourselves using instruments alone to descend towards the runway. The torrential rain continued ... The wind buffeted the airframe and the gusts made it difficult to maintain an accurate heading. Just as it came to the point where we would have to overshoot and try again or go elsewhere, the runway lights appeared straight ahead out of the mist and a landing became possible despite the 20-knot plus crosswind.'

Relieved to be safe on the ground at last, they were met by the others, who had arrived much earlier by car, with the question 'What kept you?'

Meanwhile the quietly adventurous Margaret and David Hare had gone 15 miles further the previous day, landing at Andrews Field, the most southerly airstrip on the continent, to find that their red Piper Aztec, G-TAPE, known to everyone as Red Tape, had become the first aircraft ever to have flown to that remote spot from London.

From Cape Town, the group flew north-east, over the mountains of Lesotho to the battlefields of Rorke's Drift and Isandhlwana. They were treated to a 'spellbinding' tour by David Rattray of these two Zulu War encounters of 1879, where a total of 14 Victoria Crosses were awarded.

The next stop was the military base at Waterkloof (Pretoria) for a dinner hosted by the South African Air Force and sponsored by British Aerospace. At the dinner, Lt-General R.J.Beukes, Chief of the South African Air Force, was made an honorary member of

1

1   The Victoria Falls, known locally as *Mosi-oa-Tunya* or 'The Smoke That Thunders', photographed from James Gibson Fleming's Cessna 182.

2   Lord Kitchener's gunboat, the *Melik*, lying in dilapidated condition in Khartoum. Built in Chiswick in 1896 and shipped to Sudan in pieces, the *Melik* was a decisive weapon at Omdurman and in the recapture of Khartoum. The ship was used as a club house by the Blue Nile Sailing Club from 1926, but came to be regarded after Sudanese independence as a symbol of colonial oppression. The *Melik* is now rotting on a sand bank, awaiting rescue in her turn.

3   John Steel, a flying QC and active Air Squadron member, at the Mission Aviation Fellowship Flying Event, Sywell, October 2007.

the Air Squadron, and Michael Graydon presented a Sword of Honour for officer cadets.

The Air Squadron was also thanked for raising £45,000 for the charity Mission Aviation Fellowship. Founded in 1946 by a group of airmen who had served in the war but wanted to use flying for peaceful ends, MAF today operates 130 aircraft in 35 countries, carrying doctors, medicines, building materials, emergency supplies, food and personnel into the remotest communities, 'where deserts, jungles, mountains or swamps bar the way', even when isolated by war or natural disaster. In the words of Gilbert Greenall, 'they will go in where no-one else is prepared to go.'

The party now divided again. Some began the long journey home, while others moved on for a short stay in Kenya.

On 27th April, a group that included Andrew Bengough, James Gibson Fleming, Gilbert and Johnny Greenall, Bill Hall, Mic Mac Moss, Robin Rotherwick and Christopher Sharples were staying at Delarane, a farm in Kenya. Their aeroplanes were at a nearby grass strip. At 6,000 feet above sea level, they were well aware of the dangers of 'hot and high' flying. They therefore planned to set off early in the morning, when the air was cool and take-off would be easier. There were delays, however, and it was almost noon before they were ready to go. The temperature was rising and there had been rain during the night, making the ground soft in places. Johnny Greenall, with his passenger Andrew Bengough, was the first to start up. Faced with a tricky choice between taking off downhill with the wind or uphill against it, Johnny 'made the understandable decision to take off into wind.'

The email diary takes up the story:

2

3

'We all stood and watched anxiously as the aircraft accelerated along the runway. Someone commented that the Turbine Bonanza did not seem to be gathering sufficient speed. There was an expectation that perhaps the take-off would be aborted.

'It seemed that the aircraft was never going to become airborne, but eventually we could see it lift sluggishly into the hot thin air. They started to climb and reached around 250 feet before the climb turned into a nose high gradual descent. The angle of the aircraft suggested a desperate struggle was taking place to stay airborne but the airspeed was decaying and then the aircraft disappeared in amongst the scrub and trees about a mile away.

'To the rest of the Air Squadron members and many others who had gathered to watch the departure, it was obvious that the aircraft had crashed and the fate of Johnny and Andrew hung in the balance. Most of us piled into a Land Rover and raced off to the crash site as fast as possible with everyone preparing themselves for the worst and hoping for the best. The absence of smoke was an encouraging sign as at least it looked as if the aircraft had not caught fire.

'Three minutes later we had reached the crash site by the side of the road. To everyone's enormous relief, Johnny Greenall was out of the aircraft and apparently not injured. Andrew Bengough, whilst proclaiming what a brilliant job Johnny had done, was also uninjured apart from a minor cut to his leg. The Bonanza had ended up on the bank alongside a road after smashing through a fence. One wing had hit a tree that had caused the aircraft to end up facing back the way it had been coming from. Somehow Johnny had managed to avoid

1

1 Henry Labouchere with two of the aircraft that he maintains for Torquil Norman, the DH Dragonfly (left) and the DH Dragon. Henry is an engineer specialising in the restoration and maintenance of vintage aircraft. He has flown more than 100 different Tiger Moths, including his own which he bought in 1970. His skills as a pilot were honed in crop-spraying work in Australia in his youth, flying at altitudes of 18 inches to 50 feet above the ground. He has also flown professionally in Sudan and Morocco, worked in films, taken a Puss Moth to Australia with Tim Williams ('bolting it together all the way'), and co-piloted Torquil Norman's Dragonfly to the USA and back in 1996/7. He joined the Air Squadron in 2001. 'My immediate reaction was, God they're far too grand for me, I don't know what I'm doing here. And I still think that, but I've got used to them and they've got used to me, and they're the most marvellous bunch of mates you could have anywhere in the whole world. Any of them would go to the ends of the earth to help you if you were in a muddle.'

2 Johnny Greenall in the cockpit of his Beech Bonanza at RAF Kinloss, 1998.

high voltage power lines that were just a hundred yards away and had pulled off a crash landing without anyone being injured.

'The smell of aviation fuel was evidence of the ruptured fuel tanks. As a turbine aircraft it used jet fuel, which is much less flammable than the avgas used by most light aircraft, and this may have been a deciding factor in the absence of the horrors of a post-crash fire.'

Three days later, Christopher Sharples reported from Khartoum that 'Johnny Greenall seems to be back on top form after his traumatic time and is now flying with his brother Gilbert … Johnny spent much of yesterday dealing with officials in Nairobi sorting out the paperwork and insurance issues. The various pieces of his aircraft have been put on a lorry and have apparently already been sold by the insurance company, probably for spare parts.'

Over the next few days, the remaining aeroplanes flew home. Bill Hall was last back, touching down at White Waltham on the evening of 6 May.

Christopher Sharples closed his email account with a few statistics:

'Countries landed in or overflown (25): France, Spain, Morocco, Western Sahara, Mauritania, Mali, Burkina Faso, Ghana, Togo, Sao Tome, Angola, Namibia, South Africa, Lesotho, Botswana, Mozambique, Zimbabwe, Zambia, Democratic Republic of Congo, Tanzania, Kenya, Sudan, Egypt, Greece, Italy.

Distance: 14,200 Nautical Miles or 16,400 Statute Miles or 26,300 kilometres.

Total hours flown by all aircraft: 1,250.'

Chapter 5   Awards and Charities

Awards and Charities

1 Giles Goschen flying his 1943 Piper Cub L4, an ex-US Army WWII battlefield liaison aircraft. With a cruise speed of only 70 knots, it is one of the slowest aircraft in the Air Squadron.

2 An air cadet ready to go flying in a Squadron member's Tiger Moth.

3 Maxi Gainza briefs an air cadet on the controls of his Yak 52 before taking him flying.

2

3

The first Sunday in July is an important date in the Air Squadron calendar. In the historic setting of the Royal Air Force College, Cranwell, members gather for a ceremony that celebrates the achievements of air cadets from schools, colleges, and cadet units around Britain.

The ceremony is simple. In a hangar on the Cranwell airfield, three squads of air cadets stand to attention in precisely drawn-up squares. To the right is the Band of the Royal Air Force College, white-gloved, gold-braided, their brass instruments glinting. Facing the cadets is a podium and a line of chairs for spectators. In the centre stands a solitary youthful figure – the winner of the Sir John Thomson Memorial Sword, the outstanding air cadet of the year.

With a few well-chosen words of encouragement, the awards are presented. First the Air Squadron Trophy for the best Combined Cadet Force (RAF) Section, then the Sir John Thomson Memorial Sword, finally the Geoffrey de Havilland Flying Foundation Medals. The band strikes up and the cadets march, past the spectators and away, to loud applause.

After lunch, the cadets go flying in Air Squadron aeroplanes – modern Pipers, Cessnas and Beeches, but also vintage models such as Tiger Moths and Dragons. Once they are up above the windswept Lincolnshire countryside, cadets are allowed to take the controls – an unforgettable experience for everyone. Taking the young flying, says Bruno Schroder, 'doubles the pleasure you have yourself'. The cadets themselves, says one teacher, are 'on fire

with excitement' at the afternoon's adventures.

While the cadets are flying, parents and guests take a tour of the College, where officers have been trained since 1920. Here, among squadron banners and portraits of legendary figures such as Douglas Bader, Frank Whittle and Hugh Dowding, visitors gain a vivid sense of the history and traditions of the Royal Air Force – to which many of today's generation of air cadets will soon make their own contributions.

The cadet scheme offers more than a convenient recruiting system for the armed forces. Michael Graydon explains: 'The formal view is that this is a good thing to do because it's good for young people. It's about making them appreciate what flying is about and giving them an interest in aviation in the wider sense... I think it's doing a huge amount for the youth of this country. I'm involved a lot with schools, and we call it 'life skills' now – a very important ingredient for young people: not just academic qualifications, but skills to cope with life.'

In addition, the Air Squadron's encouragement of the cadets has 'widened the centre of communication so that not only are the parents of the cadets involved but you also have a sponsoring organisation with influence – people who have the ears of politicians and people in the City.'

The success of these awards can be judged most clearly from the reactions of the cadets themselves. Flying Officer Vivien Seymour, of the Royal Grammar School High Wycombe, wrote on 10 July 1996: 'Our cadets felt very privileged to fly in your wonderful aircraft and were in awe of

1 1 July 2007. Cadets at RAF Cranwell for the presentation of the Sir John Thomson Memorial Sword examine John Steel's Cessna 182 before being given the chance to take the controls in a flight experience sortie.

2 Alan Curtis presents the Air Squadron Poignard to the winning member of the Red Devils Free-fall Parachute Regiment Team at Old Sarum, 2008. The presentation took place at the 'Support Our Paras' day, an event that raised £75,000 to help the families of the four Parachute Battalions' Afghanistan casualties, and a further £25,000 for 'Hope & Homes for Children'.

1

2

the tremendous hospitality and interest in them shown by your members. Visits to RAF units are always great highlights in our programmes but last Sunday was made doubly special by the kindnesses shown to everyone. During our journey home the boys were already planning their strategy to maximise their chances of winning your magnificent trophy next year. We all had a day to remember forever.'

In addition to the cadets day at Cranwell, the Air Squadron sponsors several other awards, presented on different occasions during the year. The full list, in order of their founding, is as follows:

– The Air Squadron Trophy for aerobatics (awarded by the Air Squadron 1967-84, subsequently by the British Aerobatic Association)

– The Air Squadron Trophy for home built aircraft (awarded since 1970 by the Popular Flying Association – renamed the Light Aircraft Association in 2007)

– The Air Squadron Trophy for cadets (awarded by the Air Squadron since 1985)

– The Geoffrey de Havilland Flying Foundation Medals (awarded since 1988 by the Chairman of Trustees)

– The Sir John Thomson Memorial Sword (awarded by the Air Squadron since 1995)

– The Millennium Sword for the United States Air Force Cadet of the Year (awarded by the USAF since 2000)

– Gold and Silver Medals – 'to constitute permanent keep-sakes for Trophy winners; to recognize service to the Squadron, and to mark

flying achievements by its own members'. Winners include Torquil Norman and John Houlder for solo flights across the Atlantic, Bill Hall for his African journey in 2002, David Hare for his flight around the world in 2001, and Bruno Schroder for thirty-five years of outstanding generosity and commitment.

– The Air Squadron Poignard, awarded annually for 'the most meritorious member of the Red Devils Free-fall Team' (first presented to the Parachute Regiment at their Arnhem Dinner in 2001)

– The Sword of Honour for the outstanding cadet in the South African Air Force (first presented by the Air Squadron in 2003)

– The Geoffrey de Havilland Flying Foundation 'John Cunningham' Scholarships for air cadets (funded by the Foundation and organised by HQ Air Cadets at RAF Cranwell since 2002. The four scholars also compete for the John Cunningham Bust for flying achievement, and the John Hogg award for all-round achievement)

– The Sword of Honour for the outstanding cadet in the Polish Air Force (first presented by the Air Squadron in 2006).

THE AWARDS
The Air Squadron Trophy for aerobatics

This was the original Air Squadron trophy – a Georgian silver-gilt sauce boat, bought for £120 by Peter Vanneck and James Baring in Bond Street in 1967. It was first awarded as a prize for aerobatics. A competition was set up by the Tiger Club and the Royal Aero Club, and the Air Squadron was invited to provide the

1 Old Warden, 11 July 1987. Peter Vanneck presents the Air Squadron Trophy to Queen Mary's Grammar School, Walsall.

prizes. This new competition followed the end of sponsorship by Lockheed for a UK aerobatics prize in 1965. Since then there had been no national event allowing British pilots to gain practice for international competitions. Many countries had state-funded training schemes for these events, but Britain was dependent on unsponsored private entrants.

The first Air Squadron aerobatics competition was held at Staverton on 1st July 1967, and won by an Australian, David Allan, who received the trophy from Douglas Bader. Competitions have continued to be held each year since then, with various changes to the rules and purpose, and occasional disruptions for weather. Since 1985 the competition has been run by the British Aerobatic Association.

Barry Tempest, twice a winner of the trophy, says, 'it is, with the arguable exception of the Neil Williams Trophy, quite the most elegant trophy the British Aerobatic Association has. I won it on a couple of occasions and my wife Diana nearly wept when it had to be returned.'

The British Aerobatic Association website (www.aerobatics.org.uk) describes the competition as follows: 'Originally a 5 minute free programme was flown. During the initial 25 years of the BAeA it has most often been a nominally Intermediate 4 minute, sometimes a fuller contest acting as Intermediate Nationals, as in 1974 and 1975, and more recently as an Apprentices contest.'

The list of winners 1967-2008 can be found at Appendix C.

The Air Squadron Trophy for home built aircraft

Funds were given by the Air Squadron in 1970 to establish an award for the best home built aircraft at the annual Rally of the Popular Flying Association. Christopher Paul, PFA President at the time, arranged for the purchase of 'a very beautiful solid silver cup on a polished light oak base, about ten inches high, hallmarked George V.' The trophy was first awarded in 1970, to Roy Watling Greenwood for a Druine Turbulent 'which was quite unbelievably good'. The competition attracted 40 entries, and has continued to run successfully ever since. The list of winners 1970-2006 can be found in Appendix D.

The Air Squadron Trophy for air cadets

In 1983 a new Air Squadron trophy was proposed, to be awarded to the best school CCF Air Section. Simon Bostock, who organized the first competition, has written this account of its first 16 years:

It was at the Air Squadron Winter Dinner of 1983 that Martin Barraclough floated the idea of presenting the Air Squadron Trophy to air cadets. For some years, aerobatic pilots had competed for it, but with sponsorship providing budding pilots with both means and incentive, the Air Squadron Committee now sought an alternative cause. Martin suggested that we reward keen young cadets in Air Training Corps (ATC) and Combined Cadet Force (CCF) units with an annual proficiency award. An added bonus would be to fly cadets of the winning unit in Squadron members' Aircraft. The Committee charged me (I was then a serving Squadron Leader) with approaching

Headquarters Air Cadets and providing proposals by the next Winter Dinner.

Group Captain Hives, Senior Air Staff Officer at the Headquarters, said that ATC cadets already had an annual proficiency award, but he enthusiastically embraced the idea of an award for CCF units, with the added attraction of flying experience. He charged Wing Commander Stansfield to work with me on the detail. It was agreed that the proficiency competition and selection of the winner would be entirely the responsibility of HQ Air Cadets; that the Trophy presentation day would be organised by the Air Squadron; that an aviation museum would provide the ideal location, thereby giving the cadets an added interest; that early July would fit in best with school calendars, and that cadets could fly in Air Squadron members' aircraft, subject to compliance with HQ Air Cadets regulations. It was also agreed that HQ Air Cadets would get the cadets to the presentation and accommodate and feed them as necessary.

The Air Squadron Committee ratified the proposals at the 1984 Winter Dinner and charged Simon Ames and me with organising the first presentation day at Old Warden on Saturday 6th July 1985. Simon Ames arranged a lunch at the Hare and Hounds close by, and the Trophy presentation followed in the afternoon. Tony Haig-Thomas organised the flying of cadets of the winning CCF Section from Bedford Modern School, with pilots drawn from the ranks of the Air Squadron and the Shuttleworth Trust. It was a great success.

The formula was repeated in 1986. The Air Officer Commanding Air Cadets, Air Commodore Peter Taylor, attended, and Air Chief Marshal Sir Denis Smallwood,

1 Stephen Partridge-Hicks in a Yak 50. Stephen first flew in 1972 with the School CCF. He started flying hang gliders in 1976 and was part of the 3-man British team that won a Gold in the FAI World Hang Gliding Championships of 2002. "In 1998 I bought my first jet, a Jet Provost 3, and was taught by the illustrious and hugely entertaining Tony Haig-Thomas. The JP3 was finally scrapped and replaced with a Strikemaster in 2006. I also share a pair of Gnats with three friends and we fly the three jets regularly and display them from their base at North Weald." He has owned an RV4, and built an RV8 which with his Microlight and Yak 50 he keeps at home in in Suffolk. He is currently restoring a Mk 17 Seafire and learning to fly helicopters.

2 In 2001, David Hare piloted his Piper Aztec D in the London to Sydney Air Race. David and his co-pilot Robert Miller won six world records for various stages of the race. With his wife Margaret as co-pilot, David continued his flight around the globe, stopping at numerous Pacific islands and Alaska before crossing the North Atlantic to reach London with two hours to spare before the Air Squadron dinner. David and Margaret have also flown this aircraft on Air Squadron trips to Pakistan, South Africa, Poland and Italy.

3 One of the last ever built Cessna T210Rs being flown by Basil Hersov in South Africa. Basil shares the aircraft with his son James and flies all over Southern Africa, including the Skeleton Coast and to a small strip at Hermanus where they have a summer home.

4 John Hoerner bought a Piper Aztec in 1988 and learned to fly in Oxford and Cannes, doing US ratings in twins, IMC and seaplanes. As senior executive at Debenhams he declared Friday 'stores day' and used his Aztec to make unannounced visits to the company's shops all over the UK. More recently he has used his Beech 200 King Air in his supervisory work for Tesco in Central and Eastern Europe. John is particularly proud of the Air Squadron's encouragement of cadets and young fliers.

5 Henry Labouchere at the controls of Torquil Norman's recently restored DH Dragon. This DH 84 Dragon was designed in 1932 as one of the first airliners, built for Edward Hillman who had a bus company. Hillman had asked de Havilland to produce a 'twin engined Fox Moth' that would carry eight people. It cruises along at 85-90 knots and is the forerunner of the famous DH Dragon Rapide.

6 James McAlpine in his Enstrom 480B, built in 2003.

7 Casey Norman flying a DH82 Tiger Moth, built in 1940. Casey, son of Torquil and nephew of Desmond Norman, lives in the Cotswolds and flies from RFC Rendcombe.

8 Tim Clark in his Beech Baron.

INAUGURAL AWARD OF AIR SQUADRON TROPHY

Mr Simon Ames (centre), watched by CWO William Chadwick (right) and members of the RAF section, see Lt-Col D. G. Roberts, Contingent Commander, receive the Air Squadron Trophy on their behalf.

2

then the most distinguished RAF member of the Air Squadron, presented George Herriot's School with the Trophy.

Next year saw Queen Mary's Grammar School, Walsall, receive the Trophy from Air Commodore Sir Peter Vanneck, one of the founders of the Air Squadron. Also for the first time, fuel sponsorship was provided, on this occasion by BP Oil. In 1988 another dimension was added when Group Captain John (Cat's Eyes) Cunningham, Chairman of the Geoffrey de Havilland Flying Foundation and famous wartime ace and test pilot, presented selected cadets of the winning school (Bedford Modern for the second time) with medals For Achievement. These are still awarded to this day.

The Presentation day had now settled into an established routine: lunch at the Hare and Hounds for Squadron members, followed by a brief presentation ceremony on the airfield, photographs and then cadet flying, the aim being to give each cadet at least one flight and a chance to handle the controls. On average the Squadron provided between 40 and 50 flights in a variety of aircraft, some quite exotic – Adrian Swire's Rapide and Tony Haig-Thomas's Harvard to name but two – but finding pilots was a struggle. They were required to have 60 hours first pilot in the previous 12 months, an impossible target for most private pilots. Fortunately, I was able to negotiate with HQ Air Cadets a relaxation to 25 in the previous 12 months and 4 in the previous 56 days.

Judd School Tonbridge won in 1989 and Birkenhead School in 1990, when the organisers and pilots faced an unusual challenge: the United States Base at Chicksands

3

close by had an air display, requiring stringent de-confliction procedures. It was a credit to all that these worked faultlessly. This event saw another development: cadets from the second and third placed schools also attended to receive Flying Foundation Medals and fly.

In 1991 Old Warden altered its annual programme, scheduling a Shuttleworth Collection flying display on the preferred Air Squadron Trophy day. The confliction was likely to be repeated in future years, so with profound gratitude to all the staff at Old Warden, the Squadron took its leave. It was the RAF's turn, and I persuaded the Station Commander at RAF Cosford and the Officer Commanding Birmingham University Air Squadron to take on the day. It was a splendid success, with the magnificent museum there throwing open its doors, giving the victorious cadets of Adams Grammar School an added treat. Two days later I handed the baton to Air Vice-Marshal Ian Macfadyen and departed for a year in Pakistan.

Ian and Simon Ames selected RAF Halton for 1992, and in 1993, having returned from Pakistan and now working at Strike Command, I stuck with it. Winners respectively were Monmouth and Birkenhead schools. A further move followed next year to RAF Benson, with London University Air Squadron the hosts. In perfect weather the cadets of Lancing and the runners up enjoyed a splendid afternoon's flying, but it was to be marred by profound shock and sadness. Air Chief Marshal Sir John Thomson, the most senior of the serving Royal Air Force officers in the Air Squadron and a tremendous ambassador for both, had been prevented from attending by illness. As the Squadron was closing up shop after one of the most successful

events in the history of the presentation day, Air Commodore Timothy Elworthy, Captain of the Queen's Flight, walked across the grass to inform those still there that John had died. It was utterly shattering news, particularly for me; as Group Captain Plans at Strike Command, I had worked closely with John, my Air Officer Commanding in Chief, on this and other Air Squadron events.

Benson hosted the presentation day again in 1995, with Group Captain Terry Holloway, in post at Strike Command, contributing much to its organisation. Maidstone Grammar School began what was to prove a formidable run of success. This day also saw the inaugural presentation of the Sir John Thomson Memorial Sword. In his memory it had been decided to commission a sword and to award it annually to the cadet judged by Headquarters Air Cadets to be the outstanding cadet of the year. Lady Thomson made the presentation and has continued to do so every year.

For 1996, Simon Ames and I – now an air commodore and Commandant of the Central Flying School at Cranwell – agreed that Cranwell should host the day, but the trick was to tempt sufficient pilots to fly to the wilds of Lincolnshire. With Group Captain Terry Holloway, we arranged an aerial treasure hunt, starting at Old Warden on Saturday, stopping over-night in Cambridge and concluding at Cranwell in time to present the Trophy and fly cadets. To set the event off Tony Haig-Thomas organised lunch at Old Warden, and Michael Marshall kept up spirits with a dinner at his Cambridge College. The weather was perfect and the treasure hunt a resounding success. An added bonus of staging the event at Cranwell was the presence

1

2

1 The proud winner of a Geoffrey de Havilland Flying Foundation Medal standing in front of Peter Vacher's Hawker Hurricane at RAF Cranwell.

2 The winner of the Sir John Thomson Memorial Sword 1997, Lee Ahern from Wellington College, standing between Air Vice Marshal John Thompson, CO of RAF Cranwell, and Jan (Lady) Thomson.

there of Headquarters Air Cadets, who shared the burden of organising the day. They with Simon Ames took care of the ceremonial aspects while I continued with the arrangements for the cadet flying. The Red Arrows hangar was selected for the presentation; the Royal Air Force Band formed up to provide the music, and the parents of cadets and Air Squadron members were treated to a splendid parade. Queen Mary's Grammar School, Walsall, were the winning CCF Section, and only the second school to have won the trophy twice. Lunch was taken in the splendour of College Hall, and a tour was arranged for those not involved with the afternoon's flying. Finally, to liven up the whole occasion, Robs Lamplough gave a spirited display in his Spitfire.

Cranwell had proved such a success that the Air Squadron Committee decided to hold the event there permanently. I retired from the Royal Air Force in 1996, and though I continued to organise the flying,

Simon Ames and Headquarters Air Cadets now took on all the administrative and ceremonial arrangements. Maidstone Grammar School won again in 1997, 1999 and 2000, with Dulwich College denying them the consecutive hat trick in 1998. The presentation in 2000 provided a particular challenge, since many Air Squadron pilots were returning from the Squadron's millennium tour of the USA and Canada. With customary efficiency and determination, Simon Ames managed, nevertheless, to gather just sufficient pilots and aircraft, and the event went off without a hitch.

The event had become, and remains, a major event in Cranwell's calendar.

I finally stood aside in 2001, handing the organisation of the flying to Air Commodore Julian Stinton.

The Air Squadron Trophy winners for the years 1985-2008 are listed in Appendix E.

The Geoffrey de Havilland Flying Foundation Medals and Flying Scholarships

The Geoffrey de Havilland Flying Foundation was created in August 1966, shortly after the death of Sir Geoffrey de Havilland, as a memorial to his aviation achievements. Its purpose was to 'advance the development of the art and science of aviation in all its forms, particularly (though not exclusively) for the benefit of young people'.

The founders were Peter de Havilland, the youngest son of Sir Geoffrey; C Martin Sharp, a shareholder in the company; Eric Greenwood, a former Chief Test Pilot of Gloster Aircraft; and Colonel Freddy Gough, MP for Horsham, who was Chairman of the Royal Aero Club at the time. The first Secretary was Brigadier Desmond Curme, who established a small office in Victoria Street and was responsible for the launch and first two years. In 1968 he retired to Jersey, to be replaced by Simon Ames, Chief Executive of the British Light Aviation Centre.

In its early days, with strong financial help from the aviation industry, the Foundation embarked on a programme of scholarships for young people, helping them to add new qualifications to their flying experience or pursue aeronautical studies. Sir Alan Cobham became President and Whitney Straight, at that time Chairman of Rolls Royce, was Chairman of the Council. De Havilland Test Pilot John Wilson and the company's PR Manager John Scott joined the Trustees. In 1980, Group Captain John Cunningham was appointed Chairman of Trustees, a position he held until his death in 2002.

John Cunningham was keen to retain links with the flying services. During the late 1980s gliding scholarships organised by the Royal Navy and Fleet Air Arm at RNAS Lee-on-Solent were established for cadets contemplating a naval career. Achievement Medals for cadets showing leadership and airmindedness were also introduced. These were presented at a joint ceremony with the Air Squadron's annual awards for CCF cadets.

As the British aviation industry declined, so too did its support for the Foundation. It became clear that the Foundation needed a link with an organisation that would help to secure its future. The Trustees, with the full approval of John Cunningham, agreed with a proposal prepared by Simon Ames that the Foundation should become the charitable arm of the Air Squadron. Its name, and its status as a separate entity, would remain unchanged because of its special mandate and registration with the Charity Commissioners. John Cunningham was invited to become an Honorary Member of the Air Squadron. He attended the annual ceremony to present the Achievement Medals and was immensely popular with the cadets.

Towards the end of his life John Cunningham asked Simon Ames to suggest a new Chairman for the Foundation. Simon proposed Ian Macfadyen, an admired senior RAF figure, winner of the Sword of Honour at Cranwell in his youth. John Cunningham happily agreed and Ian took over in 2002.

Since 2002, with generous bequests from the estates of John Cunningham and John Hogg, the

1

2

3

4

1 Robin Rotherwick overhead Cornbury Park in his Columbia 400 which he flew back from the factory in Bend, N.W. America with John Steel. This was the fastest fixed gear propeller-driven aircraft when built, achieving 235 knots at 25,000 ft and capable of carrying four passengers, baggage and full fuel. Robin has been a regular on most of the short and long distance Air Squadron expeditions since joining in 1995.

2 Tom Storey in his Van's RV-9 which he built from a kit between 2005 and 2006. Tom has built or re-built six aircraft over a 40 year period, including Alex Henshaw's record-breaking Mew Gull.

3 Johnny Greenall, brother of Gilbert, flies helicopters and fixed wing aircraft and is here flying his Beech turbo Bonanza. A passionate horseman as well as pilot, he was a professional jockey for many years.

4 William Williams-Wynne joined the Air Squadron in 1974. Chairman of the Europa Club for five years, he sold his first Europa to Wilksch to re-engine with their prototype diesel engine. He now owns a second Europa fitted with a Rotax engine, and also flies a Czech-built Eurostar.

5 Eddie Liverpool making an approach to land his Bell 206B helicopter, built in 1978. Eddie started flying in 1966, progressing to twin-engined aircraft in 1982 and obtaining his helicopter rating in 1988. He took part in several Air Squadron flying competitions and visits, notably Stuttgart (1987), Texas (1989) and Pakistan (1997) when he co-piloted 'Red Tape' with David Hare. He sat on the first Executive Committee of the Air Squadron (1987), and captained the team at the Wallop Challenge in 1993. In his professional life he has been managing director of Melbourns (subsequently Camerons) Brewery, and director of a commercial property company. He has been a Member of the House of Lords since 1970, and in 1997 became one of the 92 Elected Hereditary Peers.

6 Greville Vernon in his Cessna 182, which was built in 2005. Greville organised the Air Squadron visit to Ireland in 2008.

7 Carletto O'Donnell with his wife Lucy and his Aerospatiale SA341 Gazelle. He was brought up in the Bahamas and obtained his PPL in 1977. A third generation pilot after his father and grandmother, the philanthropist Josephine Hartford Bryce, he has time and ratings in more than 30 aircraft types. His trips include crossing the US in 1978, the Chevalier Preston Air Rally in 1989 (commemorating the opening of the Imperial Airways East African route to Johannesburg), Milan to Havana in a Piper Mirage (1995), and numerous flights around Africa, the Caribbean and South America.

8 Charles Masefield's P-51D Mustang, N6365T, was built in Montreal in 1944 and won the King's Cup Air Race on 19th August 1967 at Tollerton, Wolverhampton. In 1969 the aircraft was painted in US Air Force livery for the filming of the movie *Patton*. Charles flew the Mustang from Gatwick to Madrid on February 1st 1969 and then flew it in the action sequences of the film, shot near Madrid in February and March of that year. In the process he established a lifelong friendship with the actor George C. Scott who played Patton in the movie.

fund has grown from £65,000 to £500,000. It now pays for four flying scholarships each year, taking cadets up to Private Pilot Licence level. Tuition is provided during the summer holidays by Tayside Aviation in Perth. At the end of the course, two prizes are given: the John Cunningham Trophy for flying ability, and the John Hogg Trophy for all-round achievement.

The Sir John Thomson Memorial Sword

This trophy was commissioned from Wilkinson Sword in 1995, to commemorate a much-loved member of the Air Squadron, John Thomson, who died on 10 July 1994 while serving as Commander-in-Chief Allied Forces North Western Europe. The premature death (aged 53) of this lively, intelligent and warm-hearted man struck a deep blow of sadness among his friends and colleagues. On July 11, James Baring wrote to Peter Vanneck: 'I was really stopped in my tracks by the news of John Thomson's death. Nothing more unexpected or worse for so many people and projects could have occurred. I was counting on him being there and highly influential for the next 20 years at least! Others can certainly try to carry on as he would have wished, but, dammit all, he was such a key man, straddling with his experience of life and aviation and intercontinental ties so many of the divisions that can otherwise cause problems. One needs not one man to replace him but half a dozen working as a team, not to mention his role as husband, father, friend.'

Marcus de Ferranti, then a fast-jet pilot in the RAF, wrote: 'His qualities were capacity for detail, calmness, and a can-do attitude. During his career, he was the officer who made things happen by taking risks, but always from the most informed possible position. As a result, he was respected throughout all services, professions and ranks. He was never condescending to subordinates, always finding time to educate, explain or just chat. This mixture of qualities, coupled with ambition, had assured his place at the top.' (Letter to Simon Ames, 11 August 1994).

Although other eminent members had died (notably Douglas Bader in 1982), none caused such a widespread sense of shock. James Baring, in his letter to Peter Vanneck, made a proposal: 'It seems to me that something really serious and permanent in the way of Air Squadron commemoration of John should be put in hand. In this way we can turn his premature loss into gain, at least to some small degree. Of course we are all going to snuff it in due course, and we don't want to create a precedent for making a great fuss, but this man had so much to give and was taken so much in his prime that I do feel we should now do something in his name.'

Many others felt the same. Simon Ames wrote to members asking for suggestions for a suitable memorial for a man who 'must take a very large slice of the credit for the very special bond that has developed between the RAF and the Air Squadron'. Several ideas were put forward: an annual publication, a scholarship, a trophy for cadets. It was a proposal by Denis Smallwood that carried the day: 'I have always been impressed

1 The Sir John Thomson Memorial Sword, awarded annually to the best RAF cadet in the Combined Cadet Force.

with the 'Sword of Honour' awarded to the best student graduating from each course at the RAF College Cranwell. Could we not institute a similar arrangement for the best cadet?'

Catalogues were ordered from Wilkinson Sword and a special presentation sword was chosen, with silver hilt and crossguard, the grip covered in blue leather and bound with silver wire; on the blade, the crests of the Thomson family and RAF Strike Command, together with winners' names in years to come, would be etched. At the same time a poignard, or 'miniature sword of peace', was commissioned, to be given to the winner as a permanent keepsake. For the cost of making the sword and poignard (£2,250 in 1995), funds were contributed by members of the Air Squadron and by Jan Thomson, widow of Sir John, who agreed to present the sword at the first ceremony.

The presentation took place at RAF Benson on 9 July 1995, in the presence of 200 guests. The recipient of the sword was described by Air Commodore Peter Stean, Air Officer Commanding Air Cadets, as follows:

'I am pleased to say that we have identified an excellent young CCF (RAF) cadet to be the first recipient of The Sir John Thomson Memorial Sword. He is Cadet Warrant Officer Ian Lakin of Queen Mary's Grammar School, Walsall. Ian comes from one of our outstanding RAF Sections... His achievements in the CCF include: Cadet Warrant Officer rank, Advanced Proficiency, Initial Gliding Training Wings, Marksman, Red Cross First Aid qualified, Army Signals qualified.' He had also passed the Air Cadet Leadership Course at RAF Halton, gained an "Exceptional" rating on his Air Cadet Pilot Navigation Training Scheme, and

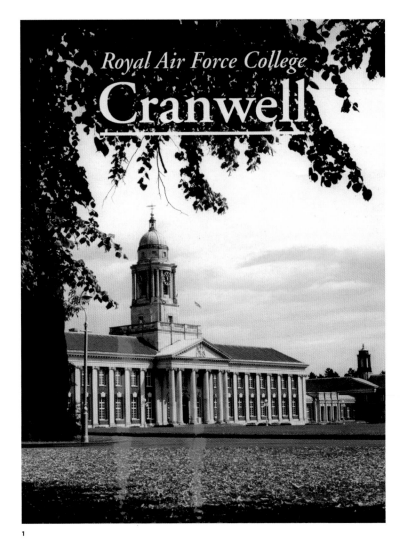

1

2

3

1 RAF Cranwell, where the Air Squadron awards to cadets are made each year in July.

2 The first winner of the Sir John Thomson Memorial Sword, Ian Lakin, from Queen Mary's Grammar School, Walsall, with his parents and Jan (Lady) Thomson, RAF Benson 1995.

3 The winner of the Sir John Thomson Memorial Sword 2006, Nicola Clark from Colston's Collegiate School, Bristol, holding the poignard that she will keep as a memento. With her is Jan (Lady) Thomson.

4

been chosen as one of 14 out of 9000 CCF (RAF) cadets for the International Air Cadet Exchange (IACE) to Sweden. With a place at Oxford to read Engineering, the Duke of Edinburgh's Gold Award and the Chief Scout's Award, he was regarded as 'a very suitable young man for this prestigious award.'

Impressive as this record is, it has been matched in subsequent years by cadets of similar brilliance. In 1999, for example, the sword was won by Nancy Owen, who was head of her school's CCF, captain of shooting, an active member of the 6th Form Council, a keen stage manager, a qualified life guard, first aider and glider pilot, a reading mentor to younger children, and an accomplished saxophonist and clarinettist. She also had a Duke of Edinburgh Silver Medal and a Royal Air Force Flying Scholarship, and planned to read Business and Spanish at university before serving as a pilot in the RAF.

All the award-winners, boys and girls from many different social and geographical backgrounds, display the same inspiring qualities of enthusiasm, hard work, leadership and dedication, as well as that most important characteristic for the Air Squadron, a love of flying. Many go on to careers in the Royal Air Force. A list of the winners of the Sir John Thomson Memorial Sword 1995-2008 can be found at Appendix F.

Overseas Awards

On 19 June 2000, at a dinner in the Mayflower Hotel, Washington, DC, the Air Squadron presented a Millennium Sword of Friendship to the United States Air Force. Every year since then, the USAF has awarded the Sword, together with a solid silver medal, to its Officer Cadet of the Year. The ceremony, at the Pentagon in Washington, is attended by numerous generals, politicians, and defence staff, as well as the UK Air Attaché, a member of the Air Squadron, and the family and colleagues of the winning cadet.

The Cadet of the Year is selected from the 5000 officer cadets who are commissioned into the USAF each year through the Air Force Reserve Officer Training Corps, supported by over 900 US colleges and universities, or through the 4-year course at the Air Force Academy in Colorado Springs.

In a letter to the Air Squadron Chairman in 2004, the UK Air Attaché in Washington, Air Commodore Jerry Witts, commented: 'America loves winners and the USAF is no exception. Recognition, awards and award ceremonies feature prominently in all aspects of US daily life. Albeit that we are in an election year, both the winner's local Congressmen attended or were represented at the award ceremony. Indeed, one of them had earlier that day arranged a personal meeting [for the winner] in the Oval Office with President Bush...

'An award's provenance also adds much to its standing. With the trophy in this case being a Sword of Honour presented by such a select organisation from the USA's staunchest ally (particularly in military aviation), the USAF Cadet

1

2

3

4

1 Nigel Prescot in his Piper Dakota, built in 1979. Nigel flew to Poland with the Air Squadron in 2006. "Who else," he asks, "has a more memorable registration?"

2 James Astor flying his shared Bolkow Monsun which he has twice taken to Italy. He now owns a Vans RV7 which he recently flew to Morocco.

3 Adrian de Ferranti (son of Sebastian, brother of Marcus) started flying in 1982, and joined the Air Squadron in 1986. Although he has mainly flown helicopters, he co-piloted Bruno Schroder's Pilatus on the South African trip in 2003.

4 John Allison joined the Royal Air Force in 1961 and trained on Jet Provosts at Cranwell 1962-4. He flew Lightnings, Phantoms and Tornados. He was a Phantom instructor on exchange with the USAF in Arizona, later at RAF Coningsby. After Staff College, his commands included RAF Wildenrath in Germany, a front line Cold War fighter station. MOD jobs followed: Secretary to the Chiefs of Staff Committee, Director of Air Force Plans and Programmes (Budgets), and Assistant Chief of Defence Staff for Operational Requirements. In 1992 he was given command of No 11 Fighter Group at Bentley Priory, before moving on to C-in-C Logistics Command, and finally C-in-C Strike Command. He was knighted in 1995 and retired with the rank of Air Chief Marshal. He subsequently became a trustee of the Shuttleworth Trust. He has been a display pilot since 1978, starting with the Battle of Britain Memorial Flight and thereafter in a civilian capacity. He still displays a Spitfire for Rolls-Royce and flies the historic aircraft of the Shuttleworth Collection. This experience, he says, 'has brought great joy into my later life. It has opened up a world of flying to me that's beyond imagination.' John Allison has also written regularly for *Pilot* magazine (see his article 'Requiem for a Phantom' in Chapter 6).

5

6

7

8

5   Egidio Gavazzi (No. 26) and Maxi Gainza (No. 50) flying their Yak 52s in the 'Vodka Formation'. Egidio's brother Paolo took the picture from their brother Gerolamo's Gazelle helicopter. There are four Gavazzi brothers, all pilots. They were generous hosts to the Air Squadron on the trip to Italy in 2007.

6   Robert Camrass at the Altiport de Courchevel in his Beechcraft Bonanza, built in 1989. Robert has flown the North Atlantic twice and took his aircraft to the Himalayas on the Air Squadron trip to Pakistan in 1997.

7   Richard Folkes, Director of Army Aviation, stands with fellow Air Squadron member Robs Lamplough in front of the Mustang in which Richard had been given 'the flight of his life' over Middle Wallop and the surrounding countryside. Richard's main task in the Army was to bring the Apache Attack Helicopter into service in 2004. He was also responsible for the Army Air Corps Association, of which Robs Lamplough has been a supporter for many years.

8   James Gibson Fleming in his Cessna 182 which he flies regularly for his farming business. He has also participated in Air Squadron expeditions to Pakistan, USA and South Africa, which he helped organise.

1

2

1 Lt-General Carlo Gagiano, Chief of the South African Air Force (left), with Basil Hersov, an Honorary Colonel of the SAAF, holding the Air Squadron Sword, 2007.

2 Jock Stirrup, Chief of the UK Defence Staff from 2006. Commissioned in 1970, he served on loan with the Sultan of Oman's Air Force, operating Strikemasters in the Dhofar War. Later postings included an exchange appointment on Phantoms in the USA, the Jaguar OCU at Lossiemouth, command of No 11 Squadron, flying Fighter Reconnaissance Jaguars from RAF Laarbruch, command of RAF Marham, Director of Air Force Plans and Programmes, AOC No 1 Group, Deputy C-in-C Strike Command, and Chief of the Air Staff (2003-6). He has also been Commander of NATO's Combined Air Operations Centre 9 and Director of the European Air Group. He joined the Air Squadron in 2001 and was appointed KCB in 2002.

3 Poland 2006: Michael Graydon presents a Sword of Friendship to Lt-General Stanislaw Targosz, Commander of the Polish Air Force.

4 Martin Barraclough presenting the Air Squadron Sword to Karen Fisher, the winning US cadet in 2002. The sword was a gift to the Chief of the Air Staff of the United States Air Force in 2000. It is awarded annually to the USAF Cadet of the Year.

3

4

of the Year award is extremely prestigious.'

Inspired by the success of the Millennium Sword in the USA, the Squadron offered a Sword of Honour to the South African Air Force on the occasion of their visit to Pretoria in April 2003. This was handed to Lt-General R.J.Beukes, Chief of the South African Air Force, by Michael Graydon. It is now awarded for all-round achievement to the top graduate flying officer at the Air Force College in Pretoria. Basil Hersov, who attends the ceremony each year as the representative of the Air Squadron and as an Honorary Colonel in the South African Air Force, describes the event as 'very important, a big parade, attended by all the top officers. The Chief of the Air Force always takes the parade himself and the sword is presented by him.' As to its significance, he adds, 'The sword is greatly appreciated for its connection to Britain and the Royal Air Force through the Air Squadron.'

On the Squadron's visit to Warsaw in 2006, a sword was presented to the Polish Air Force in honour of the many Polish airmen who served in Britain in the Second World War. This too has become a prized award to officer cadets. In a letter to Jonathan Elwes, who organized the Warsaw visit, the Commander of the Polish Air Force, Lt-General Andrzej Blasik, writes of the 'very close and great friendship' that has resulted.

It is clear from such testimonials that these international awards carry great prestige, a view confirmed by Jock Stirrup, Chief of the Defence Staff.

'I have been to Poland, South Africa and the USA in my professional capacity more than once, and spoken to my opposite numbers in my present role and in my previous role as Chief of the Air Staff. I know that they value this relationship very highly indeed. The sense of interest and shared endeavour and common purpose that these awards foster is very tangible... This connection to an established organization from a country that has been a friend, through some good times as well as bad, is enormously important to them. And we must be careful ourselves not to lose sight of how important it is to them.'

The variety and significance of the awards given by the Air Squadron have grown enormously since the first trophy for aerobatics was presented in July 1967. Many members have given much time and thought to this aspect of the Squadron's life, none more so than Bruno Schroder and Simon Ames. Bruno Schroder recalls: 'Soon after I was elected in 1974 I suggested to Douglas Bader that, given that the Air Squadron had a number of well-off members, it could help other parts of aviation. Douglas replied, "The Air Squadron is just a society of friends". End of conversation. How the Air Squadron has changed in the last 35 years!'

Chapter 6   Exploits

Exploits

The professions exercised by Air Squadron members are as various as the aeroplanes they fly. In 2008 these included architect, banker, civil servant, company director, engineer, farmer, financier, fund manager, jeweller, journalist, land agent, landowner, lawyer, museum curator, music teacher, officer in the armed forces, painter, physician, property developer, public relations consultant, publisher, resort manager, shipowner, student, surgeon, textile manufacturer, toy designer, and a number of careers which defy the usual descriptions. To these we should add the professions of past members, such as aeroplane salesman, auctioneer, estate agent, newspaper owner, stockbroker and television executive. It must be remembered, of course, that most of these are the 'day jobs' – set aside on evenings, weekends and holidays for the true passion of their lives: flying.

Given the variety and dynamism of these people it is not surprising that some should have written books and articles about their exploits – or, in a few cases, had books and articles written about them. The gliding pioneer Philip Wills was an early member of the Air Squadron, and wrote one of the most highly regarded of all flying books, *On being a bird* (1953). John Allison and Maxi Gainza have been regular contributors to *Pilot* magazine, Alex Norman was Defence Correspondent of *The Spectator* for several years (and has written biographies of the Dalai Lamas), Egidio Gavazzi founded Italy's

leading wildlife periodical, *Airone,* and has written a fascinating account of his love of birds and fighter aircraft in *Desiderio di Volo,* published in Italy but yet to appear in English. Alex Henshaw wrote of his racing and test-pilot years in *The Flight of the Mew Gull* and *Sigh for a Merlin*, and Tony Haig-Thomas has just completed an amusing account of his youth as a fighter pilot in Britain and Aden, *Fall Out Roman Catholics and Jews*. Polly Vacher's long-distance flights for charity are described in *Wings Around the World*, and Martin Barraclough's early adventures as a pilot in East Africa, his four decades with the Air Squadron, and his long love affair with vintage aeroplanes are recounted in *Fifty Years Have Flown*. James Baring, true to his spirit as an internet pioneer, has published several autobiographical sketches on his website (http://revelstoke.org.uk/Strange_Adventures.html), and Jonathan Elwes has recorded two of his Tiger Moth expeditions, with excellent photographs, in *Eight Wings to the North* and *Glasmoth*. Among many articles in the press it is worth singling out a portrait of Torquil Norman by the poker-playing literary critic Al Alvarez. This was originally published in *The New Yorker*; it is much too long to reprint here, but can be found in Alvarez's book *Risky Business*.

Four early members of the Air Squadron were Battle of Britain pilots. Their courage and skill have been celebrated in an unceasing flow of historical and biographical works, although few can match the physical and psychological immediacy of Hugh Dundas's *Flying Start*. More recently the stories of key players in the Falklands War, including Michael

Beetham, Peter Cameron and Peter Squire, now form the subjects of a new generation of military histories.

Other members have appeared on cinema and television screens, sometimes in disguised (or even transvestite) form: Robs Lamplough flew as Beryl Markham in *Shadow on the Sun* and as aviators of different nationalities in *Pearl Harbor, Memphis Belle, Empire of the Sun, Flyboys* and *Dark Blue World*. (He also drove in John Frankenheimer's motor racing classic, *Grand Prix.*) Henry Labouchere has had a similarly varied cinematic career, including *A Piece of Cake* and *A Bridge Too Far*. Charles Masefield flew his P-51 Mustang in *Patton,* Caryll Waterpark performed flying sequences in East Africa for two 1950s Tarzan adventures, and Christopher Foyle turned up as a bookseller in the TV series *Foyle's War*. On the stranger-than-fiction side, Hugh Astor's work as a spymaster, running German double agents in some notable campaigns of deception, was revealed in a BBC documentary shortly after his death. ('If one man could be credited for winning the war,' said Euan Strathcona, 'Hugh Astor would be my choice.') The most popular film of the Air Squadron's war collection, however, is *Reach for the Sky*. Kenneth More's portrayal of Douglas Bader was based on a close study of the original; Simon Ames, who knew both men well, describes it as 'absolutely true to life'.

It would be fun to assemble an anthology of film sequences, and perhaps a future electronic edition of this book might include it. What follows is a selection of writings by Air Squadron members – tales that amuse, thrill or inform, told by the protagonists themselves. As well as being good

flying stories, they also express three of the qualities that characterize the membership as a whole: courage, curiosity and the spirit of adventure.

ON FIRST MEETING DOUGLAS BADER (1940)
Hugh Dundas, *Flying Start* (Stanley Paul & Co, 1988) pp 47-8

After we had landed at Fowlmere and seen our planes refuelled and made ready for action we went into a hut on the edge of the field for tea and sandwiches. There we met the pilots of 19 Squadron and settled down to wait for developments.

Quite soon the door was flung open and an extraordinary figure in squadron leader's uniform stomped vigorously into the hut. Instantly the subdued and somewhat queasy atmosphere was dispelled, driven away by the hard, robust character of Douglas Bader as he called noisily for Billy Burton, an old friend, and then greeted each one of us individually. Much has been written about Bader. I shall write much more, for we were to be closely associated during the spring and summer months of 1941. My personal debt to him is incalculable. He showed me quite clearly by his example the way in which a man should behave in time of war and his spirit buoyed me up through many dark days long after he himself became a prisoner of war.

With Bader on this occasion of our first meeting was the Duxford sector commander, Wing Commander 'Woodie' Woodhall. Then and later, in 1941, he and Bader combined together with remarkable effect – Bader as the formation leader, always, always looking for a fight; Woodhall as the controller with a cool, unruffled ability to size up the situation presented to him on the big board in his operations room and then to give directions to his pilots in a voice which invariably remained calm and sonorous, even at times of greatest stress.

I felt better, much better, after their visit. I was almost anxious to get airborne on patrol behind this fabulous character. But in fact nothing happened that day. The five squadrons sat on the ground inactive and late in the evening we flew home to Kirton. From then until the end of September we went down to Fowlmere most days, once or twice spending the night there in bunks in the dispersal hut. Almost every day we took off and patrolled the London area in our strong formation of sixty planes, the three Hurricane squadrons in a wedge below, the Spitfires above and to one side.

On the first of these sorties, after the five squadrons had assembled in proper order and were climbing away to the south and the butterflies in my tummy had begun to work overtime, Bader's voice rang out on the radio, calling Woodhouse in the control room. To my amazement the purpose of his call turned out to be the arrangement of a game of squash. Bader explained that he had intended to ask a particular person to play with him but had forgotten to do so before taking off. He asked Woodhall to do it for him. The conversation had a decidedly calming effect on my nerves and the butterflies were somewhat subdued. It was extraordinary enough that a man with two tin legs should have been thinking about squash, in any circumstances. That he should be doing so while leading three squadrons of Hurricanes and two of Spitfires into battle against the Luftwaffe was even more extraordinary. Here, quite clearly, was a man made in the mould of Francis Drake – a man to be followed, a man who would win.

TEST FLIGHT IN A LANCASTER (1944)
Alex Henshaw, *Sigh for a Merlin* (Crécy Publishing, 1996) pp 180-2

The monthly check on full performance trials now necessitated a flight to 45,000 ft or over in the Spitfire and 29,000 ft in the Lancaster. The former was completed easily and quickly unless I had to check for stability due to change to a new type

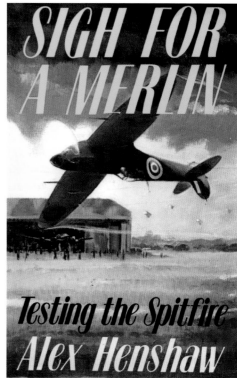

Alex Henshaw
in 1939

airscrew or some modification, but the Lancaster was more ponderous. Also for the first time I had to think of others as well as myself. This was brought home to me abruptly when once we were creeping up to around 28,000 ft: a member of the crew came forward and said, 'Eric Holden is either asleep or unconscious.' Not wishing to break off the trials, which were at a fairly conclusive stage, I shouted to Billy Buckley to check Eric out at once and they found that he had trapped his oxygen line; when this was freed he recovered quickly enough.

It made me realise the seriousness of having a crew who were not medically fit and who could pass out on me, with probably more serious consequences. From then on I made sure everyone who wanted to fly was examined by the Works Doctor. It was inevitable that with so much flying I would be unable to insist on my own crew, whom I knew well, being with me on every flight that I made, and I only assumed that new members had been carefully briefed before take-off. This rather loose system almost cost me my life and made me realise as never before the importance of a well

disciplined, knowledgeable and clear thinking team, reacting immediately to the calls made upon them by the pilot. On 17 March in Lancaster HK540 we had flown for approximately half-an-hour and had landed with a few minor snags. On the 18th the machine was flown once again and appeared to be all right; at 10,000 ft we commenced a power dive and had reached the speed of about 320 IAS when I heard a shout from my No.3 to slow up; at the same time I felt a severe jolt go right through the machine, which then pitched into an uncontrollable dive, and in spite of every effort I could do nothing about it. We were in clear weather with a thick layer of stratus below at about 4-5000 ft. As I struggled to get the machine under control I heard my No.3 shout something about the dinghy bursting out of the wing, striking the tailplane and wrapping itself round one of the fins. In seconds I was going to plummet into the cloud below so, noting that my own chute was in place, I gave the order to bale out to every crew member. To my astonishment, as I hung onto the controls, ready to make my own desperate attempt to get

out through the forward hatch, no-one moved. The new flight engineer beside me stood petrified as if welded to the machine and although I screamed down the intercom the whole crew either could not or would not listen to me. For a split second I toyed with the idea of going it alone, but when I saw the look of fear on the man beside me I knew I could not leave him, and even if I had I doubted whether I could have got past him on my way down to the hatch and snapped my chute on in time before we hit the ground.

We were now in cloud with me almost standing on the instrument panel in my frenzied attempt to pull the machine out. It would not budge and the dive got progressively steeper and faster; I realised that within seconds of us breaking out of the cloud we should be making a very nasty hole somewhere around Birmingham. Just then I felt something give; I assumed later that it was the dinghy tearing away from the tailplane, for the machine suddenly responded to the elevator control. We came out of the dive over the tops of houses on the north-east sector of Sutton Coldfield, with me in a bath of perspiration from my physical exertions at the controls and my frustration at not being able to get out of the aircraft or get my crew to make the first move. When we landed and the crew saw the extent of the damage to the tail, it was very easy to appreciate why I could not control the machine; my immediate relief was then rapidly displaced by cold anger as I began to realise that I had nearly been killed by a crew who were either deaf or stupid and unfit to fly as a test team.

I called them into my office later, when they had recovered from the shock, and told them in no mean manner what I thought. Each man swore he did not hear my instructions but, as I said at the time, 'You make bloody sure you do next time, because if you think I am going to wait and be killed because of a lot of stupid fools like you, you've got another think coming. Next time you'll find yourselves on your own.' I then told Buckley, Holden and Hastings to select carefully those who they thought would make a good flight team and to send them to me for a very thorough briefing on what to do in a similar emergency and, in particular, to ensure that they knew how to test and use the intercom.

THE SPIN TEST (1953)
Philip Wills, *On being a bird* (Max Parrish, London, 1953) pp 95-101

In 1937 the Germans held the first International Gliding Championships ever organised. The venue was their famous soaring centre on the Wasserkuppe, in the Rhön mountains.

We decided to enter a team and, as it happened, Slingsby was at the time building at his works a new high performance sailplane, designed by Mungo Buxton, who had also designed my Hjordis. The Slingsby firm very sportingly decided to take the risk and complete three of these aircraft for us to take to Germany.

I say 'risk' because, in the normal way, a new design is usually built as a single prototype, which is then exhaustively tested and modified until one is quite sure she is right; and not until then does quantity production start. There was no time for this in this case, but Hjordis, designed and built by the same people, had proved immediately successful, so everyone, including myself, had considerable confidence in the new type.

The first machine was finished in April, and I went north for her test flying, which took place from York aerodrome. She proved beautiful to look at and to handle, and everyone congratulated everyone else on her success. A month went by, and in Coronation week I again went north for her final trials, the last item of which was to be her test for spinning. Even today, when the causes of spinning and the design requirements for successful recovery from a spin are fairly well known, every machine has to be taken to a great height and stalled and spun deliberately before the designer can be quite certain that it is satisfactory in this respect. But I had never heard of a glider spinning viciously: in fact my own Hjordis refused to spin at all; and the King Kite had behaved so beautifully on all

Philip Wills (1907-78) learned to fly in 1928 and quickly became a dominant figure in British gliding. His obituary in *The Times* (18 January 1978) describes him as 'continually extending the frontiers of gliding... He repeatedly broke British distance and height records both before and after the Second World War.' While serving as Director of Operations in the Air Transport Auxiliary in the war he qualified to ferry all types of single, twin and multi-engined aircraft. From 1946 to 1948 he was General Manager (Technical) of BOAC, the British Overseas Airways Corporation. At the age of 45 he won the title of Single Seater World Gliding Champion. *On being a bird* is the best-known of his books — a clear, thorough and passionate account of the pleasures and hazards of gliding.

her trials so far that any idea of trouble never entered my head.

I was strapped into the cockpit and the celluloid cover was put on over my head. Three hundred feet of wire cable was strung from the tail-skid hook of the towing aeroplane to my own nose-hook, and we took off.

It was a clear blue day with not a ripple in the sky. At 4,500 feet I pulled the release, and the aeroplane put down its nose and dived away to the distant earth. I floated along for a minute or so in the blissful quiet which is one of the abiding joys of the sport. Then I eased the stick gently back, and she started to climb. Slowly the speed fell off until, as the needle came back to just under 40, she gave a little shudder, and the stick went dead. I kicked on full left rudder, the nose rolled over, the earth tilted majestically up from underneath until it was right ahead of me, then started to revolve.

After half a turn the speed came up rapidly, I put on opposite rudder and centralised the stick in the normal way, the earth slowed down and returned quietly to its normal place beneath me. Good! I glanced at the altimeter: still 4,000 feet up, plenty of height for one more spin, the other way.

I eased back the stick once more, she climbed, slowed, faltered. I kicked on full right rudder, she rolled over like a gannet on to the dive. I let her spin a little longer this time, all seemed well, then moved the controls again to bring her out.

Nothing happened: the earth ahead went on revolving like an immense gramophone record, objects on it growing perceptibly larger.

Quickly I put the controls back to spinning position, adjusted the wing-flaps, and tried again, firmly. Still the spin went on, my speed increasing unsteadily and the hum of the wind outside growing to a roar. There was nothing more to be done; the time, so often anticipated, had come to abandon ship and take my first taste of the delights or otherwise of parachuting.

There was so much to do that I did not feel in the least worried, only faintly ridiculous that such a thing should befall me, a respectable City business man, husband and father. There was some mistake; these experiences should confine themselves to our professional heroes. But my next movements had been practised so often in imagination that they took place almost without volition.

I reached above my head for the cord releasing the cockpit cover, pulled it, and pushed the cover upwards. The gale outside lanced in underneath as it lifted, caught it from my hand and whirled it away. The wind shrieked and tore at my clothes, caught my glasses and whipped them off. The nearing earth became a green, unfocused, whirling blur. I let go of the controls and my hands went to the catch fastening the safety straps, clicked it open, and gave a reassuring pat to the sheathed handle of the parachute rip-cord.

The machine, freed of all attempt at human control, lurched about as it span in a curious idiot way, a body without a mind. I drew up my knees, leant over the left-hand side of the cockpit, and dived head foremost over the edge.

And now a dreadful thing happened. As I went over the side, it seemed to swing round and up at me with a vicious jerk, struck me across my chest and flung me back helplessly into my seat. The spin went on.

A second time I gathered myself together and leaped over the side, and a second time I was caught and bounced childishly back: it was as if I was struggling to break through the bars of an invisible but invincible cage. The spin went on. The blurred earth seemed now very near: in fact it was scarcely two hundred and fifty yards ahead.

It is curious but true that at a last moment such as this one's body, partly exhausted by former struggles, can nevertheless gather together sufficient physical energy to make a final effort surpassing previous ones. A third time I flung myself, still more violently, over the side. This time I got well out, head-first and well forward – almost free – the whirling outline of wings and fuselage was all around me, filling the sky. There was the most appalling bang, a violent blow, and I found myself once more back in my seat, hands and feet instinctively on the controls. The world swung violently overhead, slowed, stopped spinning, stopped spinning, the machine was on its back, only centrifugal force was holding me in – but the controls were biting the air again, life had come back into them, life in them was life in me. I pulled back on the stick, she came staggering round on the second half of a loop, I steadied her, and looked down.

The aerodrome buildings were a bare three hundred feet beneath. The raging gale in the exposed cockpit sank to a friendly breeze, apologising for losing its temper. I put down the landing flaps, did a half turn and landed, not a hundred yards from the clubhouse. I looked out, and saw my wife running towards me over the turf. My recording barograph showed that I had spun down like Satan from Paradise, two thirds of a mile in one minute.

After a while I levered myself to my feet and stepped gingerly over the edge of the cockpit. As I did so I felt a violent cramping pain in my chest. Clearly I had strained my heart: you can't go doing things like this without paying for it, I thought.

I was helped into the clubhouse and lay down, waiting for the reaction. Every time I moved my heart gave a vicious tweak. Ten minutes later I put my hand to my waistcoat pocket for a soothing cigarette and brought out my metal case bent in a line across its centre to the shape of a three-dimensional 'L'.

My last jump had got my weight so far forward, had so materially altered the trim of the machine, that the hidden vice had been overcome. As the wings bit the air at high speed, the machine was swung round with such violence that we found the main wingbolts, great rods of steel holding the wings to the fuselage, all four bent. And the side of the cockpit came round and hit my chest with a blow sufficient to break every rib in my body. But instead it caught my cigarette case fair in the middle, the force was distributed over an area, and I escaped with a set of internal bruises that kept me awake for the next three weeks, a cigarette case that will never open again, and a parachute that never had been opened, but nevertheless had given me the incentive to jump.

In the outcome, I was able to describe my spin sufficiently well for the experts to diagnose too small a rudder. A larger one was fitted, the machine was tested again with many safeguards. Although subsequent events showed that this was not the full answer, we took the three King Kites to Germany with two other machines, and in the fortnight the British team did cross-country flights totalling over 1,100 miles.

I was told that I should have known that you must always bale out on the *inside* of a spin, and that if, in a right-hand spin, I had dived over the *right*-hand side, I would have fallen cleanly and instantly down the centre of the corkscrew and, once clear of the machine, released my parachute and watched the glider spin down to its wreckage.

As it happened it was fortunate I did not know this, one of the elementary rules of parachuting which no one troubles to tell you; for the machine was saved. Even the cockpit cover was picked up, but slightly damaged, a mile away. The only permanent loss was my spectacles, and perhaps a few days cut off my old age.

VENOM IN ADEN (1959)

Tony Haig-Thomas, *Fall Out Roman Catholics and Jews* (Old Forge Publishing, 2008. Copies available from the Shuttleworth Trust, which receives all royalties from the book: www.shuttleworth.org)

Sometimes the intelligence staff would tell a village that if they received arms from the Yemen they would be the centre of a proscribed area in which anything would be shot including people or animals, the latter because they represented wealth and not because they were suspected of gun running. Flag waves, proscribed areas, leaflet drops and of course, occasionally, a little demolition were the control measures used, exactly as they had been on the NW frontier of India in the 1930s. When we were 'on ops' flying was curtailed the day before to get the aircraft armed and serviceable and, when armed, each Venom had a red flag mounted on its nose so there was little secret about it. I did wonder, quite absurdly, about Nasser, the Squadron

Tony Haig-Thomas on the wing of his Grumman Avenger

odd job man who made the tea and coffee, looked half starved and came from the Yemen. As a boy I devoured all the Biggles books and remembered that in *Biggles in the Orient* my hero uncovered a treacherous spy in the officers' mess called Lal Din who, when confronted by the great B, committed hari-kari all over the floor in the officers' mess ante room. I was reminded of the Oriental saga when Nasser was looking at the armed Venoms with flags and inquired 'Tomorrow Operations yes?' 'Yes,' I replied, and was ashamed to think the thought that had briefly crossed my mind. A more unlikely spy would have been hard to find and the mess on the crew room floor would have to be cleared up by the junior pilot – still myself.

One day Andy Devine said that we were going to fly to Djibouti in French Somaliland for lunch. We took four Venoms and landed at noon for our goodwill visit; as I taxied in, I noticed three Junkers 52s, old WWII German transport aircraft, parked next to us. Even then in 1959 they looked incongruous antiques with their three radial engines and corrugated aluminium construction. I had never experienced French entertaining before. Lunch started at one and finished at four; I was very drunk without any doubt and the other three did not look much better. Our hosts drove us back to our Venoms where Andy found that they had not been refuelled and, worse still, that the drivers had finished for the day – so no fuel. After a short discussion, and bitterly regretting the use of the fuel during our impromptu four ship formation we had flown on arrival, Andy said we could make

it home without refuelling. We did, just. After take off we climbed straight ahead to 30,000' and did a long cruise descent back into Khormaksar during which I realised that if one had had too much, or much too much, vin rouge for lunch a transit from French Somaliland to Aden with very little fuel enabled one to sober up very quickly indeed.

Soon it was my turn to go 'up country' again. I liked the phrase 'up country', it certainly was the inverse of 'down town' and so accurately described the translation from our life in Aden to the South Arabian hinterland. Soldiering in the Aden protectorates was run by the RAF regiment, with tanks and armoured cars supplied and usually crewed by the Army. From what I saw of the 'RAF soldiers' they were very good. I just could not quite understand why they were in the RAF. Upon my arrival at Ataq (appropriately enough pronounced 'attack') the Flight Lieutenant in charge of the operation the next day buttonholed me. 'Ever been under fire?' he asked. 'Only in my Venom,' I replied. 'Well, tomorrow you will find it a bit different when you are on the ground.' I thought little of his remark until the next day. The master plan was for us to leave at dawn with some troops from the Aden Protectorate Levies (Protectorate Arabs, British officered) in three lorries, three armoured cars or Ferrets as they were known, and myself the ALO (Air Liaison Officer, nowadays called a FAC or Forward Air Controller). We would drive to a local village at the foot of some hills, dropping off the lorries out of rifle range, while the Ferrets and the ALO would drive forward to the

village. I was then to call in the Venoms to do high speed runs, the baddies would take to the hills and the Venoms would shoot them. The plan to me, even then, seemed a little naive. It also had a major weakness. The APL troops would be safe in the rear, the regular army, who are paid to be killed, would be in their armoured cars, leaving only myself in an open top Land Rover exposed to hordes of angry Arabs armed to the teeth. (Arabs are always angry it seems, especially nowadays, just as they are always going to fight to the last drop of blood – inferentially their own – a loser mentality if ever there was one). The battle plan proceeded like clockwork. To start with we stopped the lorries a mile from the village and I and the three armoured cars drove forward. Someone must have been in charge telling them to hold their fire because nothing happened until we halted at around four hundred yards when a hail of mercifully very badly aimed rounds came our way just as I had called in the first pair for a low run. I was amazed; as the Venoms turned in, firing at us stopped and several hundred rounds were fired at the aircraft; as soon as the aircraft were clear, firing resumed at us. I slowly became aware that 'us' meant me, since my Arab driver had jumped out and fled behind a rock. None of that for me, I was British; I was, however, sitting bolt upright in my Land Rover clutching the microphone very tightly, wearing my No.1 Service Dress hat, and becoming aware that my mouth had gone very, very dry. Bullets were ricocheting off rocks making noises just like the films and then I felt one pass in front of my face, hearing the shot

that fired it very soon afterwards. I decided to forgo my medal for conspicuous gallantry, and join my Arab driver behind the rock. Half an hour later we all retreated, drove back to Ataq and I went back to Aden and the safety of my Venom cockpit. Being shot at in the air is a non-event but being shot at on the ground is a different ball game; I almost began to respect the Army's role in life.

THE NIGHT OF THE JACKAL (1961)

James Baring (from http://revelstoke.org.uk)
James was flying to Switzerland for a skiing holiday when a thick fog and approaching darkness forced him to land in a field in northern France. Having tied down his aeroplane, he walked into the nearest village to find a telephone.

It appeared that the mayor and the Pole were the only inhabitants of the village. There was no telephone directory, and the mayor did not know how to use the telephone except for ringing one number – his brother-in-law who lived in Poix. I asked him to ring his brother-in-law and request that he inform the local Gendarmerie that I had landed here, having taken off from Le Touquet, on a flight plan to Beauvais, that I was unhurt, that the plane (registered G-APTZ) was undamaged, and that the ATC centre at Lille should be informed of this.

When that was done, the mayor opened a tall cupboard beside the kitchen table. It was empty apart from a piece of excellent cheese and a loaf. He reached behind the stove and came out with a bottle of red wine. From his trouser pocket he took a pen knife and cut some slices of bread and cheese which we proceeded to share while we discussed life in general.

We were getting on famously when half an hour later the door burst open and four or five Gendarmes rushed in, at least two of them armed with machine guns. It seemed clear that I should put my hands in the air, so I did so. They were shaking like leaves, and I did not want the guns to go off by accident. They searched me for weapons and then I slowly prevailed upon them to let me lower my arms and to stop pointing the guns at me. I produced a passport and the aircraft documents and flight plan. Eventually I was sitting at the table with one of the policemen going through the papers, another on the telephone, but two still holding their machine guns ready. I asked them to phone the Air Traffic Control Centre but instead they phoned the Ministry of Defence and the Elysée Palace.

It may be clear to the reader by now that all this was at the time when every gendarme and agent de police in France was on the alert for an assassin, probably English, probably arriving by air in a deserted area to avoid immigration procedures, to take out the Président de la République, Charles de Gaulle. But we know all this with hindsight. Frederick Forsyth had not yet written *The Day of the Jackal* and the elements of truth on which he drew to construct that work of 'faction' were not in the public domain. I was therefore bemused, not realising that for the gendarmes in question this was not just a matter of life and death but quite possibly of the Légion d'Honneur or the sack. I was not to understand all this until some years later.

Meanwhile I had a problem with my paperwork. On giving an account of my journey, it seemed there was an hour unaccounted for. Bear in mind that at this time they had no idea what sort of aircraft I had arrived in or how many seats it had. Instructions from the Ministère de la Défence were evidently formal – all movements and personnel had to be accounted for. Then I realised, looking at the mayor's clock, that my flight plan was in GMT, my watch still on English time – the same as GMT at that time of year, but the police were (naturally) on French time. They were also unfamiliar, I noted, with aviation, with things outside France, and quite possibly with life outside their region. And why not. I have never understood why any Frenchman or woman would bother to travel when it is so beautiful where they live. I explained the lost hour by telling them "In

England we are an hour behind". This seemed to ring a bell with my inquisitor and he accepted it. But worse was to come.

On examining the customs clearance stamps from Lympne and Le Touquet, he turned to me and said: "But there is a day unaccounted for." I stared with disbelief at the date of the Lympne customs stamp. It was true. It was the day before the date of my arrival at Le Touquet. I racked my brains for an explanation and in the meantime, to lighten the tension I joked: "In England, we are a day behind." Two of my inquisitor's colleagues were by now looking over our shoulders. He hesitated for a moment. At that moment the phone rang. "Bon." he pronounced, closing my *carnet de passage en douanes* and took the phone from the fourth gendarme.

"Oui mon… oui, je crois que… oui…. Oui je crois que…. Oui, nous l'avons verifié et…. Oui, toute en ordre et…. Oui, bien gentil… oui, je vais lui dire… oui, mon… oui, au revoir."

He turned to me, reassured: "It seems that you are who you say you are, and that your aircraft and your flight are in order. However we must now find the aircraft and guard it."

"Not necessary", I told him. "It is quite safe for the night." He looked at me severely: "You have not understood. We still have orders from the Minister of Defence to find the aircraft and guard it till someone arrives from Paris."

It was by now pitch dark, with a soft drizzle. I sat in the back of a car next to a man with a machine-gun as we sped out of the gate of the small courtyard. "Left or right?" I did not know, but answered "Right".

I tried to think of the general direction. We passed a gate into a field. "I think it is in that direction," I volunteered. The driver parked in the gateway and we got out. From the boot of the car they unloaded a portable searchlight and a heavy battery supply with a harness which one of the gendarmes put on. Three of us, myself and the man with the gun and another with the light, set off into the field. It was ploughed, and it was wet. We continued in the same direction for many minutes, crossing ditches, climbing fences, negotiating hedges. During this time I pondered on the missing day and came to the conclusion that what had happened was explainable quite simply. I had been the first person through the customs office at Lympne that morning, arriving before the customs officer. In his haste to see me on my way he had forgotten to wind the date stamp on from the day before when he stamped my carnet. I decided to keep this logical explanation to myself and hold it in reserve in case the matter was raised again.

My thoughts were interrupted by a cry from the darkness ahead. The man with the searchlight had been walking some yards in advance, probing the sky with its powerful beam which suddenly flashed around in the mist and went out. He had fallen into a ditch. I helped him out and we continued, but he was soaked from the waist down.

After about 25 minutes we came to a field with smoothish grass. By now I was carrying the searchlight on the end of the cable, about 3 metres long, attached to the battery which the soaked gendarme was still carrying. But the drizzle had turned to mist which turned to fog, so we could not

see far ahead. Suddenly I almost tripped over a guy rope which appeared on my left. It was the plane. Beautiful, tiny, red, with the green cockpit cover on, snugly tied down for the night.

"Voilà!" I cried triumphantly.

They observed it. After some seconds they started to laugh. It was the laughter of surprise, then of relief, then of happiness. They had clearly expected something different, more dangerous, more military perhaps and certainly more valuable. This was a toy.

In a matter of seconds they decided that there was no need to guard it. It was undamaged, there could have been no other occupants, it was safe where it was. "Let us return to the village," they suggested, "and report to the Chef."

I took them back – no mean feat without a compass. Crossing a ploughed field, the man with the gun tripped over a parked plough. When he stood up in the redirected beam of the searchlight he was chocolate coloured in front but blue behind. Both men were wheezing audibly by now as it had been a strenuous excursion for which they were not prepared. Since I was wearing ski-boots and waterproof clothing and about 22 years old, I was. I ended up carrying the light and the gun, for by now they had decided that I was certainly not a threat to their survival.

As we neared the village the fog cleared noticeably. The car was no longer by the gate so we walked to the Mairie. The Chief of Police from Poix opened the door as we came up the steps and his eyes fell on my two companions, one soaked from the waist down, the other mud-coloured in front but, as he came through the door, quite presentable from the rear. The Chef de Police started to shake with uncontrollable laughter. It was an important moment for diplomacy. I continued into the kitchen to speak to the mayor leaving the three of them on the doorstep, coming from where I detected the sounds of a sense of humour failure of some proportions.

A VISIT TO ALBERT SCHWEITZER (1963)
Winston Churchill, *Memories and Adventures*
(Weidenfeld & Nicolson, 1989)
After completing his degree at Oxford, Winston Churchill set off on a journey round Africa with his friend Arnold von Bohlen in a hired Piper Comanche. Winston's grandfather had advised against the trip, which he thought 'a very hazardous enterprise' for a pair of very recently qualified 22-year-old pilots. Winston Junior replied, 'When you were my age you had already come under fire in Cuba, fought on the North-West frontier of India, and were on the point of charging with the 21st Lancers at Omdurman!' His grandfather said, 'I think you may have a point... You have my blessing!'

They set off from Oxford in November 1962, returning home five months later. In early February 1963, they visited Dr Albert Schweitzer.

Our next stop, Lambaréné, set on the banks of the Ogowe River deep in the jungles of Equatorial Africa, was then still one of the more remote places on the African continent. On our three-

Winston Churchill after being flown in a Jaguar by Fl Lt "D Reg" Bhasin at RAF Coltishall, 2001.

hour flight from Brazzaville, capital of the former French Congo, we had overflown a seemingly limitless expanse of dense tropical rainforest. Had our engine failed, our best chance of survival would have been to ditch the aircraft in one of the numerous crocodile-infested streams that intersect the jungle. From Lambaréné's small airstrip we walked two miles to the river bank where we crossed by ferry to the island on which stands the village of Lambaréné. There we found someone to take us by pirogue, a dug-out canoe, to Dr Albert Schweitzer's hospital about a mile upstream.

The setting sun, as it sank behind the jungle-covered hills of Lambaréné, momentarily turned the broad waters of the Ogowe River into a shimmering sheet of burnished gold. Then, suddenly, it was night. The elderly African propelled his flimsy craft with an increased vigour. He did not like paddling his canoe after dark

for fear of being shipwrecked against the dark motionless mass of a hippopotamus. To avoid the swift current in mid-stream, he hugged the bank under an overhang of branches and trailing creepers which reached almost to the water. On attaining the upstream end of the island he altered course and made for the opposite shore. Soon we were gliding in under the palm trees that line the waterfront below the hospital and the canoe came to rest with a slight lurch on the sandy beach. Numerous small fires were flickering in the darkness; around each was huddled a group of Africans cooking their evening meal. By the light of the flames we were able to make out the long, low shadows of the hospital buildings of Lambaréné.

Schweitzer's hospital stood on the side of a hill overlooking the broad Ogowe River. It was surrounded by the impenetrable primeval forest that encroaches on all sides. Here the visitor finds

Africa as he has imagined it should be – a land of steaming, teeming rainforest where massive trees and tumultuous jungle exclude the light of day and thwart the advance of civilization. The hospital at Lambaréné was not out of character with its surroundings. To those visitors who came to Lambaréné expecting to find a clean, modern hospital, Dr Schweitzer's establishment was, inevitably, a shock. Some 500 Africans were accommodated in the long, low hospital buildings made of wood and corrugated iron. The buildings were divided by partitions into cubicles, each with its own entrance. The cubicles, in which the patients lay side by side on wooden bunks, presented a dismal picture of darkness, dinginess and squalor. Outside, on the doorstep, sat those inmates who were less seriously ill, some of them deep in contemplation. Beside them were the dead embers of the fire on which they had cooked their meal the previous evening; and, on all sides, there was a litter of wash pots, cooking pots, empty bottles and rusting tins. In the open drainage ditches that ran beside the hospital buildings slops, old bandages, banana skins and other refuse lay putrefying and stagnating in the sun. The hospital's only sanitary facilities were two 'long-drop' latrines, kept under lock and key for the exclusive use of the European staff. They consisted of two wooden huts standing side by side on an elevated platform, supported by stilts over a ditch which was a seething mass of maggots and flies. The 500 or so Africans were supposed to do their business on the edge of the jungle, but most were sick and others were lazy,

with the result that few got that far. There are certain things one associates with hospitals the world over, even those in the bush, in particular concrete floors, whitewashed rooms, iron beds, electricity, lavatories, running water, covered drains, and the distasteful, all-pervasive smell of disinfectant. But none of these were to be found in the African quarters of the hospital at Lambaréné.

Dr Schweitzer explained to me, when I questioned him on this point, that the African has a horror of European-type hospitals. Many, he told me, would sooner suffer or even die from lack of medical attention, rather than go to a modern hospital with its unfamiliar, unfriendly, antiseptic atmosphere. At Lambaréné they could bring their families with them, wear their own clothes and live the life to which they were accustomed, while at the same time undergoing medical treatment. There could be little doubt that this was why so many came to Lambaréné rather than to the Government-run hospital, not far away. Indeed some came from 200 miles or more upstream by pirogue or river steamer to be treated at Schweitzer's hospital.

Soon after lunch on the day after our arrival we witnessed what was evidently a regular hospital ritual. A dozen or so bedraggled Africans, some of them armed with shovels, lined up before Schweitzer. He called them briskly to attention – an order not so briskly complied with – and thereupon they removed their hats and, with a deep bow and grins on their faces, they intoned: *'Bonjour, Grand Docteur!'* Schweitzer, seeing us watching,

blushed slightly and then chuckled in his merry way, explaining that this was his labour force and he had to check that they were all present and correct. Most of the hospital patients brought with them at least one member of their family to act as their guardian and to cook for them. All the able-bodied men, including some of the lepers, were put to work digging or some such activity, which they performed with a singular lack of vigour. At the end of the day they were given a ration of bananas and rice and, at the end of the week, they received a *cadeau* from the Doctor of a few pennies.

One afternoon, a Sunday, we took a pirogue and went with one of the German doctors at the hospital on his rounds to the village of Abangue a couple of miles upstream. The small village, inhabited solely by Africans, was one of the most delightful that we saw in all of Africa. A broad grass path lined on either side by clean, well-constructed huts led up from the landing-place where brightly-coloured butterflies flitted by the water's edge. The first hut had a great fishing net hung up outside to dry in the sun. The owner invited us in and proudly showed us the masks – most sinister in appearance – that he was making for the Saturday night dances that took place in the village. Next door was a man who repaired clocks and radios. Further along a man with a sewing machine was sitting outside his house mending some clothes. The huts, which were built of palm trees, had big windows and were furnished with locally-made tables and chairs. In one of the huts there were two pretty girls reading through a pile of notebooks. They told us that they were both married to the local schoolteacher and were correcting some French homework done by the children. The father of one of the girls was sitting outside the house relaxing in the sun. We sat down on the ground beside him and had a long talk which ranged from local politics to the price of a wife which, at the time, was £15. As he explained: 'It's all right for you Europeans to lead a bachelor existence, you have servants to look after you and cook for you. We do not. Instead we have to buy a wife. But it's no use having just one wife. You need at least two, so that if one gets sick there is still one to look after you!'

As I discovered in the course of our stay, there had, for several years, been a battle raging between Schweitzer and those members of the hospital staff who were anxious to see built an air-conditioned operating theatre. They quite justifiably pointed out that the existing one, with its gauze sides, let in the dust from outside and became so hot that two nurses were required constantly to mop the surgeon's brow to prevent the sweat falling into the open wounds of the patient on the operating table. The doctor had, at last, reluctantly accepted the necessity for this and the concrete foundations for the new building had been laid and posts installed to bring mains electricity to the village to provide lighting and air conditioning for the operating theatre. However, Schweitzer, perhaps due to his distaste for the modern world and newfangled equipment, had mischievously postponed the project in favour of an extension to the guest accommodation. But, as one of the staff remarked philosophically to me: 'Everything is relative. There is no point having a modern, air-conditioned operating theatre if the

patient, as soon as he returns to his cubicle, is going to pull the dressing aside and poke around with his finger to see what has been done to him. Although we use the latest drugs and the most modern surgical techniques, it is really eighteenth-century medicine that we are practising here.'

The doctors and nurses at Lambaréné were mostly Dutch, Swiss or German, and many were highly qualified. However, except for a couple of the nurses who had been with the doctor for a very long time, most of the staff came for a period of just two or three years. Among those working at the hospital at the time of our visit were a young American couple in their mid-twenties, he a doctor from North Carolina, she a nurse. After reading of the work of the Great Doctor in the tropical forests of Africa, they had decided to devote their lives to assisting him in his work at Lambaréné. They had sold everything they had in America and taken a boat for Africa. Sadly, within a year of their arrival, they were planning to leave, feeling that all initiative towards improving conditions at the hospital was being stifled and they were clearly sadly disillusioned. This couple were perhaps the exception. The majority of the staff found their work deeply fulfilling, not only for the vast amount of practical experience they were able to accumulate but, above all, because they were working among people desperately in need of their skills.

Schweitzer's reputation was so great that at the snap of his fingers untold resources from the great American charitable foundations, no less than from his many admirers throughout the world, could have been made available for

the modernization of his hospital. Yet it was evidently his wish to keep Lambaréné as he had originally conceived it. He had built the hospital and the nearby leper village largely with his own hands from such materials as could be obtained locally. He had been thirty-eight years old when he had first arrived in Lambaréné and already he was a doctor four times over, in theology, philosophy, music and medicine. He had written two authoritative works, one on Bach, the other on organ-building, besides a handful of other books on Christ and civilization. An academic career full of promise seemed to lie before him. Yet, as he pointed out in his autobiography, he deliberately turned his back on it: 'in order to devote myself from that time forward to the direct service of humanity'. He was very conscious of this 'act of renunciation' and, later in his book, made the assertion that: 'There are no heroes of action: only heroes of renunciation and suffering. But few of them are known, and even these not to the crowd, but to the few.' Perhaps the most obvious exception to this rule was Schweitzer himself.

When he had first come to Lambaréné there was no other doctor for hundreds of miles around and an epidemic of sleeping sickness was raging. For want of medical attention the local people were dying on all sides from this and other diseases. Founding a hospital in the heart of the jungles of Equatorial Africa was a remarkable achievement and one that required enormous courage and dedication. That had been in 1913.

But half a century had passed since then. Africa had changed immeasurably in those fifty years: Schweitzer and Lambaréné hardly at all. He had weathered well. During all his time in tropical Africa he never contracted any serious disease – a tribute to his remarkable constitution and stamina. Pith helmet on, he would stand for hours beneath the equatorial sun directing some new building project or resolving a dispute in the hospital. And, in the evening, when darkness had fallen on Lambaréné and all was silent, except the sounds of the jungle, the glow of a paraffin lamp could be seen shining out from the tiny room where, amid a rummage of papers, books and tools, he would sit at his table writing late into the night, in the cause of civilization and peace. At least so long as the *'Grand Docteur'* lived, Lambaréné remained a corner of Africa unspoiled by the advance of the modern world – a backwater cut off from the mainstream of the African Revolution.

FLYING A SPITFIRE (1970)

Martin Barraclough, *Fifty Years Have Flown* (Bound Biographies, 2004) pp 121-5

Ever since I learned to fly I harboured the dream of flying a Spitfire and declared to anyone prepared to listen that I would give my right arm to do so. In the 1960s, however, the prospects of fulfilling this dream were almost non-existent as the final Spitfires came out of service with far-away air forces and went onto the scrap-heap or into museums.

In 1965 I had tried to persuade Norman Jones, Chairman of the Tiger Club, to buy for us the last Mk 9 Spitfire that had been brought back from the Dutch East Indies by a firm called COGEA at Ostend in Belgium. The aircraft was fully airworthy and was for sale with a host of spares, including radiators, undercarriages, etc., for a now incredible £2,500. But Norman didn't think that it would be wise to let the Tiger Club loose on a Spitfire – someone was bound to crash it! None of us saw the coming boom in vintage aircraft and the making of so many films, such as *The Battle of Britain*, for which airworthy Spitfires and ME 109s would be in great demand, so the opportunity of a life-time was allowed to slip by.

In England the number of airworthy civilian Spitfires could be counted on the fingers of one hand. True, there were two in the RAF Battle of Britain Memorial Flight, but they were certainly

not available to be flown by civilians, let alone more than a handful of aspiring RAF fighter jocks. By the end of the 1960s there were only four airworthy Spitfires in civilian ownership.

Patrick Lindsay, the Flying Scot, was putting together his private air force. Patrick, who was Christies' senior auctioneer, with an encyclopaedic knowledge of art, had a passionate interest in racing cars and vintage aeroplanes and was assembling a major collection of each at Folly Farm in Berkshire. He bought a Mk 1A Spitfire from Air Commodore Alan Wheeler, who was the Aviation Trustee of the Shuttleworth Trust at the time and, despite living in a disused railway carriage, owned the Spitfire on his own account (which is probably why he had to live in a railway carriage). Actually the Spitfire cost Alan nothing as it was thrown in for £200 when he bought the Shuttleworth's Mk V from the RAF, and he later sold the crate in which it was stored for £200.

There were two two-seaters. One, the prototype 502 trainer, and registered G-AIDN, was owned by John Fairey, son of Sir Richard Fairey, who I did not know at the time. A second two-seater, a type 509, serial number MJ712, and registered G-AVAV, had served with the Irish Air Corps, and in 1966 was sold to Tony Samuelson at Elstree. She eventually went to Willie Roberts' collection at Strathallan.

Finally there was a Mk 9, MH434, now probably the most famous airworthy Spitfire in England. Originally test-flown by none other then Alex Henshaw in August 1943, the aircraft was delivered to, and saw wartime service with, 222 Squadron. In

1947 she was sold to the Netherlands Air Force and sent to the Dutch East Indies. Re-delivered in 1954 to COGEA in Ostend she was used for target-towing and in 1963 was sold to 24 year-old Tim Davies in England. Tim flew her from Elstree aerodrome, registered as G-ASJV, and painted in a smart blue, white and silver civil livery, until she was bought by Hamish Mahaddie for the making of the film *The Battle of Britain*. When filming was over all the aircraft were sold and MH434 went to Adrian Swire.

Adrian flew with us in the Tiger Club and I also knew him in shipping circles. In 1970 I had persuaded Dene Shipping to diversify into aviation with a 30% holding in the newly-formed Invicta Airways at Manston. Invicta, brain-child of Wing Commander Hugh Kennard, had bought the last Vikings from the Queen's Flight, as well as two DC4s, to fly package tourists to the bulb-fields in Holland. I tried to interest Adrian in extending Swire's ownership of Cathay Pacific Airways to encompass the emerging package holiday business through a shareholding in Invicta. We drove down to Manston in Adrian's Volvo sports car and, having inspected Invicta's aged fleet, he wisely declined to invest – but he did ask me if I would like to fly his Spitfire.

This was a hugely exciting prospect and I accepted with alacrity, but how was I going to fly a single seat Spitfire when I had no heavy metal experience, and how was I going to be absolutely certain not to bend it? "No problem," said Adrian. "Ray Hanna will check you out." Ray had just left the Red Arrows, and was uncomfortably doing a staff job. Later, like many ex-RAF pilots who wanted to earn a living by continuing to fly, and wanting to join a compatible Pacific-based airline, he went out to Hong Kong and signed on with Cathay Pacific. But from time to time Adrian needed someone to display his Spitfire – it was after all in great demand at air shows – so Ray obliged, and the great relationship between the Hannas and MH434 began.

At no time did it ever cross my mind – or Adrian's – that we might be able to track down one of the airworthy two-seaters for me to have a dual check-out. There were no pilots' notes for the aircraft and I was still unhappy that, despite the thorough brief that I knew I would get from Ray, I would miss something critical and make a cock-up. The prospect of bending one of the last airworthy Spitfires in England was unthinkable, and Zaza was just pregnant with our first child – an added incentive not to get it wrong! So I decided, as a discipline, to write a complete set of pilots' notes for MH434. Using the RAF handling notes for similar marks of Spitfire, I painstakingly wrote a completely new set of notes, making diagrams of fuel and oil systems, compiling fuel consumption tables, photographing and labelling the main cockpit views. I produced three copies of the notes, one for Adrian, one for Ray and one for myself, and committed the whole lot to memory. Finally, I condensed the notes into a set of cockpit checklists.

The great day arrived, 15th June, 1970, and Ray flew MH434 into Redhill in the late afternoon, when the circuit would be quiet. In front of the Tiger Club hangar and a dozen fellow pilots I strapped in; Ray gave me some last-minute reminders on the starting sequence, jumped off the wing and I fired up. Temperatures and pressures all OK, chocks were waved away, and I fish-tailed my way down the N/S runway, gently feeding power into the great rumble ahead of me, and back-tracked westwards down the active runway. In 1970 there was no air traffic control, indeed not even radio, at Redhill, and pilots took off and landed when they saw it was clear to do so. I did my take-off checks by the book, checked the approach for any landing aircraft, lined up and gently fed in the power. I don't recall much tendency to swing but then virtually all my flying had been in tail-draggers, so applying opposite rudder was instinctive and almost before I knew it we were airborne. Change hands on the stick to get the gear up – make the moves positive to ensure correct retraction – and up we went – I was flying a Spitfire!

For twenty-five glorious minutes I climbed, dived, made low – not too low – passes, zoomed up and thrilled at the sheer joy of it. I didn't roll or loop – it was too precious an aircraft, too much of a liberty for me to take – I just enjoyed flying a Spitfire. All too soon came the need to land and to get it right for the first, and only, time. Curved approach for visibility past the great Merlin engine, select gear down – check green 'DOWN' light, flaps down, fine pitch, straighten up with no forward vision ahead of the gentle rumble – looking side to side as the stick came back and then she was on three points and rolling straight. What a joy – what a relief!

I taxied carefully back to the hangars, lined up and shut down, the great four-bladed screw slowing to a halt. I had taken off, flown, landed and brought her back undamaged. Ray was there with his characteristic grin but it wasn't as big as the grin on my face. I doubted then that I would ever have the opportunity to fly a Spitfire again – and indeed I never did – the days when there would be more than 30 airworthy Spitfires of varying marks flying over England were still a long way off and the cost was always beyond my pocket. But I would, for the rest of my life, be able to say, "I have flown a Spitfire," and Adrian, bless him, didn't even want my right arm.

EVACUATING CASUALTIES IN THE FALKLANDS (1982)

Peter Cameron. From *Above All, Courage. The Falklands front line: first-hand accounts* by Max Arthur (Sidgwick & Jackson, London 1985) pp 62-3

Having learnt from the past experiences of Darwin and Goose Green, for the final battles I basically put a Gazelle flight in direct support of each of the fighting units, so 3 Para, 42 Commando and 45 Commando each had two Gazelles in direct support. I kept the Scouts in reserve. I told the flights to have liaison officers forward so that they worked out in advance exactly how we were going to do the casevac procedures, ammunition forward, and where we were going to fly it to.

In the Battle for Darwin and Goose Green we had discovered that because the Marines and Paras were so young and fit, every single casualty we took out survived. If a chap was without a leg, or had a stomach wound, the important thing was to get him off the battlefield fast. Important also was to give the injured a little hope. The chap on the ground would say, 'Don't worry, mate, there will be a chopper here for you in fifteen minutes.' As soon as it arrived we would load the injured on, just get them on – there was no place or time for stretchers. Everyone where possible would help themselves. Men with only one arm were holding drips for people with no legs and someone was probably holding a drip to him. Even in these conditions there was a great sense of camaraderie. The aircrewmen were also Royal Marines Sergeants and Corporals and with good experience of basic infantry work, so they were able to appreciate what these lads had been through. 'Don't worry, lads, we'll have you in the dressing station within ten minutes,' they would say; then as soon as they got to the dressing station the doctors would get their hands on them and carry out immediate surgery, and were able to say to them, 'Don't worry chaps, you'll be on the *Uganda* by teatime.' I think that factor kept a lot of them alive, it gave them milestones of hope. Some of those lads were very young, just boys, 17, 18 and 19 years old, just young, fit lads, and that is how they survived.

We didn't get terribly involved in the night approach. It was a silent attack on Harriet, Two Sisters, Longdon – they all went on concurrently. We started getting involved in the early hours of the next morning. I must say the aircrew were remarkably brave. I flew forward that day as well and there was artillery falling all round me but

Peter Cameron about to enter the cockpit of a Sioux AH Mk 1 at RNAS Sembawang, Singapore, circa May 1968. Peter trained as a Royal Marines Commando and with the introduction of light helicopters into commando service in 1964 he became the first Royal Marine to learn to fly with the Army Air Corps. Often embarked in HM Ships, including aircraft carriers, his service with the Royal Marines took him world wide, including operational deployments to Borneo, Northern Ireland and the Falkland Islands, where as the Commanding Officer of 3 Commando Brigade Air Squadron, he was awarded the Military Cross. He retired with the rank of Lieutenant Colonel in 1991. He went on to serve as an Army Air Corps reserve pilot until 1997.

Jonathan Elwes in his Tiger Moth, Poland, 2006.

quite remarkably we didn't get hit. It was just pure luck, because every time we flew anywhere near the front line, we would immediately draw fire. So the great thing was to get in there quick and get out equally fast. The units had to be really ready with their casevacs or whatever it was they wanted because we never hung about. It was in/out, and if they weren't ready we went away again and called them on the radio, saying, 'For God's sake, get ready – I'm coming in again.' Because every time, except for the reverse slopes of Two Sisters and Harriet, we drew fire. It was very difficult. One of the conclusions we came to after the war was that we must have some sort of protection for the aircrew against small arms and against flak if we're going to be required to fly in a forward area to get the ammunition in or casualties out during or after a battle, or during a counter-attack. We were vital but we are vulnerable.

In the twenty-four-hour period after the battles, we actually casevac'd something like eighty-five casualties and only one died en route. The aircrewman tried mouth-to-mouth but unfortunately we lost him.

THREE TIGER MOTHS TO MOSCOW (1989)
Jonathan Elwes, *Glasmoth* (Quiller Press, 1989)

It was the era of 'Glasnost' and 'Perestroika'. In 1987 Mathias Rust had landed a light aircraft in Red Square; two years later his jail sentence was commuted, and he and his plane were sent back to Germany. Meanwhile, Mrs Thatcher said that she "could do business" with Mr Gorbachev, who was about to visit Britain. The stage was set...

In April 1989 Jonathan Elwes secured support from both the British Prime Minister and the Soviet President for a flight from London to Moscow by three Tiger Moths. The pilots (Jonathan Elwes, Nicholas Parkhouse and Roger Fiennes) soon found that they had become a small but demonstrable part of the dramatic political change sweeping the continent. In all, they flew 33 sectors in three weeks, and were feted at every stop beyond the Iron Curtain. The Tigers were granted a 15 minute exclusive landing slot at Moscow's Sheremetyevo Airport, in the full glare of publicity, having their flight effectively 'adopted' by Gorbachev who, despite widespread unpopularity amongst the powerful Soviet elite, was dismantling the status quo. The Tigers featured regularly on TV right across the USSR as a visible symbol of 'Glasnost'.

The team had many adventures on the way, caused mostly by the rigidity of the Soviet system. The system swept them along without option, including a directive to cross the city of Moscow at no more than 100 metres, lower than many buildings in the city. However, they were honoured and welcomed throughout the visit from the moment they crossed the Soviet border when they were escorted by a Mil helicopter filmship and saluted by a MiG 27 'Flogger' interceptor flying just above them.

Two edited extracts from the book follow...

10 April 1989, Prague – Wroclaw – Warsaw
In Prague we were entertained by the last Russian General in command of the city. Eventually, after a four hour weather delay, we departed and flew across the Sudety Mountains en route to Wroclaw at a cautious 4,500 feet. It was turbulent and blowing some, with awful visibility. Without any GPS or other electronic help, navigation had to be precise because the East German border lay a mile to port, and a large Russian airbase a mile to starboard. The Russians wouldn't talk to us, and when we had to make radio contact to cross the Polish FIR boundary, we couldn't raise a dicky bird... until at last Anatoly Gorbatov, my navigator, was able to contact a friendly Aeroflot pilot far above us who relayed to Wroclaw. He also linked us to our Polish escort pilot in a Zlin, who was circling at a pre-arranged point way below us in the murk.

On arrival in Wroclaw our three Tigers were immediately surrounded by a large number of soldiers, full of curiosity. Such close contact with Warsaw Pact military was almost unheard of at that time, and with hindsight it was a clear pointer towards the dramatic collapse of the Soviet Union later that year. They pored over our biplanes and their enthusiasm delayed us yet more. The Polish Colonel, who piloted the Zlin, rushed us through the formalities and urged us to depart to Warsaw as soon as possible because a big reception awaited us.

Flight planning in three languages can cause misunderstandings. Add a touch of Polish flair and things can really get exciting. The weather was calm at Wroclaw and we were assured that we would face no headwind en route to Warsaw. The Tigers were not equipped for night flying and reaching Warsaw before nightfall was going to be tight, but with Lodz as the agreed alternate, we took off without any misgivings.

As we approached Lodz the wind started to get up – 10, 15, 20 knots, right on the nose. There was no way we would reach Warsaw in daylight, but persuading our escorting Colonel was not easy. Every message went from English to Russian, to Polish, and back again. However, we got *his* message very clearly. Lodz was our alternate alright, but we were strictly forbidden to land there. Lodz Niet, niet, niet! Messages to explain that the Tigers had no cockpit lighting and therefore the pilots couldn't read instruments at night, let alone change radio frequencies or see the other three aircraft, cut no ice whatsoever.

We spread out and kept glued to the tiny red and white lights of the Zlin which served as our artificial horizon. I can remember shouting to Anatoly, "For God's sake, get him to slow down," as the Colonel appeared determined not to miss a moment of the party, flying two or three knots faster than our absolute maximum. Then salvation. "Don't worry," said Anatoly, "the Poles have arranged for Babice to be lit up by World War Two searchlights!" Suddenly, having been glued to the tiny lights of the Zlin, we saw the sky lit up some 30 miles ahead over Babice airfield, where a classic Polish reception awaited us.

After landing we were blinded by the glare of TV camera lights and needed a bevy of wing-walkers to steer us to a large hangar where the Poles cheered us in. The vodka flowed copiously. Then just fifteen minutes after arrival the whole airport, searchlights and all, was plunged into darkness by a massive power cut. I wondered how we would have landed if the lights had gone out twenty minutes earlier. "Don't worry," said the phlegmatic Anatoly, "they would have steered us to the International Airport where there is a special generator for power cuts."

On the following day Nick, Roger and I flew a low level display for our Polish hosts and for about 25 veteran Polish RAF pilots, who had only recently been allowed into the public gaze; another sign of the times. Later I had the honour of flying with General Skalski, one of their top wartime fighter aces, who had been imprisoned and at one stage left on death row for his exposure to the wicked West.

14 April 1989, Bryansk – Kaluga – Moscow
We set off for the little town of Kaluga, home of Russia's first rocket engineer. On the outskirts of the town there were hundreds of attractive multi-coloured bungalows. By now we were used to skimming over roof tops, but we must have astonished the local residents as we flew overhead. Another reception awaited us: pretty girls in traditional dress, gifts, crowds and TV interviews.

A quick turnaround and we were lined up for the last leg to Moscow, all set to arrive at Sheremetyevo on time. Then at the last minute departure was delayed because a bank of fog had rolled across the route between Kaluga and Moscow. It was a four hour delay. Roger passed the time playing chess with an old babushka in a ramshackle hut. He was relieved when permission to take off was eventually given: he was losing heavily. News came through that the authorities in Sheremetyevo, Moscow's 'Heathrow', had actually reduced their landing minima to 150 metres ceiling and 1,000 metres visibility to facilitate our flight. We were literally 'ordered' to take off.

I looked at my tiny eight by four inch 12-volt battery which ran the radio and prayed fervently that it would not let us down. Both Nick's and Roger's radios had been unserviceable since their encounter with the Polish soldiers in Wroclaw, but nobody knows whether there was any connection with this event, or if it was mere co-incidence. We had no navigation instruments other than old P-type compasses – but on the other hand our navigators were on their home turf. Damn it, we had to go! Anatoly was very nervous, not of the flying, but because as the most senior navigator in Aeroflot he was responsible for our flight and for our arrival exactly as instructed in Moscow. After all, airliners from all over the world were in holding patterns to allow us a 15-minute exclusive landing slot, rather like a Royal Flight.

The fog had lifted no more than 50 metres. After a stream takeoff we went into line astern and found the railway track that ran along the perimeter of the airfield. Hanging on our props, we followed the line at no more than 60 knots, assured by Anatoly that the ceiling would gradually lift as we approached

Moscow. We flew over a forest following the railway line not too many feet above the tops of the trees which were poking through the fog. It was appalling weather but we left just enough latitude to turn back on our line feature if we were forced to retreat. At last we reached the Moscow River and turned onto a new course which would take us right into the city. We carried on in line astern for about 40 minutes along the river. It was exciting nap-of-the-earth flying, following every meander of the river, hopping over little hills and back inside the river banks. It was sparsely populated but every now and then there were smart dachas along the riverside. Wherever possible we gained height but never achieved more than about 200 metres.

About 80 miles from Kaluga we made our first radio contact with Moscow – excitement was mounting. We went right through (not over) a missile site in the outskirts and soon came across a major road that headed straight as a die towards the heart of the city. Moscow Approach ordered us to remain below 100 metres as we picked up the city's ring road which we were to follow. We were at that stage flying below the tops of apartment buildings. There were people along the pavements waving at us and some staring disbelievingly at our biplanes from the flats alongside us. All three pilots were busy glancing like dervishes to the left and to the right making sure that we didn't fly into overhead cables or some other obstacle. And then, there it was, Sheremetyevo Airport. We flew straight over the VIP terminal at 100 metres in vic

formation, then a circuit in echelon followed by a break and stream landing. What an experience!

REQUIEM FOR A PHANTOM (1993)

John Allison, *Pilot* magazine, November 1993.
John Allison made his final flight in a Phantom on 31st October 1993. He wrote this article 'in its entirety and in final form' that evening at home. Later he recalled, 'The editor and owner of Pilot, *James Gilbert, who generally liked my stuff, did not much care for the style of this particular article, dismissing it as "mawkish sentimentality". However, he published it anyway and it was probably my most acclaimed piece. One or two people told me it made them cry.*

'It does still speak to me of how I felt about the demise of the Phantom in RAF service. The political and industrial imperatives that favoured the Tornado F3 over the Phantom were obvious, but in my opinion it was a poor decision for the RAF, as the F3 was considerably less effective. I note that the Luftwaffe did not purchase the F3 variant of the Tornado. Sixteen years later, it is still operating its Phantom F4Fs and will be doing so for a few more years yet.'

XV497 is singing to me as we roll along Wattisham's taxiway. Actually, the gentle hum I can hear is just internal noise in the aircraft's electrical system, picked up through the intercom. It is an endearing characteristic common to all Phantoms.

Indulging for a moment in the pathetic fallacy (that is, endowing inanimate objects with the power of conscious thought), I fancy that *XV497* is singing because she is happy. It is a nice day and we are going flying.

Doesn't she know? Doesn't she even suspect? Hasn't she noticed the steady disappearance of her brothers and sisters over recent months? Hasn't she seen most of them lying rejected and forlorn on the station dump, waiting to be cut up and carted away? In fact, did she but know it, only she and *XV460*, trundling along behind us, now remain.

The voice of Ian Wright, my navigator, breaks into my reverie: "Pre-take-off check-list". All is business now as, for the last time, we chant the familiar litany of challenge and response. As we take the runway I lower half flap, put on the pitot heater, turn on the stab augs and the anti-skid, and bring both engines up to 85 per cent cold power. She strains lightly against the brakes. We are ready.

What *497* doesn't know is that she is leaving home for good. The shelter that has housed her is cold and lifeless now, just a shell, empty of men, equipment or machine. But at least she is escaping that terrible graveyard.

I release the brakes, bring the power up to 100 per cent, rock the throttles outboard then push them smoothly forward into max reheat–a gutless pause as the nozzles open, then 40,000 pounds of thrust push with sustained, irresistible force. Ian chants the speeds, ever faster, "100 knots, 135 GO, 165." At this, fifteen seconds after brake release, we are airborne on twin columns of flame. It is *XV497*'s final take-off.

Quickly, I raise the gear and flaps. At 300 knots I cancel the burner, select tanks to outboard and turn downwind. Soon Group Captain Tony Alcock,

Wattisham's Station Commander, and Flight Lieutenant Pete Yeats, his navigator, in *XV460*, join up in formation. We make several fly-pasts for the cameras of the press down on the airfield. Then I pull off and leave Tony to say goodbye to his station in his own way.

Holding at 8,000 feet in the Wattisham overhead at endurance speed, I return to my fancy. What is *497* thinking? Probably she is thinking: *'This is boring. Why aren't we going hunting, or fighting? Let's see. Last time this pilot flew me we did air combat. He seemed all right then. In fact he worked me hard and the fuel only lasted 45 minutes. Perhaps the old guy is finally getting past it.*

'Hunting and fighting is what life is all about. That was a good fight we had then. I remember we came in high, out of the sun. We chopped the burner at ten miles to cool down and defeat the IR threat. The boss rolled inverted and pulled. We dropped like a stone. But the other man was good. He saw us and his energy was high. He came up to meet us and we passed beak to beak.

'The boss tried a great sweeping reversal, up, up and over, reheats biting hard. The opposition was just a dot, way below. We had potential energy as we arced over the top in light buffet, but he had loads of kinetic and as we plunged down, he met us again, head on, swimming towards us at a closure of well over 1,000 mph, suddenly growing and flashing past, too fast for thought.

'Then we were the low man, and he above. And so it went, no quarter given, always seeking the fleeting opportunity for a missile shot – brilliant, exciting, knackering.

'Why are we loitering around here when we could

be fighting?'

We drop down and join the other Phantom to pose for a cameraman in an accompanying Hawk. It is important to record this last flight, but it is pansy stuff. I would like to be hunting or fighting too. We could be out over the sea, searching on the radar for that first glimpse of a target, assessing speed, direction and manoeuvre, planning a stealthy approach. With a flick of my left wrist I could surge *497* from loiter speed to supersonic in less than half a minute, flashing across the wave tops in a blur of speed. Then with just a tiny pressure of my right hand I could set her surging up at a dizzy angle to punch into trails five miles high only a minute later. Surely such performance cannot be redundant?

Our next port of call is Duxford, where we join up with a Corsair – another F4 from a much earlier generation – for some publicity shots. The flying is not demanding and again my thoughts stray. What will *497* be making of this?
'Boy, this is a weird trip. Whatever next! I reckon the old guy has flipped. I remember him in Germany in the early eighties. We flew together quite often and he was perfectly normal then. Now, that was good hunting country – low level in the Eifel and the Ardennes nearly every day and the sky full of Jaguars, Harriers, F-16s and F-4Fs to stalk and attack.

'We nearly bought the farm once, though. We were tooling along, minding our own business, when the nav screamed "PUSH". We were at 250 feet but the boss pushed hard anyway and a Jaguar flashed over the top of us, so close we felt and heard the shock of its passage. We were lucky to survive that one.

'Oh, it's good to be alive and airborne, even on a dull trip like this!'

I am looking across at the Corsair and reflecting that it is a quarter of a century or so older than *497* and, unlike her, has absolutely no military utility. Yet it will fly on, a treasured historic artefact worth about half a million pounds, whereas poor *497* would only fetch her value by weight as scrap metal. But that Corsair, I know, was rescued from a military scrapyard in a derelict state. Perhaps *497* might make a similar return from the grave, if she survives long enough for her real value to be appreciated.

I appreciate her now. I respect her worth, purposefulness and capability. I love her grace, power and beauty. With the affection of long friendship I tolerate her quirky handling. Her trembling airframe talks to me through my fingers and my feet and through the sounds of the airflow around the cockpit. If ever an aeroplane had character, it is the Phantom.

The photography done, we set course for Coningsby, *XV497*'s final home as a grounded airframe. As we cross the Wash, perhaps the grey waves remind her of the long perilous transit to the Falklands in 1988 and back again in 1991 – hour after hour of droning into nothingness over a seemingly endless sea.

As we approach Coningsby, I would have her remember us both at our best:
'Ah, Coningsby! Nice to see the old place again. That reminds me, the old guy and I flew together from here a time or two in the early seventies, when we were both young and in our prime.

John Allison with his Miles Gemini, 2007.

'It was great to be a Phantom then because we ruled the skies, before those upstart F-16s came along with all that turning performance and forced us to change our tactics. We were still doing ground attack as well as air defence and Phantoms were the best in the world in both roles. Still, they've given me a digital weapons control system plus hands on throttle and stick and, with my steel strap mod I reckon I'm good for years of hunting and fighting yet.

'I wonder why we're going to Coningsby?'

It is still a lovely day. I can see half of Lincolnshire spread out beneath us, but I am not enjoying this any more. I glance at the fuel gauge. For perhaps another fifteen minutes I can stave off the inevitable, can keep *497*, and all my memories, alive, can commune with her, savour her. But after that, my ability to protect her will be at an end.

She is only a machine. Only? She, and her kind, have been the primary tool of my profession, the primary means of my self-expression and personal satisfaction. What am I? I am many things – husband, father, Royal Air Force officer,

Royal Air Force pilot. What kind of pilot? I am – I was – a Phantom pilot. I am diminished by her passing because no other aircraft could ever mean so much. I have flown many types of aeroplane, but the Phantom has been the aeroplane of my life.

Ian is much younger, but the Phantom has been his flying life too, and he feels it just as much. Subdued, we talk about it a little.

We join the circuit at Coningsby. I fly a few patterns – nothing special, not tight or showy, but smooth and relaxed. I hope 497 is enjoying them. I am caressing her. But I have no more thoughts to invest in her. She is just a machine, isn't she? I turn downwind for the last time, as hundreds of pilots before me have done in this now-worn cockpit. And as a younger John Allison did nearly twenty years ago, I carry out the pre-landing check-list.

Then I drop full flap, pull off a little power, raise the nose a tad and roll into the final turn. The angle of attack settles 'on the doughnut'; the rate of descent looks right. The approach is perfect. But it ought to be – I have done this on and off for most of my working life. As we curl towards the runway I reflect that the aeroplane has twenty seconds left to experience the sweetness of flight, then fifteen, ten, five and we are into the flare.

I pull off a little power; the wheels brush the ground. I bring the throttles to idle, killing all that thrust. I feel the main oleos compress as the lift comes off the wings; I let the nose settle to the ground and pull the drag chute. XV497's final landing is done. For me it is a bereavement, but traitor that I am, I shall fly a Tornado next week. For XV497 it is the end.

But there is ritual to be observed yet. As we slow down, turn off the runway and taxi in, Ian is reciting the familiar phrases of the 'After landing' check-list – I will know them till I die – and my hands are dancing round the cockpit in unquestioning response. We come to *temperature controller – full hot*. Why am I doing this? There is no need to purge a system of moisture when the system will never run again. I do it anyway. Ritual is important in flying and *XV497* will be treated as a working aircraft to the very last second.

We are marshalled in to the parking spot. The aircraft is chocked. I only have one engine running now, keeping the systems alive. Still she hums happily, still entire, purposeful and working. I have unstrapped already (as the ritual permits) severing most of the umbilicals that bind man and machine. Just the personal equipment connector, bringing me oxygen and intercom, remains. There is nothing more to do except shut down the left engine and climb out. My hand hovers over the throttle. *XV497* is still humming sweetly, machine-like, oblivious of her fate. I have only to pull the throttle through the idle cut-off gate, thus closing down the HP cock and denying fuel to the engine. It will spin down, the remaining on-line generator will cut out, unconsciousness will swiftly overwhelm the system, the hydraulic pumps will slow, then stop, the lifeblood coursing through the aircraft will be stilled. Death.

I could bring resurrection simply by reaching for the start switch, but no man of my kind will ever again sit in this cockpit. Tomorrow other men – technical men – will come and disembowel her,

taking away useful parts like engines, radios and navigation systems. These men will not be despoilers; they will do their task carefully, dismantling not hacking. They will not enjoy it because the purpose of their working life has been to care for aeroplanes and prepare them for flight, not for the grave. But behind these men are other men – the shadowy phalanx of the nation's book-keepers, who have done their sums and their duty and have ruled that *XV497* and her kind can no longer be afforded. Poor them; they know only their ledgers and their computer printouts. They have never even touched this marvellous machine, let alone bound themselves to her, trusted their life to her, tamed her with skill of hand, gloried in her power and magnificence.

XV497 hums on, unknowing, waiting, still alive, still potent, not obsolete, not life-expired, just unwanted.

Feeling like a murderer, I lay my hand on the throttle and gently close the HP cock. The hum dies. Goodbye Phantom.

FLYING A MIG-25 (1997)

Maxi Gainza, 'Foxbat', *Pilot* magazine, February 1998 (extract)

220 km out on a south-easterly heading – hardly ten minutes since take-off and already topping Concorde's cruising altitude – we banked 60° right to reverse course in a 2.5g turn, trading the excess fraction of a g for climb. The Foxbat turned all right, even if it devoured air-space. Rolling

out, we raised the nose 5° over the horizon. My eyes went to the variometer needle, now pointing upwards like a conductor's baton drawing out an endless *finale* no human voice or instrument could possibly hold; to the ever-winding, yet slowing, altimeter; to the visibly-falling fuel gauge; to the reassuring wink of the oxygen-flow indicator. When I next looked out, already passing Mach 2.2 and 20,000 metres, the sky had dramatically darkened.

"Come on, Vladimir," I cried, space fever catching on, "give me a record!"

The dazzle from the sun on my left was so searing I had to lower the inner tinted visor to protect my eyes. But as I looked the other way, the sky was such a mesmerizing ocean blue that I flipped it up again to behold it in all its spell-binding glory, straining to catch sight of the first star to shine at me in broad daylight.

Our nose had dropped a degree or two, but we

were still climbing in excess of Mach 2.3 when, passing 26,000 metres, Vladimir cut the afterburners.

"Sorry Maxi," he said, sounding disappointed. "Temperatures." One look at the JPT gauge confirmed that one needle was up against the 820° C redline; the other only a hair away.

I was sorely tempted to pull the stick back on him, but the heat from the canopy dissuaded me. Instead, I reached for my pocket camera and finished the film while Vladimir gently unloaded in a long, flat parabola, suddenly banking 30° as if to adjust course or, for all I know, simply to show off the Foxbat's astounding controllability, milking 0.4g for the turn out of the ever-thinning air molecules that miraculously kept the engines burning and our cockpits warm and pressurised. No fly-by-wire, no manoeuvering thrusters: just plain, mechanically-actuated aerodynamic controls. But then I was in the hands of one of Russia's top test pilots, the kind who can fly a Foxbat a good 20 kph below its stalling speed range of 220-260 kph, and our indicated air-speed – if it did mean anything at that height – was still over twice that.

Wings level again, we coasted steadily on up, nose slowly falling to the horizon, engines pressing on at 100%. Somewhere during the climb the altimeter watch I had strapped to my suit to monitor cabin pressure had gone off the scales – I was later told it would have been the equivalent of 7,000 metres – yet I don't recall my ears blocking nor being short of breath as the oxygen pressure-feed automatically increased. I was too tightly strapped in to feel myself floating when we reached zero g, so I let go the

camera – carefully – and watched it do a few lazy tumbles. Then I put it away and just stared ahead.

The horizon was a fuzzy band of baby blue, with just a hint of a curve, hemming in the cottony brightness of the storm clouds far below. Elation was not the word: I was too calm. Perhaps a mountaineer feels this way atop Everest, only I was three times higher and hadn't strained my lungs and limbs for it. A Promethean fire had carried me this far, and now, at last, I could silence the nagging "why do it?" which had been preying on my conscience, just by being here. With the ride so smooth, the engines so faint, the universe so compellingly close, I sensed the peace that passeth all understanding: the soul's inkling – a memory? – of its true home. My umbilical cord to earth stretched to a painless breaking point, draining my humbled mind of every conscious thought, except of loved ones. And even these were dimming before this overwhelming threshold to infinity.

An eternity later – probably far less than a minute – I eased my human burden back on the seat as we regained 1g and commenced our descent with the nose a few degrees below the horizon and the variometer plummeting almost to its lower stops. Plunging through 20,000 m we eased the nose up to the horizontal, thus slowing our descent to a mere 80 m/s, (*16,000 fpm*) at Mach 2.2. Only at 16,000 meters did we throttle back to 70% flight-idle and let the nose drop to 15°. The TAS split-needle on the Machmeter began lagging the Mach indication as the speed of sound increased in the thickening air.

Shallowing the descent through 12,000 metres,

Vladimir performed a double roll, then invited me to do the same. I made a tentative one to the left, getting the feel for the controls through that tall stick, then whipped it up for a double roll to the right, convinced that the Foxbat wouldn't bite. Break-in force lacked the hair-trigger lightness of a Mig-29; but once initiated, the rolls proceeded smooth and briskly, with plenty of aerodynamic feedback.

Levelling off briefly over high cloud Vladimir asked the plane back and rolled us inverted to skim over them. Rolling out again, he asked me to wait half a minute – I guess to restore oil circulation – then let me have a go myself. Head-down supersonic at 10,000 metres, skimming cloud-tops at the sharp end of the mightiest Cold War Soviet plane – it takes some beating!

LEARNING TO FLY AGAIN

Egidio Gavazzi, *Desiderio di Volo* (Sironi Editore, 2005) pp 25-8, translated by Alex Martin.

I explore the woods at Il Borro, alert to every sound, following an ancient impulse to take animals by surprise. Their alertness, however, is superior to mine. I have only modest success. One day I almost manage to touch a roebuck, another I think I see a wolf. Wild boar, perhaps the most populous animals in these parts, are too wily to be caught off guard. Even so, they are not exactly shy. Every time I plan to fly, I have to drive along the airstrip and fill the holes they have dug during the night.

This is a time when my mind is deeply occupied with arcane things. I notice that the woods, the village, are full of 'presences'. The Romans were right to believe that the souls of the dead roam the woods. *Animula vagula blandula, … Quae nunc abibis in loca…*, Hadrian's verses come back to mind. I go about those *loca*, those woods, seeking contact with the world of the shades. I register the 'aura' of the firs against the winter sky, or at least I believe I do. It may be my retinas playing tricks. There is always a rational explanation.

These excursions into the paranormal have one practical result. One afternoon, when I am learning to fly again, I quietly climb into a plane hidden in the gloom of the hangar. There is no one about. I have plenty of time. I begin the complex ritual that I learned at the Institute of Applied Psychodynamics in Milan – applied in this case to flying. I put myself into a light trance, known as 'the alpha state', and set myself back at the controls of the aircraft I flew more than twenty years ago at Vergiate. In the reality thus evoked I go through all the pre-flight checks. Then I roll down the runway, take off, fly, manoeuvre, and return to the field.

The aeroplane has not moved. The sparrows continue to chirp undisturbed among the roof-beams. And when I return to this world, it is as if I really have just landed. Nothing is forgotten. Somewhere each event of our lives, no matter how small, is recorded. It is a question of groping for it in the dusty archives of memory, where it lies buried under layer upon layer of subsequent experience, and bringing it up to the surface as if it were a thing of yesterday; like slipping a file from the bottom of a pile and setting it on the top.

Whether this immense deposit of experience is located in the brain, in the unconscious (wherever that may be), or even in an outside space common to all, as some people claim, is of no importance. The important thing is that it works. *'E pur si muove.'* My hands perform the familiar gestures, led by recovered reflexes; they move on their own, without hesitation, to switches, levers, controls, in the correct sequence. And so my return to flying occurs, not in the skies of the Val di Chiana, but in an immaterial, personal and timeless universe, to which only I have the keys. Auto-suggestion? Perhaps. We make two types of mistakes when we deal with the paranormal: believing too much,

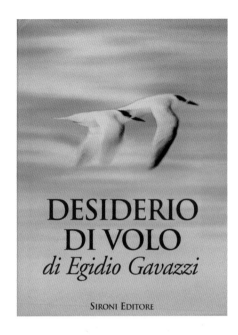

**DESIDERIO
DI VOLO**
di Egidio Gavazzi

Sironi Editore

and believing too little. At all events, the instructor allows me to go solo after just four landings.

My satisfaction is short-lived. I know how to pilot a plane but have no idea how to go from place to place. I know nothing about navigational instruments and less about the radio; nor can I cope with the labyrinthine complexity of 'air spaces,' those menacing immaterial entities that still send shivers along my spine today. The patient process of re-learning begins. The fact that I already know how to fly puts me in a very odd position. The true novice is someone who knows nothing, like a child going to school for the first time. Whereas I feel like a wild man – fully-grown, capable of survival, yet ignorant of the complex rules of communal living. Like Jimmy Button, the native of Tierra del Fuego brought to England aboard HMS *Beagle*. My longest flight, in fact my *only* long flight, was made thirty-three years ago. This was the 'distance trial' required for my pilot's licence. Milan–Venice – practically transcontinental! The choice of Venice was a

kindness to the student. Idiotic as he might be, it would be hard to mistake Venice for another city.

It went like this, as I recall. I drew a line on the map from my departure airfield to my destination. I took the bearing of this line at its mid-point, as prescribed, to eliminate errors due to map projection. Having calculated the 'true course', I corrected it for the difference between true north and magnetic north as indicated on the map, bringing the figure up to date with a formula that took into account the time lapsed since the year of publication. I then subtracted the compass deviation particular to each aircraft, which I read off the relevant card. Finally I tackled the awkward problem of 'triangles of velocity', to correct drift due to cross-winds during my flight, using figures supplied by the meteorological service of the Italian Air Force.

Eventually I took off. At once I adopted the tactics of a well-schooled cheat, and 'caught the train' – found the Milan-Venice railway line, and followed it unswervingly, as my instructor had ordered. Despite glorious weather, I still managed to lose my way, only finding it again when I spotted Padua cathedral, which I happened to recognize from the label on a bottle of VOV, a liqueur of which I was curiously fond. Radio, in those days, was an unimaginable luxury.

Giorgio Giorgi gives us lessons in radio communication. The classroom reminds me of a village school. Educational posters on the wall, dating from the 1930s, show the anatomy and inner workings of the basic flying instruments. On a shelf lies an Isotta Fraschini engine,

unfortunately incomplete. Giorgio sits at the teacher's desk, the students at cubicles with earphones, like interpreters at an international conference. It is dark outside. By day Giorgio is an air traffic controller at Firenze Peretola. The evening is fragrant with lime blossom. A resident nightingale is in full voice. The teacher, like a true Tuscan, is incapable of ending a word with a consonant, so I am puzzled when he sends me to 'Scipolle' – which turns out to be Schiphol in Holland. We are 'flying' in the summer night, following our antiquated instrument charts, guided by Giorgio's vernacular English while the nightingale sings on without a pause.

I like the atmosphere, and the night favours dreaming. Now he sends me to Lamezia Terme. I see myself, disciplined and competent, at the controls of a commercial airliner, streaming high over the island of Ponza, the black sea beneath me scored by a silver streak of moonlight reflected through scattered veils of cloud. Meanwhile the real moon is out there, visible through the window, lending authenticity to my fantasy. Then, on the stroke of midnight, we are packed off home like Cinderellas. I climb into my MG and drive away along the forest track, the wind in my face, hoping to catch a fallow deer or a porcupine in the beam of my headlights.

About a dozen pupils attend these lessons. Five of them form a special little group. They are selected by Alitalia and taught under contract by the local aero club, which is obviously a place of some repute. They are splendid young men, the sort any father would be proud of. So intent and committed, they allow nothing

to distract them from the lessons – fearful, it seems, of spoiling themselves, of compromising their integrity.

Then, one morning, they are gone. A telegram has arrived from Rome. Not a telephone call, a telegram, as in the Great War, stating that the Alitalia courses are suspended. The flying club is in mourning. An old pain flickers to life again inside me.

TRANSATLANTIC LEOPARD MOTH (1999)
Torquil Norman, *Pilot* magazine 15 March 2001 (extracts)

Flying old aircraft is my passion and when I was a Navy pilot back in the fifties I developed a fondness for flying over water – so much flatter than mountains (although, they tell me, almost as hard when you hit it!). Since I retired from my toy business I have had more time to indulge this passion and make longer trips.

Long-distance flights in old aircraft put the world into perspective and help keep me sane. I feel comfortable around old planes. I was brought up on them and understand their technology. They are like old friends whose idiosyncrasies I know and appreciate.

I decided to fly my D.H.85 Leopard Moth to Oshkosh, in 1999, as a personal millennium thank you to Geoffrey de Havilland, a man who has given me so much pleasure in my life.

The Leopard Moth was built in 1933 and has a 143 hp Gipsy Major. It was de Havilland's favourite touring aeroplane. It was fast for its era, had a long range and was wonderfully stable. Normally, it carries three people with the pilot in the front, but for the Oshkosh flight I took out the back seats and put a 35-gallon long-range fuel tank in their place. This gave me about eighty gallons in all - perhaps 11 ½ hours endurance under normal conditions. About 2 ½ hours out of Reykjavik I did something I had never done before. I used the pilot's relief tube in the immersion suit. This sounds easier than it is, especially since I was at about 400 feet over mist at the time, and of course old planes have no

autopilot. It was a tricky business: with one hand I had to keep the aircraft steady; with the other I unzipped and then unrolled a wide, foot-long rubber panel in the suit. This creates a long tube into which to manoeuvre an organ – which at that point was about two inches long – and connect it with the cutely named container, 'Little John'. The result was not entirely satisfactory – about 10% of the fluid never made it – but the sense of relief was so enormous that I didn't care.

The weather was fine when I arrived at Reykjavik and, although it was drizzling the following morning and the ceiling was down to 500 feet, there was high pressure over Greenland, so I set off for Kulusuk on the east coast at about 8.30 a.m.

Again there was a headwind and I was at my 'normal' 65 knots, but after a couple of hours it died down and my speed increased. As the cloud above me broke up, I decided to climb and test the winds at higher levels. At 5,500 feet I was doing ninety knots; at 10,000 I was up to 100 knots. I could see Greenland from over 150 miles away in perfect sunshine. I calculated that in these conditions I could get clear across the ice cap to Söndestrom, on the west coast, in about 8 ½ hours – less than I had flown the previous day. So I altered my flight plan via a relayed radio message and was given approval to cross the ice cap at 12,000 feet.

I have discovered on these trips, and in fact on any flying occasion – I'm tempted to say on any occasion in life! – that complacency is a huge mistake. Nearly every time you succumb to it, the great poker player in the sky has a card up his sleeve and he has a way of playing it with such subtlety you often don't understand the strength of his hand until you have raised the ante too high!

On this occasion I was blissfully happy as I passed over the gravel strip at Kulusuk and climbed gently towards the ice cap for the crossing at 12,000 feet. The sunshine was brilliant, visibility unlimited and I was doing about 120 knots groundspeed. So when the first delicate wisps of cloud appeared after about 100 miles I didn't think much of it. But the cloud started to get higher and I was forced to climb to 13,200 feet to stay above it.

I have been flying for about fifty years, so it would be reasonable to assume that obvious problems, such as anoxia, would have been in the forefront of my mind. Not a bit of it – sheer stupidity ruled! I am deeply ashamed to be writing these words, and only do so as a cautionary tale for those who may follow.

I couldn't really go higher than 13,200 feet, the mixture was leaned a long way and the airspeed indicator was showing about 75 mph, which seemed a reasonable gap above the 54 mph stalling speed (the Leopard has no flaps). As the cloud came over me, my reaction was, 'It looks like fine ice crystals and, hell, I'm only an hour and a half from Söndestrom and my groundspeed is a spectacular 123 knots!' So I pressed on into the cloud. The ice cap at that point is about 9,600 feet high and the freezing level was about 5,000 feet, so this was all happening far above icing levels. I watched a thin layer of rime ice build up steadily on the struts but it

was only after about forty minutes in cloud that the stupidity of what I was doing began to dawn on me.

By then, the ice had built up to about one-third of an inch, and I had just made up my mind to turn around and go back to Kulusuk when I flew into what looked like rain, but presumably were super-cooled water droplets. These can turn instantly into clear ice, which can be lethal. From where I was sitting, the effect was dramatic. One moment, I was looking out at a frosty aeroplane with a propeller in front, the next, the windscreen had gone completely white and I was sitting in a closed box unable to see anything at all except the instruments.

At this point a butterfly the size of Concorde took off in my stomach and I realised my decision to turn back was long overdue. I started to bank gingerly into a gentle turn, while trying not to stall the aircraft. The artificial horizon and the turn-and-bank indicator were operated by suction from two venturis below the fuselage and I wondered what effect the ice was having on them. At that height in cloud there was no question of recovering from a stall, and much as I love ice in dry martinis, there was far too much of it about and it was far too close. I kept my portable GPS in my crotch between my legs, which was safe and secure in normal conditions, but it meant taking my eyes off the instrument panel for vital seconds to maintain the correct heading.

Out of the whole trip, two episodes, on top of the early backfires, still fill me with fear. This was the first. I still don't know how I made it round without stalling, but soon I was heading back

to Kulusuk at about 65 knots. I sat glued to the instruments, with the cockpit covered in ice, for nearly an hour. Finally I broke out into brilliant sunshine again, watched the ice clear and landed at Kulusuk after nearly nine hours, having passed over it 2½ hours before. The trouble with these trips in slow aircraft with limited instruments is that the best you can hope for is clear weather for take-off and landing. This usually means lousy weather somewhere in between. You have to assume that you can fly under (or near the bottom of) any weather fronts, and you take comfort from the fact that you are below the icing level and over water, not mountains.

So when the forecast showed low pressure clearing Goose Bay and a warm and cold frontal system in the middle, I felt I had little option but to go for it. Although there was some mention of embedded cu-nims, which was slightly off-putting, I set off the next morning in fine weather. I reckoned I would encounter the first front about two hours out. In fact it was over 3½ hours before I hit it and by then I was almost beginning to hope that it, and the cu-nims, might not be there at all.

No such luck. The cloud thickened steadily and I tried to keep between layers as long as possible, climbing to nearly 10,000 feet in the process. Eventually, I was forced down to 1,000 feet, with the sea visible below. Though the ride was bumpy, I had the unusual luxury of a following wind and I began to think that it might all work out quite reasonably. Needless to say, I was wrong.

The warm sector lasted maybe half an hour

Bill Hall and his much-travelled Robin Aiglon.

before I hit the cold front and found myself flying at 100 feet, still able to see the waves, but unable to climb without disappearing into cloud. It was cold and dark and gloomy, and I thanked my lucky stars that I had had the sense to use the relief tube an hour before.

After an hour on the deck, I worked out that I was about 35 miles from the coast of Labrador and that, come what may, I had no alternative but to climb. I was praying that the forecasters had been right about the low pressure system moving away from Goose Bay.

As I was steeling myself to start the climb the second nerve-racking incident of my journey occurred. An enormous iceberg flew past me out of the mist, just to my left and a few feet below. It was gone in a second, but it certainly got me started smartly into the climb.

After that, things started to look up. The gloom was beginning to lighten and suddenly I saw patches of blue sky above me. I flirted briefly with the icing level when a thin coat of rime ice started to appear, but in a few minutes I burst out into perfect sunshine above the most extraordinary cloudscape I have ever seen. The cloud top was formed into gigantic smooth white waves; it looked like breaking surf, although each wave was about 2,000 feet high. I was surfing happily along the edge of one of these waves when I was suddenly hit by tremendous turbulence. The aircraft was barely controllable. It was flung from one wingtip to the other, while I tried not to bang my head all over the cockpit and tightened the seat-belt with all my might. I had visions of my luggage, the fuel tank on the rear seat and everything else behind me tearing loose and clobbering me on the back of the neck.

Eventually, the turbulence eased off and I let down, still in windy conditions, over the estuary and flew the last thirty miles into Goose Bay. The 7½ hours since Narsarsuaq felt like 7½ lifetimes.

That is really the end of the story. I had flown the old Leopard Moth from Wick to Goose Bay in four long days. Thanks to the undersized immersion suit, my feet were excruciatingly sore and two toenails were missing. My back ached and I was short of sleep. But when I stepped out onto the tarmac, I felt an incredible feeling of elation. I forgot all my stupidities and the prospect of nothing but dry land ahead was wonderful.

LANZAROTE TO CAPE TOWN (2002)
Bill Hall, www.airsquadron.org

20 April, Lanzarote – Nouakchott
I don't get a romantic view of the African coast coming slowly into view because the ground is covered by a cloud layer at 2000ft or so. As I proceed south this breaks up and a good textbook desert with crescent dunes is revealed. Nouakchott merges with the sand which laps up the streets like water. I land at the very quiet airport and as my engine stops a man rushes out, greets me and helpfully informs me that I have no clearance for Mauritania and for a fee he would fix it (in fact Mauritania only ever replies to clearance requests if they object). I ignore his request and, in spite of further threats, nothing comes of it. Every one else is friendly; a middle aged French woman mans the met office where there is good information. I chat to the Fugro watch keeper (apparently oil has been found). A group of military men in fatigues approaches to ask my business and seem satisfied with my explanation. After only one hour on the ground I'm on my way.

Nouakchott – Bamako
I route via Kayes since this takes me over a more populated area at the cost of a couple of miles extra distance. The desert slowly gets greener with first a few trees then bushes and by Bamako it's only semi desert. There is patchy VHF coverage and when I

get within 100nm of my destination I am informed of CB activity but luckily on the far (eastern) side of Bamako. I descend into what feels like an oven; the air is hot, dry and filled with red dust that accentuates the red gloom as sunset approaches. Within 5 minutes of my landing a hot dust-laden wind blows strongly at right angles to the runway causing an Air France flight to overshoot. I carefully make my way through the blowing dust and G-BIRT is tucked up next to some sorry looking Wessex helicopters that look like they last flew in 1975.

I am getting into the ITCZ thunderstorm zone so I want to make as much progress as early in the morning as possible so I strike up a deal with a tall fireman to collect me at 3AM from my hotel. I then go to the hot sandy Hotel Faso where I have an excellent pepper steak (at least the French ex-colonies have good food) and retire for a couple of hours to my oven-like room. The early start fails due to an area of thunderstorms on the satellite picture (the met office is well equipped) so I get a few more hours sleep.

21 April, Bamako – Lome

In the morning the thunderstorms are no longer a factor so I take off for Lome. The ground gets slowly lusher, there are more and more carefully laid out towns that look very much like the ones that Babar the elephant used to live in. Even in the morning I have to dodge a thunderstorm building 100 miles north of my destination. When I get in range of Lome they tell me I have no clearance, I assure them I have and quote the number and am then informed that it's for last month! But there is no real problem and

I am allowed to continue. Lome is hot, humid and very quiet as I park next to a 707. After a short pause a USA government pressurised Beech twin arrives and disgorges a group of men in fatigues who salute and shout at each other briefly before silence descends again. A man in uniform approaches, salutes, and gives me a hand-written form for the information that should have been in my clearance. I go into the flight planning office hoping to continue to Libreville that day but a violent group of storms in the Gulf of Guinea stops that idea.

I ask the friendly staff to recommend a hotel and am directed to the Hotel Napoleon. This is a small privately owned place run by a Frenchman in a very relaxed style overlooking a lake. I am invited to drink wine with a couple of local pilots (French again) who sing the praises of their Viscount (the last one flying they say). An extremely attractive receptionist smoulders in one corner while lively French chitchat goes on all about. The pilots give me two useful bits of information: Be careful with Nigeria – if you are forced there without clearance (e.g. with engine problems) there is an automatic $20,000 fine. The last people who went to Libreville without clearance got thrown straight into prison.

22 April, Lome – Libreville

At this stage I do not have clearance for Libreville (Overflight have not received an answer). So the only thing to do is to send a request over the AFTN network from the Lome flight planning office. This appears to work and after a couple of hours a reply

is received that gives permission. Meanwhile the thunderstorms out to sea are still there but seem to be shrinking slightly. In my opinion a shrinking thunderstorm probably won't kill you so I depart. This time I am right and the storms are negotiated. The problems start when I get in radio range of Libreville who tell me in no uncertain terms that I have no clearance and am not welcome – perhaps I should go to my alternate. Friendly alternates are rather thin on the ground in these parts so I protest my innocence and read out (in French) the message I had received in Lome. My accent is not too good and after a short pause they again suggest I go elsewhere. I start to look at my maps to decide what to do but after a few minutes Libreville relent and say that I can proceed inbound. I do not know why they changed their mind – perhaps they found my clearance or just decided they would let me in.

On landing I am met by two customs officials in French Gendarme uniform who want a General Declaration form. I am then left alone. Libreville airport is busy, there is lots of coming and going overlooked by large French men with crew cuts and radios. Several big hangars are servicing turboprop and jet aircraft. There is even a flying club but the C152s outside it have flat tyres. A sad looking jet seems to have landed a bit too much sideways and is propped up on pallets.

I stay at the Hotel Atlantique which is one of those hotels that pilots end up at (similar to the Loftendir at Reykjavik). It is on a good tropical beach, walking distance from the airport and only slightly scruffy. Again the French influence gives good food.

23 April, Libreville – Pointe-Noire

I now make a mistake. There had been no problems with fuel so far and, lulled into a false sense of security, I do not carry a full fuel load for the short hop to Pointe-Noire. The three hour flight is over lush jungle and a tangled river system that steams in the morning sun. The relaxed mood is soon spoiled when Congo ATC ask me for a clearance number that I don't have. I fall back on saying "romeo tango, standby" and (thank god) they are apparently too busy to ask again. At Pointe-Noire they are resurfacing the runway; there is no nonsense about closing the airfield, one simply avoids the obviously wet bits of tarmac and steamrollers. Along the side of the runway there are aircraft with people living in them. Washing hangs from their wings. On the ramp there is a hive of activity, Antonovs with Russian registrations jostle with each other for parking positions carrying who knows what to god knows where. Passengers and well-wishers mill around in front of my propeller. I quietly find myself a parking place under the wing of a jet, shut down and am relieved as no authority takes any interest in me. I flag down a fuel truck touting for business and ask him where I can find avgas; he politely informs me that there is no avgas here. Without letting my considerable consternation show I enquire who I can ask about this (often someone has some drums in a shed) and he points me towards a hangar several hundred meters away with "Aviation Service" on it. Wondering what a few weeks in Pointe-Noire would be like, I walk over there to find a tidyish hangar with a couple of piston aircraft parked outside and two Frenchmen doing something complicated to a large polyethylene tank. The boss (M. Ryman) confirms that there is no avgas; he also states that he was in Libreville yesterday and there was none there either (in which case what have I got in my tanks?)

I am now faced with a choice of either going back to Libreville and taking on a full load of fuel before flying from there to Ondangwa (not attractive because of my lack of Gabon clearance), I could stay in Pointe-Noire or I could fill up here with motor fuel and go south to Namibia. I choose the latter course. Even if the practice is not condoned by the CAA, I feel that my engine was originally designed for 95 octane fuel, there should be enough lead in the avgas still in my tanks to keep the valve stems happy and mogas formulated for use on the equator would be unlikely to produce any vapour lock problems.

M. Ryman helpfully changes some dollars for me and lends me two 60 litre jerry cans. My gold stripes work their magic as I nod politely at the customs man (whose attention I *really* don't want) and make my way to the taxi rank. A little later the gold stripes enable the taxi driver to queue barge at the petrol pumps where I cause much interest and buy the cheapest fuel of the whole trip. I am assisted by a couple of helpful lads who, for a small consideration, help wrestle with the 100lb jerry cans in the (by now) noon equatorial sun, the whole process being watched with interest by a crowd of Russians from the shade of their aircraft's wing. Two trips are required and by the end my helpers and I are covered in sweat and petrol but I feel much happier since I now have a chance of leaving Pointe-Noire intact.

Pointe-Noire – Ondangwa

I file a flight plan to Windhoek since this is in the Jeppesen as a 24H airport. A visit to the weather office provides no information at all which is a slight worry since it is now after midday and I have over 9 hours to fly requiring a night arrival. I have the Iridium phone so I ring my brother Martin and ask him to email the TAFs to my phone. Luckily the messages don't arrive for some time so I don't see the very bad (and wrong) forecast for my destination. After waiting for a steam roller to get out of my way I take off heading south towards Angola and am soon dismissed by Pointe-Noire ATC in disgust at my lack of HF. The fuel seems to work ok, though I am careful not to allow the engine to get pure mogas and I don't lean to the ragged edge. I get high oil temperatures but this is normal in G-BIRT when climbing out on a hot day, particularly if the engine is warm from an earlier flight.

Luanda seems to be a global crossroads, jets of all nationalities keep the frequency busy and I am easily able to get a relay. ATC are surprised at my estimates and ask for my indicated airspeed; they find my reply of 95 knots hard to believe (this is a maximum range trip and I am throttled right back).

As I pass Luanda I see weather building ahead and within the hour, as daylight and radio contact fades, I am confronted by a building line of thunderstorms on my track. There follows a tense few hours as I try to remain out of cloud enough to see and avoid storms in the darkness (I have no radar or Stormscope). Fortunately there is a moon and at night one can often see which are the bad places by the amount of lightning. After what seems a long time I leave the bad weather behind and fly on for lonely hours over Angola, no lights to be seen and even the 126.9 broadcast frequency is quiet.

While still over Angola my DI suddenly starts to spin and the attitude gyro drunkenly leans to one side – it appears that my vacuum pump has failed. This is not an immediate emergency since the weather is now clear, I still have the electrically powered turn indicator that drives my wing leveller and GPS gives a good heading reference. If this failure had happened earlier while in and out of the clouds amongst the storms it would have been much more worrying. I give Christopher Sharples a ring and he sends out an email with some of the events of the day.

It is with some relief that I make contact with Windhoek Control, but as I cross the border ATC asks me if I'm aware that Windhoek is in fact not a 24 hour airport and I would have to pay to keep it open. After a bit of discussion it's decided that the best (cheapest) option is for them to open Ondangwa (300 miles north of Windhoek) for me. This is done and I make my first night landing for some years.

At Ondangwa the tower operator is very helpful, he gets the immigration man to come in and books me into a hotel who say they are sending a car. He then goes back to bed since he has to be up at 7AM. Unfortunately the promised car never arrives in spite of repeated calls to the hotel. I have a long, rather surreal, conversation with the woman airport guard. We sit together in the warm, insect-filled night, she cradles her AK47 and tells me about relatives in Wales. She feels that most men (present company excepted) are untrustworthy swine and break girl's hearts. Perhaps it's the rifle on her lap that stops me going into too much detail about how much trouble women can be. Eventually, after midnight, I give up and spend the rest of the night, rather uncomfortably, in my aeroplane.

24 April, Ondangwa – Upington
I am woken by a beautiful clear African sunrise. Namibia feels very different to where I have been. I am quickly refuelled and on my way to Upington in South Africa. The sky is a hard blue, decorated with a smear of cirrus and I get an excellent view of the Etosha Pan in the unlimited visibility. There is even a tailwind and I soon land on the longest runway in the southern hemisphere. This was built to allow heavy fuel loads to be carried in apartheid days when South African flights were not allowed to stop anywhere. The refuelling equipment is certainly impressive and looks like it could easily make G-BIRT spherical if mishandled.

It's now 48 hours since I have seen any washing facilities, I notice that people seem to be keeping at a bit of a distance and my beard is coming on nicely. Upington is a good respectable town and immigration is not sure they like the look of me, however they can find no real reason to stand in my way and I spend the night in a small town hotel.

25 April, Upington – Stellenbosch, Cape Town
Cape Town has a fairly complex set of controlled airspace so I file IFR. In the event there is no problem and I have a relaxed flight over spectacular scenery. My transponder even gets some exercise. At Stellenbosch airfield I am greeted by a group of South African Air Force officers. It's only later that I learn that I was in fact expected at Cape Town International where the press, VIPs, girls etc were waiting to receive me.

ALL WENT QUIET – FLYING TO THE NORTH POLE (2003)
Polly Vacher, *Wings Around the World*
(Grub Street, 2006) pp 60-64

The mountains of Spitzbergen were fast disappearing under my wing. All that I could see was endless miles of ice interspersed with odd ribbons of open water called 'leads'. It was spectacular, but how would my little craft manage in these low temperatures?

I was frighteningly aware that I was all on my own and that I was flying over vast stretches of ice-covered ocean. My head was full of those 'what ifs' and I tried not to fixate on how Golf November would cope. But if I did come down, if the engine did fail, would I manage? Could I camp on the ice? Would I be found? Would I die?

One cannot be scared for ever. I was busy in the cockpit and my hourly routine kept me occupied. It was important to keep track of the fuel already consumed and the amount left so I did the fuel calculations and checked the instruments. Then I did vigorous leg exercises to prevent deep vein

WINGS AROUND
THE WORLD

The exhilarating story of one woman's
epic flight from the North Pole to Antarctica

POLLY VACHER

thrombosis, ate a muesli bar and drank some water and so each hour passed. Adrenalin was on permanent fast flow.

In the polar areas the aircraft compass becomes inaccurate and may topple. Satellite navigation by the cockpit Global Positioning System (GPS) then becomes the only means of finding your way. Should the GPS pack up when suspended by a tiny airframe and one engine over the North Pole, which way do you go? All roads lead south, so how do you find the correct line of longitude down which to fly? Without GPS I could use the rest of my fuel and perhaps the rest of my life going round and round in circles. All is flat and there are no landmarks to navigate by.

At this stage, I could still turn round and return to the safety of Longyearbyen, and so I might have done had I heeded that little voice that was nagging away. I ignored it and glanced at the names on my wings, drawing comfort from those that I knew. I wondered what they were doing 'back home'. Even if the GPS did fail I still had the sun, that one constant which was impervious to magnetic energy and could not fail. At that moment I felt only too grateful to Arthur Moore, the retired RAF navigator who had patiently taken me through the mysteries of the Mk II Astro Compass which I now had mounted on the dashboard of Golf November.

Every half hour I was taking sun-sights and calculating my position. Fortunately the weather was gin-clear aloft so at least I could see the sun. Using the astro compass required a complicated routine. The instrument was awkwardly placed. I could not see the true heading indicator from where I was sitting without the use of a long dentist's mirror. I then had to calculate my position using an almanac, checking the time and date on a set of tables. After all this, the result was perfect. The sun navigation matched exactly with the GPS. It was comforting to know that I had this back-up.

The miles ticked slowly behind me. I had a headwind of approximately 30 kts which meant that I only covered the earth's surface at 98-100 nautical miles an hour which was painfully slow. I willed Golf November on and gloried in the sun sparkling off the ice and the blue leads. The reality of it was that I was on my own and there was no-one there should something happen to my engine. Gradually we reached 88°N then 89°N. I became very excited.

Would the GPS read 90°North?

No-one could tell me the answer to this, not even Bendix-King, the manufacturers and sponsors. In fact it *did* read 90°N for about 5 seconds. I was so excited that if there had been a table to dance on in my small cockpit, I would have surely done so. Instead, I picked up my satellite phone and called my husband, Peter, back in Oxfordshire.

"I'm on top of the world," I screamed down the phone against the engine noise.

"For heaven's sake, head South!" he replied.

I did.

More endless miles of ice, leads and sparkling sunshine were ahead of me as I chugged my way southward. I had a crosswind now, and I had timed the flight so that the sun was directly in front of me as I turned at the Pole. Winds fluctuated and my heart rose and sank accordingly. If I had a bit of a tailwind I was going as fast as 130 kts. My heart rose and then it would sink again as the groundspeed dropped to less than 120 kts.

My spirits moved like the sea rises and sinks beneath that vast expanse of sea ice but I forbade myself to think of things like that. I knew that seals swam around beneath the ice and that polar bears sat on the edge of the leads patiently waiting for a seal to emerge for breath. The bear mercilessly pounces and it is all over in seconds. The seal is dragged onto the ice and all that remains is a red flow of blood to mark the spot.

Silence! That 'sound yet not a sound' which all pilots dread. My engine had stopped. I was over Axel Heiberg Island, one of the most beautiful and hostile places on earth. Mountains rise out of the flat sea ice in sharp peaks like whipped up icing on a cake.

Three minutes earlier the engine had coughed, indicating that my massive cockpit tank was about to run dry. This was perfectly normal. I changed onto my first wing tank and the engine purred again. I had plenty of fuel with just two hours left to run and nearly six hours of fuel in the wings.

Then the engine stopped.

I went into automatic mode. "Carb heat on, fuel pump on, change tanks,' I muttered to myself. My camera went flying. Papers flew to the floor. I rattled through the emergency check list which I had practised over and over with my 'Flying Guru', Pete Thorn. The engine sprang into life and the relief was enormous.

I had no idea whether the engine would stop again, so with sweat pouring down me and adrenalin on overtime, I detoured out over the sea ice.

"At least I have a chance of landing Golf November on the sea ice," I thought. "There would be no chance of survival over the mountain peaks of Axel Heiburg Island if it happens again."

After that every little sound taunted me as I tried to analyse why it had stopped. Was there ice in the fuel? Ice could certainly block the fuel inlet to the engine and cause fuel starvation. I looked down at the endless miles of ice below and wondered what on earth I was doing. I thought of my family and imagined their lives without me. I queried how I would manage camping on the ice or facing a polar bear......?

Unlike Axel Heiburg island, most of the North Canadian islands are flat. It is almost impossible to differentiate between land and sea ice from the air. All looked flat as I tried to pick out the small islands marked on the map. At last, the runway at Resolute came into sight.

STILL FLYING AT 90
John Houlder (2006)
Shortly before his 90th birthday, which was celebrated with a special Air Squadron dinner at Brooklands, John Houlder wrote this short autobiographical sketch. It is far from the whole story, which would merit a full-length book in itself, but it reflects in his own words the highlights of a remarkable life.

I was born on 20 February 1916 at Epsom in Surrey, England.

I was a sickly child suffering from asthma and a mastoid operation to my right ear and did not like my public school education.

Consequently at the age of 16 my father arranged for me to become an apprentice fitter in the ship repair yard operated by Cox & Company, Falmouth. I liked this work very much and shared a digs with three other apprentices. We all studied evenings three or four times per week and one of my fellow apprentices ultimately became the Chief Engineer for the Port of London Authority.

My father took me away after three years and made me learn shorthand and typing at Pitmans College, London, after which I became the personal assistant to the shipbroker who did all the chartering for Standard Oil of New Jersey (now Esso).

Again I studied in the evening and having passed first in the examination of the Institute of Chartered Shipbrokers was appointed Director of the family company, Houlder Brothers & Company, which operated a line of refrigerated vessels between London and South America.

About this time I learned to fly at Brooklands, but owing to my ear was not eligible for the Civil Air Corps which was then the way of entry into the Auxiliary Air Force or RAFVR.

Consequently, I joined the Territorial Army, Royal Artillery, and when war broke out went to Norway, Egypt and Crete.

While in Crete, General Wavell, the Commander in Chief, had lunch in our battery mess as he was a friend of Field Marshall Lord Milne, whose son was my Battery Commander. As a result of what was said at this lunch, I suddenly found myself ordered to proceed to Tobruk, which had just been captured, to be Second-in-Command of "Y Docks". This was an ad-hoc unit consisting of 100 New Zealanders and 50 Australians from the 3rd and 4th Railway Construction Group, the 1st and 2nd Libyan Labour Battalions consisting of 1,000 Libyan labourers each, a Jewish Pioneer Company and a gang of Arab lightermen from Palestine. The unloading of ships was of critical importance to the advance in the desert.

Apart from the Arab lightermen I think I was almost the only person who had seen a merchant ship before and it was a very interesting experience. After a short period I became OC.

When the siege of Tobruk began these numbers were greatly reduced and I became Major RA OC 1018 Dock Operating Company with Indian Pioneer labour. As the Germans had complete air superiority all supplies were brought in by destroyers which could only stay in port for two hours in the middle of the night.

Throughout this period we were very heavily dive-bombed, but one becomes used to it so quickly that I am convinced that dive-bombing will never destroy military morale. Everyone can shoot back. More serious, however, was the fact that our quays were within range of Italian

artillery, and ultimately I was hit by a shell which among other things permanently disabled my left arm. I was evacuated by destroyer and sent back to England, marrying the nurse who looked after me in hospital en-route.

I was awarded the MBE for my work in Tobruk. In England I thought I would be invalided out of the Army and took a job as a Civil Servant in the Ministry of War Transport, but after a few months the Army saw my records and I was called into Combined Operations, first at the Combined Operations Experimental Establishment at Westward Ho and finally at headquarters in London.

There I was a round peg in a round hole, charged with devising and testing specialist equipment for landing stores and equipment for the forthcoming operation Overlord, the landing in Normandy.

Notwithstanding that I was "home service only", I went to the beaches shortly after the landings to see how my equipment worked and, as the one-eyed man is King in the land of the blind, so I took charge of the Port of Courseulles which had not been demolished.

There was some surprise when I sent myself home after three weeks and 21 Army Group asked for me back, describing me as "an Officer of outstanding ability", but CHQ refused and in due course I was sent to India in a Sunderland flying boat to assess needs and types of equipment needed for amphibian operations in that theatre. I came home in a bomber and was conducting an experimental tow of a huge raft of American pontoon equipment behind a merchant ship when the war with Germany came to an end.

Thereafter there was a proposal that I should go to Okinawa but fortunately the war with Japan ended before this took place.

My main hobby has always been flying. Immediately after the war I did a course of aerobatics under the hood in a Tiger Moth at Luton. I cannot understand why this exercise has died out. It is very exciting and gives one complete confidence in flying on instruments.

My father then gave me a wooden Messenger aircraft which could land and take off in such a small space that it was the next best thing to a helicopter. Subsequently I bought a wooden Gemini and had it fitted with engines of much greater horsepower, then a Cessna 310, and finally an Aero-Commander 680E which I have owned for over 30 years.

Elstree aerodrome was derelict in 1950 and I took a 40-year lease on it, subsequently extended primarily to accommodate my aeroplane but it has since become a very flourishing concern and I am very active in the day-to-day management.

My Cessna 310 had an autopilot and the nearest maintenance facility was Geneva so I studied its workings and obtained a CAA X licence for Autopilot maintenance and also obtained an A licence (airframes) for the Cessna 310 and later the Aero-Commander 680E. I was invited by the CAA as a private pilot to attempt the new instrument ratings which had just been introduced in 1947. I passed and have kept it up ever since with annual renewal tests.

My main activity of course has always been ship design and operation, together with the commercial aspects of shipping. This brought me into very close contact first with the Steel Industry, then Petroleum, then Gas and finally the Offshore.

One of my designs was particularly successful (named "Uncle John") which resulted in my receiving the Gold Medal of the Institute of Marine Engineers (plus £1000 cash!), the President's Award of the Society for Underwater Technology, becoming Member of Council of the Institute of Naval Architects and member of the Board of Lloyds Register of Shipping. I was invited to become Visiting Professor to the Department of Ship and Marine Technology at Strathclyde University, Glasgow. And finally I was made a Commander of the Order of the British Empire by the Queen.

Hugh Astor

1920-1999

Hugh Astor's father became chief proprietor and chairman of *The Times* in 1922, launching it into a 40-year period of stability and prestige. Astor knew his destiny and, after a spell as assistant Middle East correspondent which covered the end of the British mandate in Palestine and the birth of an independent Israel, he worked through all the aspects of newspaper publishing before joining his older brother Gavin on the board of *The Times* in 1956.

In 1959, when Gavin Astor became chairman, Hugh became his deputy. Having relinquished control to his sons, Lord Astor of Hever left Britain in 1962 with great reluctance. It proved impossible for the Astor brothers to manage *The Times* as they wished, and in 1967 they sold it to Roy Thomson, later Lord Thomson of Fleet. Hugh Astor retained his connection with the Times Trust but diverted his business abilities to directorships in book publishing (he was a director of Hutchinsons, 1959-78), banking, insurance and similar interests.

Hugh was the second of the three sons of John Jacob Astor V, first Baron Astor of Hever, and the former Lady Violet Mary Elliot Mercer-Nairne. He was born in 1920, brought up at Hever Castle in Kent, and educated in the family tradition at Eton and New College, Oxford. In 1940 he was commissioned into the Intelligence Corps (a childhood illness had left him with permanent lameness) and served in Europe and the Far East.

He had a lifelong interest and enjoyment of the sports of the sea and air. He had taken up ocean racing after the war, was a member of the Royal Yacht Squadron, and his annual yachting expeditions were a precious recreation, allowing undersea exploration and his interest in marine biology. In 1969 and 1971 he competed in London to Australia air races, and he also enjoyed gliding.

Hugh Astor perpetuated his father's philanthropic interests, being deputy chairman of the Middlesex Hospital, 1965-74, chairman of King Edward's Hospital Fund for London, 1983-88, and also governor of the Peabody Donation Fund for almost 20 years. He served as Prime Warden of the Fishmongers' Company, and his support was quietly given to sea and airmen's charities, including the Royal National Lifeboat Institution.

However, it is against the background of his country home in Berkshire that an even wider spectrum of society will remember his unassuming kindness and generosity. He bought Folly Farm, in the Kennet valley south-west of Reading, shortly after his marriage in 1950, appreciating it as one of Sir Edwin Lutyens's most idiosyncratic and enchanting houses, with a marvellous garden designed in partnership with Gertrude Jekyll.

For perhaps 25 years Folly Farm was enjoyed by his family and friends, and in the wider context of his role as a JP and as High Sheriff of the Royal County in 1963. But during the 1970s Lutyens's reputation spiralled skywards, and architects, photographers and garden historians from far and wide began beating their path to Folly Farm's gate.

Despite his innate reserve, Astor gave his support to the Lutyens Exhibition in London of 1981-82 and he became a patron of the Lutyens Trust when it was founded in 1985. Folly Farm's glorious garden, tended by his head gardener, Dennis Honour, for over 30 years, was regularly opened for charities and a request to see the garden was almost never refused.

Perhaps on some crowded afternoons he was reminded of the "Hever Days" of his childhood, when his father entertained the entire staff of *The Times*. On rarer occasions, when the house was open, many will recall their hosts' dignified bemusement as a dozen people stood in his bedroom discussing the ingenuity of Lutyens's cupboards, or when a visitor announced that Folly Farm was his birthplace, in its guise as a maternity home during the Second World War.

Hugh Astor's stewardship of Folly Farm, for almost half a century, came naturally to him, but his graciousness in sharing his family's home - which just happened to be an architectural icon - leaves thousands of individuals, and the cause of architectural heritage in general, deeply in his debt.

The Independent, 13 July 1999

The Hon Anthony Cayzer

1920-1990

Tony Cayzer's business career spanned a period of great change in the shipping world in which his family have been, since the mid-nineteenth century, so deeply involved.

As chairman of the Liverpool Steamship Owners Association for 10 years in the Fifties and Sixties and chairman of the Chamber of Shipping of the United Kingdom in 1967, deputy chairman of the British & Commonwealth Shipping Company and a director of Overseas Containers, among other companies, he played a large part in what has been called the merchant shipping revolution. Adaptability and flexibility were the key to continued prosperity and readiness to diversify into activities hitherto unthought of – aviation, in which Cayzer had a deep personal as well as a business interest – engineering, hotels, banking and insurance. In all these changes Cayzer's open-mindedness and readiness to venture into new worlds were of great importance.

In 1967 he was appointed a trustee of the National Maritime Museum at Greenwich and he became chairman nine years later. He proved in many ways a model chairman, ready to discuss, to advise, to give of his time and the benefit of his broad acquaintance for the furtherance of the objects for which the museum was founded. He helped particularly with public relations and his lunches at Greenwich were rarely refused.

This was a period in the museum's history when the great developments initiated under Leslie Runciman's chairmanship and continued during that of Sir Charles Madden were coming to fruition. The situation demanded that everyone should be quite clear as to their roles. Despite his background as an arbiter of power Cayzer never thought to usurp the director's responsibility for initiating policy and managing its execution. Nevertheless, he identified closely with the museum and its people in many ways. His annual garden parties for the staff at Great Westwood, his house in Hertfordshire, are still remembered very happily by those who served with him.

Cayzer constantly professed to standing in awe of some of the senior academic staff and it was interesting to watch their mutual interaction. One of his great interests, a legacy of his Liverpool days, was the history of the development and operation of the conference system of cargo liner operations. He had this complex business at his fingertips and he was able to make a unique contribution as a trustee by proposing and playing a large and active part in the creation of a gallery – most unfortunately now dismantled – devoted entirely to the explanation and interpretation of this very important but somewhat esoteric subject for the ordinary visitor to the museum.

It was a fascinating experience to work closely with him and his associates in the creation of this gallery. His readiness to adapt to the role of specialist professional adviser and consultant was all part of his open minded approach to life.

The Independent, 9 March 1990

John Cunningham

1917-2002

An address by Simon Ames at St Nicholas Church, Harpenden, 30 July 2002.

In his foreword to the excellent biography of John, Raymond Baxter wrote that "No pilot had made a more spectacular and significant contribution to the aviation history of his time than John Cunningham." His story is the stuff of greatness, he wrote, and the book is a worthy telling of a noble tale. Coming from a man whose carefully chosen words, always superbly articulated, have put the stamp of authority on countless aviation events described on television and radio for over half a century, we may find it easy to give our whole-hearted agreement to the way in which John's life was so aptly summarised by an illustrious contemporary who knew him well.

In a rather Churchillian way, the awesome hand of destiny helped to shape John's preparation for an outstanding list of achievements that are the markers of his emerging career.

John began his working life just as the sky was becoming a remarkable battleground and command of the air was vital to achieving victory. It may not have been so apparent at the time - but we see it so clearly now - that the conquest of the air in both war and peace attracted a special breed of dedicated men and women. John Cunningham is an outstanding example of this breed. In a flying career of 45 years, he deservedly became a living legend.

His early days as an apprentice at the de Havilland Technical School in the mid-1930s gave him the essential engineering grounding and, of course, he made the very best of it. During that period, he was offered the opportunity to join 604 Squadron of the Royal Auxiliary Air Force and to learn to fly. This was to change the course of his life and help to shape his future career path in the aviation industry.

Every single word that has been written or spoken about John's service in the Royal Air Force in WW II serves to confirm his strong leadership qualities, his determination and professionalism. His squadron, No 604, was destined to establish trials for the development of radar-equipped night fighters. Later, John was on record as saying "Night fighting is a highly specialised game. You had to have an inner strength and determination, you had to set a standard for everybody around you. It had to be made to work and we were the ones that had to master it." Doesn't that tell us so much!

It was that spirit of determination and endeavour that enabled the RAF's embryonic night fighting concept to make a remarkable contribution to the war in the air, the details of which are well chronicled. John became a national hero, even a household name after the media branded him "Cat's-Eyes" when the Air Ministry needed to conceal the existence of airborne radar from the enemy. At the age of 26, John became one of the youngest Group Captains in the Royal Air Force and his outstanding valour in the air with 604 and 85 Squadrons won him the DSO and two bars, also a DFC and bar.

After the war, although destined for air rank he left the RAF and returned to de Havilland where he saw the jet revolution beginning to gather momentum. When Geoffrey de Havilland Junior lost his life in 1946 flying the swept wing research aircraft, the DH 108, John became Chief Test Pilot and embarked on testing a wide range of aircraft from the Vampire to the Comet , which he flew for the first time on 27th July 1949, the day of his 32nd birthday. Before that, it was the Hornet, the Sea Hornet and the Venom. Then came the Sea Vixen, the Dove and Heron and several versions of the Trident and others. His appointment as Chief Test Pilot, a challenging one by any standards, continued for well over 30 years until his retirement in 1980.

Remarkably, John had been in the cockpit all his working life. He had played a major role in pioneering the de Havilland business. He loved the culture of the great family of de Havilland people which has been so strongly and joyously maintained up to the present day. In looking back at John Cunningham - the man - here are some of the words either spoken or written about him over the years.

Jimmy Rawnsley, who was teamed with John for most of the war years as his navigator, wrote, "John Cunningham was always in control of himself, even under dire circumstances, and master of his machine as if it were part of him body and mind."

In the context of the huge range of aircraft going through test programmes in 1949, it was said that "His fitness, resilience, professionalism and self control enabled him to work seven days a week as an ongoing schedule. This alone set him apart from others and contributed to his legendary status."

In the late 1950s Captain Sir Geoffrey de Havilland wrote: "John is test pilot, demonstration pilot, salesman and ambassador - all in one. He can fly thousands of miles for many days and at the end of each flight can be charming, unaffected and apparently as fresh as ever when discussing points raised by a host of officials, press and others."

In his retirement John was as busy as ever with countless activities linked to service and industry associations. His natural modesty and distaste for personal promotion made him unaware of the inspirational effect he had on people and on the public at large. As Chairman of Trustees of the Geoffrey de Havilland Flying Foundation, he attended the annual ceremony to present the Foundation's Achievement Medals to elite young schoolboys in the RAF section of the CCF. After one recent ceremony, while chatting to the lads of the winning group, a bright-eyed youngster addressed him rather quizzically - "Are you really THE Cat's Eyes Cunningham, Sir?" John looked slightly abashed. Rather falteringly he replied, "Well, yes, actually, I am." The effect was magic.

A final recollection. The scene is a press conference for a Comet 4 delivery. One reporter, looking for a different angle, asked John when he was going to get married. Pointing to the Comet on the tarmac outside the window, he replied, "That's my wife out there. She's very beautiful, isn't she, and she only drinks paraffin."

And one final thought: in view of the eminence

of John's long career and his very substantial contribution to the UK aviation industry as a whole, it remains something of a puzzle to his many friends that his life's work was not rewarded one step further by a grateful British public with a Knighthood. If it had been bestowed, certainly it would have been richly deserved. John Cunningham - your family, your friends, your colleagues and your many admirers from around the world salute your outstanding life achievements. The legend you leave behind will surely live for evermore.

Alex Henshaw

1912-2007

Alex Henshaw, who has died aged 94, was an outstanding test pilot whose name will forever be associated with the Second World War's most famous aircraft, the Spitfire; between 1940 and 1945 he test flew some 2,360 individual Spitfires and Seafires (the naval version of the aircraft), amounting to more than 10 per cent of the total built.

By 1939 Henshaw was already celebrated as a pilot, having won the King's Cup Air Race and broken the record for a flight to Cape Town and back. When war broke out he volunteered for service with the RAF but, while waiting for his application to be processed, was invited instead to join Vickers at Weybridge as a test pilot.

At first he was put into Wellingtons and the Walrus; and, frustrated by the amount of administrative work, he was about to leave the company when he met Jeffrey Quill, the chief test pilot of Supermarine, who offered him a job.

After test flying Spitfires at the company's Southampton factory, Henshaw moved in June 1940 to the Vickers Armstrong (Supermarine) factory at Castle Bromwich, near Birmingham, where he was soon appointed chief production test pilot for Spitfires and Lancasters.

It could be dangerous work. Henshaw suffered a number of engine failures, and on one occasion, while flying over a built-up area, he crash-landed between two rows of houses. The wings of his aircraft sheared off, and the engine and propeller finished up on someone's kitchen table. Henshaw -

who sustained only minor injuries - was left sitting in the small cockpit section, which fortunately remained intact.

Only on one occasion was he forced to bale out, when the engine of his Spitfire exploded. Henshaw was thrown out of the aircraft by the blast and became entangled in his parachute, which was badly torn and held together by a single thread on its perimeter; the thread held, and he landed safely.

Castle Bromwich was not ideally suited to have an aerodrome; it was often blanketed in fog and a heavy industrial haze, closing the airfield for routine flying.

With 320 Spitfires being produced each month, however, test flying had to continue, and Henshaw developed his own technique for landing: as he made his approach he would use the columns of condensation rising from the four cooling towers at nearby Hemshall to locate the airfield and align him with the runway. No other pilot was authorised to fly in these conditions, and Henshaw sometimes tested 20 aircraft in a day.

Once he was asked to put on a show for the Lord Mayor of Birmingham's Spitfire Fund by flying at high speed above the city's main street. The civic dignitaries were furious when he inverted the aircraft, flying upside down below the top of the Council House.

Often he would be called upon to demonstrate the Spitfire to groups of visiting VIPs. After one virtuoso display Winston Churchill was so enthralled by his performance that he kept a special train waiting while they talked alone. Henshaw, for his part, considered Churchill "the greatest Englishman of all time, the man who saved the world".

Henshaw also tested other aircraft, including more than 300 Lancasters - he once famously barrel-rolled the big bomber, the only pilot to have pulled off this feat. But his great love remained the Spitfire, which he described as a "sheer dream".

For his services during the war Henshaw was appointed MBE. There were many who thought this a meagre reward for his contribution.

The son of a wealthy businessman, Alex Henshaw was born at Peterborough on 7th November 1912 and educated at Lincoln Grammar School.

As a boy he was fascinated by flying and by motorcycles, and with financial support from his father - who thought it safer to be in an aircraft than on a motorcycle - he learned to fly in 1932 at the Skegness and East Lincolnshire Aero Club.

After his first solo his father gave him a de Havilland Gypsy Moth, and he made rapid progress as a pilot; the following year he felt competent to enter the King's Cup Air Race as one of the youngest-ever competitors.

The King's Cup was the most prestigious air race of the period and attracted enormous public interest. In 1934 Henshaw was invited to take part in his Miles Hawk Major. His prototype engine failed as he crossed the Irish Sea, and he was forced to ditch.

The next year he bought an Arrow Active, an aerobatic bi-plane. While he was performing an inverted loop, however, there was an explosion and the aircraft caught fire; Henshaw was forced to bale out, using the parachute he had been given on his birthday four weeks earlier.

In 1937 he won the inaugural London-to-Isle of Man air race in atrocious weather. Finally, in 1938, flying a Percival Mew Gull, he won the King's Cup at the age of 25, setting an average speed of 236.25 mph, a record that stands almost 70 years later.

Early in 1939 Henshaw made his record-breaking solo flight from England to Cape Town and back. In the spring of the previous year, accompanied by his father, he had surveyed possible routes down the eastern and western sides of Africa.

On February 5 1939 he took off in the Mew Gull from Gravesend to fly the western route. The aircraft had nine hours' endurance, and his first stop was at Oran, in Algeria, before a 1,300-mile leg across the Sahara. Without navigation or radio aids, he made further stops in the Belgian Congo and Angola before reaching Cape Town, having flown 6,030 miles in just under 40 hours, a record.

After 28 hours in Cape Town, Henshaw set off on the return journey, following a similar route. Just after lunch on February 9 he landed at Gravesend, four days, 10 hours and 16 minutes after his departure. Having completed one of the greatest ever solo long distance flights, he was on the verge of collapse, and had to be lifted from the tiny cockpit.

He had broken the homeward record, established in a twin-engine aircraft flown by two pilots, by seven hours, and the out-and-return time by almost 31 hours. Henshaw's epic flight was, however, overshadowed by the imminence of war and, unlike those pioneers who preceded him by a few years, he received no public recognition.

After the war Henshaw went to South Africa as a director of Miles Aircraft, but returned to England in 1948 and joined his family's farming and holiday business. He redeveloped six miles of Lincolnshire coastline which had been requisitioned during the war; the project included an 18-hole golf course.

A residential estate at Sandilands bears the name Henshaw for the main avenue, while all the roads and streets are named for the various aircraft he flew.

In his youth he received a Royal Humane Society award for saving a boy from the River Witham, and in 1953, he was awarded the Queen's Commendation for Bravery following his rescue work during the great floods.

Henshaw remained in great demand at aviation functions to the end of his life. In his 90th year he gave a masterly presentation, without the aid of notes, at an event in London to commemorate 100 years of flight. During the evening Prince Philip invested him as a Companion of the Air League.

In the summer of 2005 he donated his papers, art collection, photographs and trophies to the RAF Museum, where he paid for a curator to catalogue and promote his collection, which reflects the "golden age" of flying.

To mark the 70th anniversary of the first flight of the Spitfire, in March 2006, the 93-year-old Henshaw flew over Southampton in a two-seater Spitfire, taking the controls once airborne. His pilot commented that Henshaw could have landed the aircraft but for the prohibitive insurance conditions.

Henshaw was a tough-minded man, but was

also an approachable and patient one who took a great interest in promoting "air-mindedness" in young people, for which the Air League awarded him the Jeffrey Quill Medal in 1997.

The Royal Aeronautical Society elected him an honorary fellow in 2003. He was a vice-president of the Spitfire Memorial Defence Fellowship in Canberra, Australia.

He wrote three books about his experiences: *The Flight of the Mew Gull*; *Sigh for a Merlin*; and *Wings over the Great Divide*.

Alex Henshaw died on February 24. He married, in 1940, Barbara, the widow of Count de Chateaubrun. She died in 1996, and he is survived by their son.

The Daily Telegraph, 28 February 2007

The Duke of Leinster

1914-2004

The 8th Duke of Leinster, who died on Friday aged 90, put aside family misfortune, scandal and tragedy to pursue a successful career in business.

He was premier (indeed sole) Duke, premier Marquess and premier Earl in the Peerage of Ireland. His family, the FitzGeralds, were at one time the most powerful in that country. It was they who built the colossal Maynooth Castle, outside Dublin, as well as Leinster House (where the Dail is now housed) and Carton, in Co Kildare, one of the grandest Palladian mansions in the British Isles.

They acquired many titles over the centuries; in addition to the Dukedom, the Dukes of Leinster held the titles of Marquess of Kildare, Earl of Kildare, Earl and Baron of Offaly, Viscount Leinster, and Baron Kildare.

The FitzGerald family history is illustrious, bloody and packed with incident. John FitzGerald, 6th Baron of Offaly, was a valiant soldier who assisted King Edward I in his Scottish campaigns and was created Earl of Kildare in 1316. Legend has it that, during a fire at Woodstock Castle, Kildare, the Earl, then a baby, was left forgotten in a turret and would have been burnt had not the castle's tame monkey broken its chain and carried him to safety. Later, as a sign of appreciation, the Earl adopted the monkey for his crest and supporters.

Both the Marquessate (of 1761) and the Dukedom (of 1766) were of George III's creation and were conferred on the 20th Earl of Kildare, who had married a great-great-granddaughter of Charles II. The Earl had already been created a Viscount of Great Britain in 1747, by virtue of which he and his heirs had the right to sit in the House of Lords. It was he who commissioned and built Leinster House, the stateliest of Dublin's Georgian mansions, to reflect his eminent position in Irish society.

The 8th Duke's father, Edward, was a compulsive gambler and ne'er-do-well. Born the third son, he inherited the Leinster titles in 1922 following the death of his eldest brother Maurice in an Edinburgh lunatic asylum, his second brother having been killed in action in 1916. Bankrupted three times - in 1918, 1922 and again in 1936 - before he inherited the titles, the 7th Duke had sold his life interest in the £800,000 Leinster estate for £67,000 and £1,000 a year for life, to Harry Mallaby-Deeley, a financier and Conservative MP, on the understanding that Mallaby-Deeley or his family would draw the income from the estate until the Duke's death.

The Duke hoped by this arrangement to be in a position to settle his debts. Instead, unable to dig himself out of penury, he ended up living in a tiny Pimlico bedsitter where, distraught, depressed and utterly penniless, he eventually committed suicide in 1976.

The 7th Duke had been married four times. His first wife, May Etheridge, was the daughter of a commercial traveller who had graduated from her home in Brixton, via the Gaiety chorus, to a leading role in a West End show. There she captivated the young Lord Edward FitzGerald, who defied his family and married her in 1913. Their only son, Gerald FitzGerald, was born on May 27 1914.

Beset by financial problems, their romance soon wore thin, and in 1922 the couple separated. From then on the young Duchess was not allowed to see her son and grew increasingly depressed. She had to write to him through a firm of solicitors, who answered all her inquiries with a formal "The Marquess of Kildare is in good health". In 1930 she was found in a gas-filled room in Brixton, but was brought back to life just in time. Prematurely aged and stricken in health, she died in 1935 aged 43.

Gerald FitzGerald spent most of his boyhood being cared for by Lady Maurice FitzGerald, an aunt of his father, at Johnstone Castle, Co Wexford, where he enjoyed riding and hunting. He became the Marquess of Kildare in 1922 when his father inherited the Leinster titles.

After leaving Eton, Gerald became a cadet at the Royal Military College, Sandhurst, and took a commission in the 5th Royal Inniskilling Dragoon Guards, with whom he served as a major in the Second World War. He was invalided out of the Army after being wounded in Normandy.

Owing to his father's financial mismanagement, the trustees of the family estate entrusted Lord Kildare with the care of the family heirlooms and treasures by way of an advance on his inheritance.

After the war, he tried to make a go of farming the family estate at the medieval Kilkea Castle, Co Kildare, but it proved unprofitable; so he sold the castle and moved to Oxfordshire, where he became technical director, then managing director, of Vigors Aviation, and later chairman of CSE Aviation, both based at Oxford airport.

Family troubles, though, continued to haunt him. In 1976 police were called to his house in Oxfordshire to restrain his father, who had tried to remove a painting by Joshua Reynolds and a tapestry, valued at more than £100,000. Gerald succeeded to the titles on his father's death the same year, but was prevented from receiving the Queen's Writ of Summons by a claim lodged by Leonard FitzGerald, a San Francisco school teacher, that he was the rightful heir as the son of the 7th Duke's elder brother, Maurice.

Maurice had supposedly died unmarried in the lunatic asylum in 1922. The claimant argued that it was another man who had died and that Maurice FitzGerald had emigrated, married, had children and died in California in 1967 at the age of 80. In the end the claim was rejected, but not before the Writ of Summons had been delayed by eight months.

In 1999 the Duke failed in his attempts to prevent a half-brother being formally recognised in both Debrett's Peerage and Burke's Peerage. This man, Adrian FitzGerald, was the illegitimate son of the 7th Duke by Yvonne Probyn, great-niece of Sir Dighton Probyn, VC, Keeper of the Privy Purse to Edward VII.

The Duke of Leinster was a keen fieldsportsman. He was Master of the North Kilkenny Foxhounds from 1937 to 1940; of the West Percy Foxhounds in 1945-46; and of the Portman Foxhounds in 1946-47.

He married first, in 1936, Joane McMorrough-Kavanagh; they had three daughters, one of whom died in infancy. The marriage was dissolved in 1946, and later that year he married, secondly, Anne Eustace Smith, with whom he had two sons. His eldest son, Maurice, Marquess of Kildare, who was born in 1948, succeeds to the peerages.

The Daily Telegraph, 7 December 2004

The Hon Patrick Lindsay

1928-1986

The Honourable Patrick Lindsay, second son of the 28th Earl of Crawford and 11th Earl of Balcarres, who died on January 9 aged 57, was the senior picture director of Christie's, the fine art auctioneers. He combined this work with a life that was filled with adventure, danger and sporting activities.

He was made a director of Christie's in 1955, and after becoming their picture director a few years later he conducted most of the important sales of Old Masters and English pictures held by the company since the early 1960s. In an age when the auction of a picture for a million pounds was almost unheard of, he knocked down a Velazquez for £2,310,000 in 1970. In April, 1985 he broke all auction records on Christie's behalf when Mantegna's "Adoration of the Magi" was sold for £8.1 million.

He was generally acknowledged as one of the most persuasive auctioneers of his time. Strangers, attending one of those sales, marvelled at his calm, almost carefree delivery. To anyone who knew a little about his other lives, his sangfroid came as no surprise. For more than 40 years' skiing, sailing, flying, travelling and motor racing, the elegant, soft-voiced impresario cheerfully involved himself in his own long series of games played, often, eye to eye with death.

After his birth in November, 1928, his mother was told that he had a rare, almost certainly fatal, form of peritonitis. His victory in that first struggle earned him a mention in *The Lancet*. The marks and scars he gathered later would have filled an orthopaedic encyclopaedia. Whatever the injury, however narrow the escape, his invariable reaction was to get up and play the game again.

A highly developed competitive spirit was already evident when he played cricket, the Field game and soccer for Eton and, on leaving, saw active service in Malaya with the Scots Guards.

The seeds of a passion for aircraft and flying were sown a little later in the Oxford University Air Squadron.

After leaving Magdalen, he spent what he later called "easily the most stimulating time of my life" studying in Tuscany at the feet of the great art historian Bernard Berenson. As a child he had often listened, enthralled, while his father, a great expert, expounded on the family collection at Balcarres, from which Patrick was later to auction a famous Duccio.

With that early education, the time in Tuscany laid the foundation on which his long service to Christie's was securely based – service also to the nation's heritage for his connections and persuasion saved numerous pictures which would otherwise have gone abroad.

Beauty and adventure were his enduring passions and whenever possible he pursued them simultaneously. Apart from pictures, the beauty he treasured most was that of a fast elegant machine. Playing alternately the parts of collector, auctioneer, driver and pilot he carved for himself a unique position in the twin worlds of historic cars and aeroplanes.

To him a machine, however rare or long its history, was only worth having if it worked.

Of his cars the best known was Remus, his two-litre, supercharged E.R.A. Originally one of a pair, Remus and his brother Romulus were owned and driven in the 1930s by Prince "Bira" Birabongse of Siam. Wearing the red shirt which became his familiar trademark, Lindsay drove Remus – which could still manage speeds up to 160 mph – in races for pre-and post-war historic cars on tracks all over the British Isles and Europe.

Together, they won the Richard Seaman Memorial Trophy nine times and in 70 races since 1973 their record was 30 wins.

His own car collection began with a 1930 Rolls-Royce Phantom given him by the Maharajah of Jaipur – on condition that he drove it home. He did so – through the Khyber Pass and across tracks in Afghanistan that were more desert than road. Years later, he set out on a similar journey in reverse driving a 1933 Bentley with Keith Schellenberg and Norman Berkeley in the London-to-Sydney rally. Lindsay broke his shoulder in a crash on the Afghan-Turkish border and the three friends narrowly escaped a worse fate when unfriendly tribesmen robbed the car.

Mixing work with pleasure, he involved Christie's in sales at Lord Montagu's National Motor Car Museum at Beaulieu. At Los Angeles in 1979 he sold a 1936 Mercedes-Benz for $400,000, then a world record price for a car, and, all over Europe and the United States he encouraged and conducted the sale of historic cars and planes.

Of aeroplanes his pride and joy was the 1940 Spitfire, and the rarest feature of his collection was an S.E.5 from the First World War and, from between the wars, a specially rebuilt Hawker Fury.

With planes as with cars, work and pleasure mingled and in 1981 he flew his Spitfire up to Strathallan in Perthshire to sell (for £260,000) a Hawker Hurricane and 27 other historic aircraft.

Into this full life, Lindsay managed to fit several adventurous journeys and regular fund-raising work on behalf of charities. The Courtauld Institute, the Dulwich Gallery Appeal, the Shuttleworth Remembrance Trust and the British Engineerium at Brighton all had his active support and, in 1984 he raised thousands of pounds for the Muscular Dystrophy Fund by repeating Blériot's cross-channel flight on its 75th anniversary.

He flew an exact replica of the original machine, wearing a tweed coat with collar and tie in the style of the pioneer airman, and made the crossing in an identical time.

Down the centuries the Lindsays have been distinguished for their cultivation of the arts and for their courage as soldiers. Patrick personified this combination of gifts as nobly and gracefully as any of his ancestors. His judgement, independence of mind and pursuit of the ideal were always conducted with aristocratic dash and courtesy, matched by a rare ability to laugh at himself.

He is survived by his wife Amabel, eldest daughter of the 9th Earl of Hardwicke, and by their daughter and three sons.

The Daily Telegraph, 1986

Bluey Mavroleon

1927-2009

Manuel Basil Mavroleon was born on April 17 1927, the son of Basil Mavroleon and his English wife Violet (née Withers). The name "Bluey" arose from his interpretation, as a small child, of his first names, and it stuck with him for the rest of his life.

His father, a Greek ship broker, ship builder and owner, was a great Anglophile; his vessels were built in British yards and his fleet sailed under the British Flag.

Accordingly he sent his son to an English prep school, Wellesley House, at Broadstairs, Kent – Bluey arrived armed with a huge scale model by Basset-Lowke of one of his father's early freighters, ensuring his popularity with pupils and masters alike.

Mavroleon *père* foresaw the outbreak of war, and moved with his family to Los Angeles and then to Canada, not returning to London until 1942. Bluey then spent two years at Charterhouse, leaving at 17 to join the Grenadier Guards.

To his lasting regret he was commissioned just too late to see active service, but his three years with the colours left him with an enduring love of his regiment. He regarded British traditions as the greatest bastions of freedom in the world.

After time at sea as a deck hand on one of his father's ships and a spell in France, at Grenoble and Tours, ostensibly to polish up his French, Bluey Mavroleon became a director of his father's new company, London and Overseas Freighters. He was appointed managing director in 1965 after his father suffered a heart attack.

In 1975, after the Labour government imposed punitive taxation and nationalised the Austin and Pickersgill shipyard in Sunderland, in which his family had a substantial investment, Bluey announced that he was leaving Britain to live in Switzerland. "Certain things are happening in this country that make my eyebrows shoot up," he declared. He none the less remained on the board of London and Overseas Freighters, although he relinquished the role of managing director. He eventually resigned from the board in 1985.

For all his business acumen and sporting skill, Mavroleon will be best remembered for his generosity, his infectious humour and near-professional artistry as a comic actor – at parties he would entertain fellow guests with a song and dance routine, and his friends believed that, had he not been supported by a family fortune, he might have pursued a career in showbusiness and become a household name.

Mavroleon's first wife, Ruth, was a London policeman's daughter. They married in 1951 and divorced three years later. In 1956 he married Gioconda de Gallardo y Castro, with whom he had two sons, Carlos and Nicholas. The marriage was dissolved in 1961, and he married thirdly, in 1963, Camilla Paravicini, the granddaughter of Somerset Maugham; they had two daughters, Syrie and Sacha, before this marriage too was dissolved.

In 1982 Mavroleon married Caroline Tomé, and it proved a long and happy union. They entertained many of their friends at St Moritz, where Mavroleon was a long-serving vice-chairman of the Corviglia ski club.

Their hospitality extended to his houses at Rolle, on Lake Geneva, and (in the summer) to Porto Helli in Greece – the harbour there was home port to an armada of small craft which he sailed and skippered expertly under the Blue Ensign of the Household Division Yacht Club. He also flew helicopters and fixed-wing light aircraft. He was a member of White's.

Bluey Mavroleon is survived by his wife, his son Nicholas (a former husband of the actress Barbara Carrera) and his two daughters. His son Carlos, a journalist working for CBS who had converted to Islam, died in mysterious circumstances in a hotel room in Peshawar, Pakistan, in 1998.

The Daily Telegraph, 17 March 2009

Desmond Norman

1929-2002

An aircraft designer and test pilot who made Britain's bestselling transport aircraft, the Britten-Norman Islander, Desmond Norman designed half a dozen outstanding new British aircraft, building and flying the prototypes himself. The Islander, his most famous aeroplane, is still in production after 37 years, a tough and reliable light transport aircraft lifting ten passengers or a tonne of freight. It has been called the Land Rover of the skies and more than 1,200 have been sold in 120 countries.

Nigel Desmond Norman was born in London in 1929, the second son of Sir Nigel Norman, Bt, and Patricia Moyra, née Annesley. He was born into aviation: his father built airports, founded Airwork and let young Desmond handle his de Havilland Leopard Moth. Sir Nigel also commanded the RAuxAF 601 Squadron in which, in the 1950s, Desmond and his brothers Mark and Torquil would serve as fighter pilots.

At Eton in 1945 he kept a Manx Norton motorcycle in the town and would ride it — a sackable offence — in full school dress with tails flying and Brooklands exhaust cans blaring. He was caught at least once but always charmed his way out of trouble. He stroked the Eton VIII at Henley in 1946 and, at 6ft 3 in, excelled in the boxing ring and rugby lineout.

At the de Havilland Aeronautical Technical School where, between 1946 and 1950, he qualified as an aeronautical engineer, he would arrive at work on his motorbike wearing a suit with silk waistcoat and watch chain. In such attire he set up a speed record of ten minutes for the seven

miles from the de Havilland factory at Hatfield to the Tech School at Salisbury Hall. Never recklessly brave, as his undented test-piloting career would prove, he posted fellow students to wave him through critical crossroads. Occasionally, after weekends in London, he would arrive at the Tech School hangar in a taxi, dismissing the cabbie with sweeping generosity to the cheers of fellow students arriving on their bikes.

In 1954, after a spell as export assistant with the Society of British Aerospace Companies, Norman founded Britten-Norman in partnership with his friend John Britten, a fellow DH Tech School graduate. "Brains" Britten, who died in 1977, was quieter and less flamboyant than Norman, assuring their successfully complementary 25-year partnership. After designing the BN1, an ultra-light sporting aeroplane, they and Jim McMahon formed an air-spraying company, Crop Culture, for which they developed a rotary atomiser called Micronair — still a standard farm implement around the world.

Crop Culture's fleet grew from three war-surplus Tiger Moths to more than 70 aircraft and it became the biggest company of its kind in the world. Its business took Norman to the remotest parts of every continent, where he observed the need for a new light transport aircraft to replace ageing wood-and-fabric biplanes like the de Havilland Dragon Rapide. The rugged all-metal BN2 Islander was the result.

Norman always said that the Islander was inspired by the 1932 DH84 Dragon and its creator Sir Geoffrey de Havilland, the designer and test

pilot who was one of his heroes. Norman always spoke appreciatively of de Havilland's engineering training, particularly its emphasis on practical hands-on factory experience.

He and Britten designed and built the Islander — appropriately on the Isle of Wight — as a general-purpose light transport aircraft powered by two propeller engines (Lycoming piston or Allison turboprop). The elegance of its design is typified by the simple bench seats, which are accessed and vacated via three wide doors, no space being wasted on an aisle. The benches can be stacked in the back to make room for cargo.

Norman made the maiden flight of the prototype Islander at Bembridge on June 13, 1965, with Britten as co-pilot ("It's always a good idea to tell the chief aerodynamicist he's going on the first flight," said Norman). That flight was the first of more than 20 million which have been made to date by Islanders of various models, including military Defenders and triple-engine Trislanders. The Islander is the bestselling British transport aircraft in history, and the last in production. Today Islanders are assembled in Romania and completed in Bembridge, IoW.

By the 1970s Islander production lines had been established in Belgium and the Philippines as well as on the Isle of Wight and in Romania. When world recession struck and output exceeded orders, costs overran revenue and Britten-Norman was taken over by the Fairey Group.

Shrugging off the industry politics, though wondering what could have been done with a fraction of the public money he saw lavished on the big companies, Norman relinquished executive control. He stayed on for a while as marketing director but, happiest when designing and building new aeroplanes, he left in 1976 to form NDN Aircraft, based at the family home on the Isle of Wight, with his wife Bo as a director.

He built the NDN1 Firecracker, a high-performance single-propeller military trainer which he took up for its first flight in May 1977. The Firecracker was an immediate delight to fly, handling like a Hunter jet fighter. In 1983 he flew a more powerful turboprop version designed to meet an RAF trainer requirement. He enthusiastically demonstrated the Turbo Firecracker to its limits, with and without guns, bombs and rockets, confident that it was just what the air marshals and their graduate fighter pilots needed.

The Firecracker came up against two formidable competitors, both with heavyweight industrial and political clout: the Brazilian Embraer Tucano, supported by Shorts; and the Swiss Pilatus PC7, supported by British Aerospace.

The Firecracker won the hearts of test pilot judges and the backing of the Hunting engineering group. But the RAF picked the Tucano. Norman built three Firecrackers to an order from Specialist Flying Training of Hamble, and one is still operated by a US flying school. Connoisseurs of fine aeroplanes regard the Firecracker as his masterpiece.

Norman revisited the agricultural aircraft market, which he knew well from his Crop Culture and Micronair days. He created the NDN2

Fieldmaster, a handsome crop-sprayer which he flew in December 1981. He was especially pleased with its hedge-hopping agility and safety. He designed the hopper tank as an integral part of the fuselage, dispersing spray by using the downwash of the wing flaps. Fieldmasters have also been used extensively as forest fire water-bombers.

Norman was very fond of his BN3 Nymph, a pretty little four-seat high-wing tourer with a single piston engine which he had built and flown at Bembridge in 1968. He designed it to be kit-built by private owners, and painted the prototype a memorable purple. In later years he reacquired the Nymph and developed a new version, the Freelance, with folding wings to fit in a garage. His latest private aeroplane, the Weekender, was being designed to fit in a box towed on a trailer, ready to fly in a few minutes. He was also working on a light aircraft diesel engine to run on cheap paraffin instead of expensive petrol, and was advising the French company GECI on an air freighter to be built in Romania.

From Norman's drawing board also sprang half a dozen hovercraft and several yachts, including a 70ft schooner for the family called *Wavewalker*. (He was a lifelong member of the Royal Yacht Squadron.) On November 13 he was at Basingstoke station on his way to Coventry to advise Air Atlantique on another new project when he died suddenly.

Norman was appointed CBE in 1970. He was a chartered engineer and a Fellow of the Royal Aeronautical Society. His many awards included the RAF Sword of Honour on graduating from 6

Flying Training School in 1952.

His gallant and generous life probably cost him more money than he made, but the joy and wonder of flying aeroplanes of his own design and construction never faded. The immortally useful Islander epitomises his distinguished service to British aviation.

Norman married, first, Anne Fogg Elliot, by whom he had two sons; and second, in 1965, Boel (Bo) Elizabeth Holmsen, who gave him two daughters and two sons.

Desmond Norman, CBE, aircraft designer, was born on August 13, 1929. He died of a heart attack on November 13, 2002, aged 73.

The Times, 25 November 2002

Air Chief Marshal Sir Denis Smallwood

1918-1997

Air Chief Marshal Sir Denis Smallwood was one of those rare men who were equally successful in conducting and planning military operations. His personality and always cheerful disposition made him, too, universally popular at all levels both within and outside the service. The Royal Air Force has been remarkably fortunate in producing a number of such men.

"Splinters" Smallwood was commissioned in 1938 and his first appointment was to No 605 Auxiliary Air Force Squadon to whose atmosphere he was temporarily well suited. In 1940 he was transferred to No 87 Hurricane Squadron, of which he later took command. Owing to the somewhat artificial timescale imposed on the official duration of the Battle of Britain he did not qualify as taking part in it, but thereafter saw a great deal of intensive action and made a fine and justified reputation for himself. His DFC was awarded after the abortive raid on Dieppe on 19 August 1942 when he led three sorties in one day against heavily defended German cliff-top defences.

After a period commanding 286 Hurricane Squadron Smallwood took over a Spitfire Wing in 12 Group in the South West, eventually operating in support of the D-Day landings. For his outstandingly skilful and inspirational leadership in support of these operations he was awarded the DSO.

After further active service, when peace came he became an Air Ministry planner and began to establish a reputation for thorough and far-sighted competence. However, albeit reluctantly, in 1956 he was involved in the planning and preparation for the disastrous Suez campaign about which he found it impossible to be confident. His scathing personal opinion of that campaign, that it was a "monumental political cock-up", was not exaggerated. However at least the RAF performed its role with meticulous accuracy in an action which certainly justified all the criticism aimed at its purpose and concept.

His next command appointment was to the Bloodhound Surface to Air Missile Wing at North Coates in whose planning and development he had previously paid a major part. Thereafter he commanded the prestigious College of Air Warfare before returning to the Air Ministry as Assistant Chief of Air Staff (Operations).

His next and very significant appointment was to command No 3 Group - significant because it marked his transfer to and first experience of Bomber operations. He took to this new role with his usual enthusiasum and insouciance. It should not be forgotten that our national strategy at this stage, in the mid-Sixties, depended very much on the concept of the deterrent, practically implemented by the V Bomber force and its quick reaction alert capability. Whatever the validity of this concept he and he colleagues implemented it with the maximum efficiency and his personal performance was rewarded by further advancement to Senior Air Staff Officer at Bomber Command in 1967; Deputy Commander in Chief at Strike Command; and later Air Officer Commanding in Chief of the Near East Air Force and Commander of all British Forces in that area.

This was perhaps the happiest period of Smallwood's life and he enjoyed it to the full both on and off duty, among other things leading his RAF polo team to a satisfying victory over the local army team.

Inevitably, like all men of such talents he was doomed to return to Whitehall, to serve a long stint as Vice Chief of the Air Staff from 1970 to 1974. His capacity for friendship served well in smoothing any inter-service rivalries and he made close friends of his Army, Navy and Civil Service colleagues and also his political masters - this in spite of the fervour and skill with which he fought the RAF's corner both before and after his eventual retirement in 1976.

He was a regular contributor to the correspondence columns of this and other newspapers and unusually, perhaps, could always be counted on to hit hard but never below the belt. Throughout, although by now recognised as a man of great influence and stature, he never became conceited. Important yes, but pompous never.

His final service posting was from 1974 to 1976 as Commander in Chief of Strike Command, the RAF's last surviving operational command. Thereafter he was enthusiastically head-hunted and finished his last six years of full employment as military adviser to British Aerospace (1977-83). He had a large number of outside interests, including riding (he was chairman of the RAF Equitation Society), shooting and gundog training. He also played a major part in charitable fields, notably at Pace, a locally based charity to assist children with cerebral palsy, for which he was a most effective fund-raiser, and as a crusading chairman of the Air League and co-founder and chairman of the Friends of the Air

Force Church of St Clement Danes in London.

His personal and family life was happy. In 1940 he married Jeanne Needham, who predeceased him. She was a quieter and more reticent partner in what was a finely balanced partnership. They produced a son and a daughter and a number of devoted grandchildren.

Smallwood had the rare distinction of being knighted twice, being appointed KCB in 1969 and GBE in 1975. No one could deny that such recognition was fully deserved by the life that he led.

The Independent, 8 August 1997

Colonel David Smiley

1916-2009

Colonel David Smiley, who died on January 9 aged 92, was one of the most celebrated cloak-and-dagger agents of the Second World War, serving behind enemy lines in Albania, Greece, Abyssinia and Japanese-controlled eastern Thailand.

After the war he organised secret operations against the Russians and their allies in Albania and Poland, among other places. Later, as Britain's era of domination in the Arabian peninsula drew to a close, he commanded the Sultan of Oman's armed forces in a highly successful counter-insurgency.

After his assignment in Oman, he organised – with the British intelligence service, MI6 – royalist guerrilla resistance against a Soviet-backed Nasserite regime in Yemen. Smiley's efforts helped force the eventual withdrawal of the Egyptians and their Soviet mentors, paved the way for the emergence of a less anti-Western Yemeni government, and confirmed his reputation as one of Britain's leading post-war military Arabists.

In more conventional style, while commanding the Royal Horse Guards (the Blues), Smiley rode alongside the Queen as commander of her escort at the Coronation in 1953.

During the Second World War he was parachuted four times behind enemy lines. On one occasion he was obliged to escape from Albania in a rowing boat. On another mission, in Japanese-controlled eastern Thailand, he was stretchered for three days through the jungle with severe burns after a booby-trap meant for a senior Japanese officer exploded prematurely.

Though a regular soldier, Smiley was frequently seconded to MI6. As an assistant military attaché in Poland after the war, when the Soviet-controlled Communists were tightening their grip, he was beaten up and expelled as a spy, after an operation he was running had incriminated a member of the politburo.

After that he headed the British side of a secret Anglo-American venture to subvert the newly-installed Communist regime in Albania led by the ruthless Enver Hoxha. But Kim Philby, who was secretly working for the Russians, was the liaison between the British and Americans; almost all the 100 or so agents dropped by parachute or landed by boat were betrayed, and nearly all were tortured and shot. This failure haunted Smiley for the rest of his life.

Smiley's exploits led some to suggest that he was, along with several other candidates, a model for James Bond. It was also widely mooted that John le Carré, albeit unconsciously, had taken the name of his hero from the real-life Smiley.

Born on April 11 1916, David de Crespigny Smiley was the youngest son of Major Sir John Smiley, 2nd Bt, and Valerie, youngest daughter of Sir Claude Champion de Crespigny, 4th Bt, a noted jockey, balloonist, all-round sportsman and adventurer, also famed for his feats of derring-do.

After the Pangbourne Nautical College, where he excelled in sport, David went to Sandhurst in 1934. He served in the Blues from 1936 to 1939, based mainly at Windsor, leading the life of a debonair man-about-town, owning a Bentley and a Whitney Straight aircraft. Before the outbreak of war, he won seven races under National Hunt rules. In his first point-to-point with the Garth Hunt, he crashed into a tree, suffering serious injuries. Over the years Smiley was to break more than 80 bones, mainly as a result of sport; on two occasions he broke his skull, once in a steeplechase and once when he dived at night into an almost-empty swimming pool in Thailand.

After the war, he held the record for the most falls in one season on the Cresta Run in St Moritz; bizarrely, he represented Kenya (where he owned a farm) in the Commonwealth Winter Games of 1960.

After war broke out, the Blues sailed for Palestine, where one of Smiley's first jobs, as a lieutenant, was to shoot his troop of 40 horses when it became clear they were of no use in modern combat. His introduction to warfare was against Vichy French forces in Syria. For his nocturnal reconnaissance work in ruins near Palmyra he was mentioned in despatches.

Later in 1940 Smiley joined the Somaliland Camel Corps, arriving at Berbera the very day it was decided to evacuate British Somaliland. Returning in frustration to Egypt, he persuaded General Wavell, a family friend, to recommend him for the newly-formed commandos, in which he became a company commander with the rank of captain. Sneaking from Sudan into Abyssinia, Smiley operated for the first of many times behind enemy (in this case Italian) lines.

In 1941 he returned to his regiment to command a squadron of armoured vehicles being sent from Palestine to raise the siege of Habbaniya, 60 miles west of Baghdad in Iraq, where the king and regent had been overthrown in a pro-German coup led by Rashid Ali. Under Colonel John Glubb, he led a charge alongside Bedouin levies in full cry (they were known to Smiley as "Glubb's girls", because of their long black locks). After helping to capture Baghdad, Smiley's squadron was sent to Mosul with the task, among other things, of capturing the German ambassador, who escaped.

His squadron then moved east, to capture the Persian capital, Tehran, followed by "two weeks' celebration with plenty of vodka, caviar and women". After a spell in Palestine, Smiley led a Blues squadron of dummy tanks into the Western Desert pretending first to be British Crusaders and then, on a further foray, American General Grants, which were repeatedly attacked by Stukas. When Rommel broke through, they withdrew to Cairo. Three months later Smiley commanded a squadron of armoured cars at the battle of El Alamein – his last bout of conventional warfare.

After training at a school for secret agents in Haifa and taking a parachuting course with his friend David Stirling and his Special Air Service (SAS) near the Suez Canal, Smiley joined the Special Operations Executive (SOE), the organisation set up at Churchill's instigation to "set Europe ablaze" by helping local partisans sabotage the Nazis' infrastructure. He was parachuted with his life-long friend Neil (Billy) McLean into the mountains of Albania, then occupied by the Italians (and later by the Germans). For eight months he organised the fractious partisans in a series of ambushes and acts of sabotage (bridge demolition, sometimes by climbing under them at night while German troops were patrolling above, became a Smiley trademark). He was awarded an immediate MC. In early 1944 he was again parachuted into Albania, with McLean and Julian (later Lord) Amery, to liaise with the royalist guerrillas loyal to King Zog.

After leaving Albania, where his activities brought Smiley a Bar to his MC, he was transferred to the Siamese section of SOE, known in the Far East as Force 136, where he liaised with guerrillas operating against the Japanese who ruled the country through a proxy government. It was then that he was injured by the premature explosion of a booby-trap meant for a Japanese officer.

After recovering in Government House in Calcutta, where he consorted with both Nehru and Gandhi, he was parachuted behind enemy lines into eastern Siam, shortly before the dropping of the atomic bombs and the surrender of Japan, whereupon he organised the liberation of several prisoner-of-war camps, including the one on which the film *The Bridge on the River Kwai* was based. Though only a major, he personally took the surrender of the 22nd Division of the Imperial Japanese Army.

On Lord Mountbatten's orders, Smiley re-armed a Japanese company and led them against the Communists of the fledgling Vietminh (who later became the Vietcong) in French Indo-China. Among other exploits, he freed 120 French women and children who had been taken hostage by the Communists. The only British officer in an area the size of Wales, he then took the surrender of Vientiane, Laos's capital, from another Japanese general. For his activities in Siam and Indo-China Smiley was awarded a military OBE.

He later ruefully noted that, at that time, the

Vietminh were backed by the American OSS (the CIA's forerunner); Smiley was wary of what he considered to be America's naïve enthusiasm for proclaimed democrats and its hostility to the British and French empires.

After his early post-war exploits in Poland and then his efforts to roll back communism in Albania were betrayed by Philby, Smiley returned to more conventional duties in Germany and thence to command his regiment, the Blues, at Windsor.

In 1955 he was appointed military attaché in Sweden, from where he made surveillance trips with his young family along the Russian border with Finland and Norway. But the pinnacle of Smiley's post-war career was his three-year tenure as commander of the Sultan of Muscat and Oman's armed forces during a civil war which threatened to bring down one of Britain's more reactionary allies in the Gulf.

By now in his early forties, Smiley ran a gruelling counter-insurgency which gradually drove the guerrillas back from the scorching plains into their mountain retreat, the 10,000ft high Jebel Akhdar, which had never been successfully assaulted. With two squadrons of the SAS under his command, Smiley planned and led a classic dawn attack on the mountain fastness, finally crushing the enemy.

After leaving Oman in 1961, Smiley was offered the command of the SAS, but chose to retire from the British Army and file occasional reports for Raymond Postgate's *Good Food Guide*.

He was not able to relax for long. Within two years he had been persuaded to help bolster royalist forces in Yemen. Liaising with King Faisal of Saudi Arabia and MI6, who arranged for former SAS and other mercenaries to accompany him, Smiley made 13 trips to Yemen between 1963 and 1968.

Often disguised as a local, Smiley travelled on foot or by donkey for weeks at a time across Arabia's most rugged terrain. He won the admiration of his colleagues, both Arab and British, for his toughness, bluntness, and shrewdness as an adviser. King Faisal, whom Smiley greatly admired, personally expressed his appreciation.

After ending his Arabian career, Smiley moved to Spain, where, for 19 years, he grew olives, carobs and almonds, and continued to advise Albania's surviving anti-Communists, by now all in exile, before returning to live in Somerset and then Earl's Court.

To Smiley's delight, he was welcomed back to Albania in 1990, as the Communist regime, which had sentenced him to death *in absentia*, began to collapse. He forged a friendship with the country's first post-Communist leader, Sali Berisha.

Smiley was appointed LVO, and Knight Commander of the Order of the Sword in Sweden and Grand Cordon of the Order of Skanderbeg in Albania.

In 1947 he married Moyra, daughter of Lord Francis Scott KCMG, DSO, the 6th Duke of Buccleuch's youngest son. He is survived by his wife, two sons, a stepson and a stepdaughter.

The Daily Telegraph 12 January 2009

Lord Strathcarron

1924-2006

The 2nd Lord Strathcarron, who has died aged 82, was probably the only member of the House of Lords to enjoy a parallel career as a motoring journalist; when Labour abolished hereditaries in 1999 he was the longest-serving peer in the Lords.

Urbane and charming, and cultivating a slightly eccentric air, Strathcarron was an engaging amalgam of Mr Punch, Bertie Wooster and Mr Toad. Clad in full leathers, he rode almost everywhere on two wheels: a scooter in town and a high-powered motorcycle for motorways. His array of machinery over the years included a BMW shaft-drive 750cc twin, a well-tuned 350cc single cylinder Velocette and a 1,000cc in-line BMW monster capable of speeds of up to 130mph.

Strathcarron used his seat in the Lords to support and promote motorcycling, and to defend it against anyone — including government bodies — who tried to impose unnecessary laws on the biking fraternity.

As chairman of the All-Party Parliamentary Motorcycle Group (members included Viscount Falkland, Sir Marcus Fox and the felicitously-named Sir Keith Speed) he worked closely with the Motor Cycle Industry Association to create the modern basic training system for learner motorcyclists, introduced in December 1990. The system is credited with dramatically reducing the number of accidents involving young motorcyclists.

Strathcarron also strove to correct the general perception of bikers as uncouth greasers careless of other road users. Once, in pouring rain, he turned up astride his machine with helmet and goggles at the London headquarters of BP Oil and announced himself as Lord Strathcarron, only for the sceptical parking attendant to retort that he was the Queen of Sheba.

When he returned a short time later, dressed in his customary chalk-stripe suit, the same attendant asked again who he was. "I'm Lord Strathcarron," he replied, "and you're the f***ing Queen of Sheba."

Strathcarron was also a significant figure in the British motor trade; in 1960 he founded Strathcarron and Co, supplying equipment to the automotive industry.

He was actively involved at a senior level in the Guild of Motoring Writers, the British Racing Drivers' Club, the Guild of Experienced Motorists, the Vintage Sports Car Club, the Driving Instructors' Association, the Vehicle Builders and Repairers' Association, the Institute of Road Transport Engineers, the Institute of Advanced Motorists, the Institute of the Motor Industry and the Order of the Road. In the Lords and elsewhere he campaigned tirelessly for minimum speed limits.

With his third wife riding pillion, Strathcarron would holiday in Europe on a solo motorcycle, followed by his butler in a three-wheeler also containing an elderly, scrawny parrot in its cage.

Afflicted by a problem with a tendon that gave him a "claw hand", making it difficult to grip the handlebars, Strathcarron had minor corrective surgery so that he could continue to ride a solo motorbike in comparative comfort; the change, he noted however, had made it "a bit of a bugger getting out of the bath".

David William Anthony Blythe Macpherson was born on January 23 1924. He became Lord Strathcarron of Banchor when his father, Ian, a minister in Lloyd George's cabinet, died in 1936.

His years at Eton were spent drawing cars and aeroplanes rather than learning anything. He went up to Jesus College, Cambridge, but volunteered for the RAF as soon as he was old enough. In 1941 he had the first of what would be several motorcycle accidents, this one serious enough to delay his flying training until 1942, when he was sent to learn in the clearer and safer skies of Arizona.

By 1943 he was piloting Coastal Command Wellingtons on high-risk sea reconnaissance and search-and-rescue missions during the Battle of the Atlantic. After the war he flew long delivery missions around the Commonwealth, and was demobbed in 1947.

His love of flying stayed with him all his life, and he became an enthusiastic private pilot with his own Piper; he was one of the early members of the Air Squadron and flew across Europe on more or less any excuse. He finally had to stop flying 20 years ago when he failed his medical.

He was a keen motorist in the days when it was still possible to be a pioneer; he learnt to drive on his mother's 1932 Essex Terraplane, and for his 16th birthday persuaded her to buy him a three-wheeled Morgan Super Sports for £27 10s. After his RAF service he took up motor racing, and was a frequent competitor in the very early days of 500cc racing with his contemporary and lifelong friend Stirling Moss.

Strathcarron became a works driver for Marwyn and Kieft, but became more circumspect after a fellow Marwyn driver was killed when the car overturned. He advised on smaller wheels to lower the centre of gravity; the solution worked and the cars stopped turning over.

Strathcarron subsequently owned, and frequently raced, a series of exotic Bentleys, Alfa Romeos, Rileys and Austin Healeys, amongst others. He owned a superb collection of Jensens, one of every model made. He continued to race modern and vintage sports cars up to 2000, when he came first and recorded the fastest lap in the annual Lords versus Commons race at Brands Hatch.

In 1954 he was appointed motoring correspondent for *The Field*, having discovered that, as a motoring journalist, he could indulge his passion more liberally. He published *Motoring For Pleasure* (1963), in which he described his experiences in racing and motor rallies in Britain and on the Continent. He continued as a freelance journalist until his death.

In recognition of his contribution to the motorcycle industry, Strathcarron was invited to join the Club, the industry's 60-strong motorcycle club for senior figures, and remained an active member for many years, taking part in the twice-yearly weekends involving many hundreds of miles of motorcycling.

His last attendance was in May, when the Club marked a weekend in Norfolk with an official visit to the Lotus car factory. Strathcarron attended aboard a three-wheeled 1,100cc Grinnal.

In the spring of 2000 the Club had its weekend at Fort William. The chosen route took in the hamlet and railway station of Strathcarron, from which he took his title. At the Strathcarron Arms, he posed for a commemorative photograph with the two young women managing the hotel.

Strathcarron was a popular and accomplished after-dinner speaker with a treasury of anecdotes and witticisms, one of which was that he was unable to believe in re-incarnation because it would be unfair to expect to come back again as a peer of the realm.

Lord Strathcarron, who suffered his last motorcycling accident seven weeks ago when he was in collision with a dustcart, died on August 31. He is survived by his fourth wife and two sons by his second wife.

The Daily Telegraph, 21 September 2006

Air Chief Marshal Sir John Thomson

1941-1994

John Thomson was a vigorous front-line air commander and a successful staff officer in a number of key appointments in the Ministry of Defence. At the time of his death he had only recently relinquished command of Royal Air Force Strike Command and United Kingdom Air Forces. He had just been appointed Commander-in-Chief of Allied Forces North-western Europe, Nato's newest major subordinate command headquarters and its first joint command to be based in the United Kingdom.

An upright man and model of military correctness, Thomson had a keen sense of humour that softened the formidable impact of his personality. He was noted both within his own service and in wider defence circles for his intellectual toughness and formidable stamina - qualities which enabled him to master the most complex issues with swift analysis and to provide solutions to problems that were invariably sound and often striking in concept. However, in character and in his love of flying he remained the eternal fighter pilot. A skilful aviator, he was an airborne leader of the highest quality, whose example was an inspiration to all who served under his operational command.

Born in 1941, Thomson spent his youth in Northern Ireland. He was educated at Campbell College, from which he entered the Royal Air Force College, Cranwell, directly. His skills as an aviator gained early recognition in the award of the Groves Memorial Prize and the Kinkead Trophy.

After commissioning in 1962 he flew Hunters in Aden and the Gulf for the next three years, which included the Radfan action of 1964. There followed a further three years flying Hunters, this time from RAF Gutersloh, Germany, in the reconnaisance role. For some time he was also aide-de-camp to the then Air Officer Commanding in Chief RAF Germany. It was during a three-year tour on exchange with the United States Air Force at Bergstrom Air Force Base in Texas that he met his future wife, Jan.

After Staff College in 1973 Thomson led the Jaguar Project Team at HQ Strike Command and served in Air Plans. He then formed No 41 Squadron with Jaguars in 1976, newly assigned to the North Norway area in both attack and reconnaisance roles. He led the first Jaguar transatlantic deployment to Exercise Red Flag in 1978. From then on his career followed a rapid and steady upward path with successive appointments as Personal Staff Officer to the Chief of the Air Staff in 1979 and command of RAF Brüggen in Germany, then comprising four squadrons of strike/attack Jaguars, from 1981 to 1983. The Royal College of Defence Studies course in 1984 was followed by a period as head of the newly formed tri-service Defence Concepts directorate in the Ministry of Defence and then two years as Air Officer Commanding No 1 Group, which then encompassed all UK-based offensive air, tanker, transport and support helicopter units.

In March 1989 he returned to the Ministry of Defence as Assistant Chief of the Air Staff during a particularly important period in the immediate aftermath of the end of the Cold War. Much of the groundwork for Arms Control matters, and the capabilities and structure of the Royal Air Force as it is today are directly attributable to Thomson's extraordinary drive and flair throughout a difficult time.

He then moved to command RAF Support Command, responsible for all training and logistics support to the front line and again found himself at the forefront of change which led eventually to extensive re-structuring. From November 1992 he became Air Officer Commanding in Chief Strike Command, the top operational post in the service, where again he steadfastly held out for what he regarded as the right course for the modern air force. Only last week he moved on to become the first Commander-in-Chief of Nato's newest command, Allied Forces North-western Europe. Within a few days he was taken ill; his death ends the career of an officer widely tipped to reach the highest position within the service.

John Thomson was a man who managed to combine an intense dedication to the Royal Air Force with outstanding abilities in the air and on the staff. All of this was carried off with a light touch, an admirable sense of humour and a predilection for practical jokes - including a wicked talent for mimicry, which on more than one occasion reduced telephone communication among his colleagues to chaos.

Despite all the demanding and time-consuming appointments that he filled so ably during his career, Thomson was above all a family man, with deep religious convictions, traits which gave him great strength, particularly during the loss of his much-loved first daughter, Catherine, who died aged three in 1977. He is survived by his other two daughters, Clare and Annie, and by his devoted wife Jan.

The Independent, 13 July 1994

Air Commodore Sir Peter Vanneck
1922-1999

Motor Torpedo Boat commander, aviator, engineer, stockbroker, Lord Mayor of London, member of the European Parliament - Peter Vanneck excelled in all these roles. But it will be his zest for living, so astonishingly infectious, his generosity of spirit and his capacity for friendship for which he will best be remembered.

Vanneck, the younger son of the fifth Lord Huntingfield, an Irish peer, and his American wife, was seven years old when his parents gave up their magnificent Suffolk home, Heveningham Hall. Its 37 main bedrooms caused his lordship to observe, thereafter, that it is always a great mistake to be overhoused.

Following a year at Geelong Grammar School in Australia - his father having been appointed Governor of Victoria - Vanneck went to Stowe. Choosing the Navy as a career, he arrived at Dartmouth as war broke out. His first action at sea, as a midshipman on the battleship *King George V*, was the pursuit and destruction of the *Bismarck*. As an upper gun range finder, he had a grandstand view of the engagement. Vanneck's only scars were two massive black eyes, inflicted by his binoculars as the great guns recoiled.

Thereafter, he commanded a landing craft in North Africa during the Torch operations, served under the legendary Captain "Johnny" Walker, U-boat hunting in the North Atlantic, and then on the freezing Arctic convoys to Murmansk. By D-Day, he was commanding MTB 696 in the Channel and spent the following months cruising up and down the Brittany coast bombarding remnants of the occupying forces, in close liaison with the French Resistance. Recently asked about his most vivid memories of that time, he replied: "Terrible shortage of milk, brandy on the cornflakes."

Despite his courageous war record, and a further four years in the Fleet Air Arm, Vanneck's enthusiasm for a naval career was on the wane. In 1949, he resigned his commission in order to read agricultural engineering, first at Trinity College, Cambridge and then at Harvard.

Thereafter, his passions for boating and, increasingly, flying, were gratified in the Corinthian manner. Whether steering his Maltese caique, *Perchance*, or racing his beloved 5.5 metre yacht, *Dauntless*, shared with his great friends Peter Nutting and Michael Boyle, at Cowes, Vanneck was the complete saltwater addict. He was elected a member of the Royal Yacht Squadron in 1948, at the very early age of 25, remaining on the List for over 50 years. When the tiller finally lost its allure, Vanneck continued to find the scene at Cowes enchanting, never missing a day of the annual regatta.

His other love, flying, was indulged, first of all, at Cambridge University Air Squadron and then, as a territorial RAF officer, with 601 Squadron - where he began a close and lasting friendship with the Norman brothers.

When the squadron's Meteors were grounded in 1957, Peter Vanneck remained in the auxiliary air force, rising to the post of Inspector General in the rank of Air Commodore. His achievement in this sphere is best expressed by two honours. For his

flying skills, he was decorated with the Air Force Cross; and, unprecedented for someone of his rank, he was appointed a Companion of the Bath, military division.

These activities, of course, generated no income. After working, briefly, with Ransoms, he followed his stockbroker uncle's advice and entered the City, first at Phillips & Drew and then at Rowe & Pitman. In those days, of course, it was another world. On his first day as a trainee he recalled asking a partner when he should arrive in the morning, "Oh," came the response, "9.30, or 10.45 if you are coming up from the country."

Vanneck's relaxed approach to the task in hand, his self-deprecating sense of humour and enormous charm disguised a keen mind. He quickly became a partner at Rowe & Pitman and, subsequently, Deputy Chairman of the Stock Exchange, losing in the chairmanship elections to Sir Nicholas Goodison. He adored the great traditions of the City, and served as its 650th Lord Mayor.

At the age of 57, he changed course once more, retiring from the City and entering the first directly elected European Parliament as member for Cleveland. Vanneck joined a number of other Conservatives who had already had distinguished non-political careers - most notably Sir Fred Catherwood, Sir Henry Plumb, Sir Fred Warner, Sir David Nicholson, Sir Jack Stewart-Clark and Basil de Ferranti. He was known affectionately as "Biggles" by his colleagues; his Wodehousian manner captivated the continentals and his matchless diplomatic skills helped to soften the

harsher edges of Britain's EC policy.

In retirement, his appetite for life continued undiminished. Whether boating in Malta, shooting in Suffolk, "gassing", as he liked to put it, in one of his many London clubs, or extolling the merits of a fine claret or some especially exotic cocktail, Vanneck was in his element.

The Independent, 2 October 1999

Appendices

APPENDIX A
AIR SQUADRON CHRONOLOGY
1966-2008

With special thanks to Martin Barraclough, whose record of
events that he has attended since joining in 1968 provided the
basis of this list.

1966

1	February	Inaugural dinner, 2 Ilchester Place, London
17	May	Second inaugural dinner, Brooks's
25	July	Third and final inaugural dinner, Boodle's
24–25	September	Le Touquet: first cross-channel dinner

1967

22	March	Spring dinner and first AGM, Boodle's
5–7	May	Visit to Epernay
1	July	First Air Squadron (Aerobatic) Trophy, Staverton, presented by Douglas Bader
23	September	Fly-in lunch at Bosworth (home of David Constable Maxwell)
11	October	Film night at Royal Aeronautical Society

1968

10	April	Spring dinner, Brooks's
25	May	Concorde visit, British Aircraft Corporation, Filton
27	July	Air Squadron (Aerobatic) Trophy, Little Rissington
3–5	October	Visit to Cognac
14	November	Winter dinner, Claridges (£8-15-0)

1969

12	March	Spring dinner, Brooks's
10–11	May	Le Touquet
8	June	Fly-in lunch at Peniarth (home of John Williams-Wynne)
19	July	Air Squadron (Aerobatic) Trophy, Little Rissington
26	July	Stamford Game Show and Afternoon Tea at Bosworth
4–5	October	Visit to Yacht Squadron, Britten-Norman and British Hovercraft Corporation
23–25	October	Visit to Cognac
13	November	Winter dinner, Brooks's

1970

10	March	Spring dinner, Brooks's
20	May	Visit to *Queen Elizabeth II*, Southampton
15	August	Air Squadron (Aerobatic) Trophy, Sywell
4	November	Winter dinner, Turf Club

1971

9	March	Spring dinner, Brooks's
1	May	Visit to Redifon simulator, Gatwick
5	June	Air Squadron (Aerobatic) Trophy, Little Rissington
1–2	October	Visit to Epernay
17	November	Winter dinner, Penthouse Club

1972

7	March	Spring dinner, Brooks's
5	August	Air Squadron (Aerobatic) Trophy, Rochester
15–17	September	Visit to Angers, Cointreau
16	November	Winter dinner, Hyde Park Hotel

1973

6	March	Spring dinner at 105 Elgin Crescent
12–13	May	Visit to Colonsay
9	June	Air Squadron (Aerobatic) Trophy, Rochester
5–7	October	Visit to Bordeaux
27	November	Winter dinner, Boodle's

1974

5	March	Spring dinner, House of Commons
22	June	Air Squadron (Aerobatic) Trophy, Old Warden
10	December	Winter dinner, Boodle's

1975

		[Spring dinner not held]
		Air Squadron (Aerobatic) Trophy
19	November	Winter dinner, Buck's

1976

24	March	Spring dinner, Boodle's
19	June	Air Squadron (Aerobatic) Trophy, Old Warden
25–27	June	Visit to Angers and Château Brissac
30	November	Winter dinner, Turf Club

1977

8	March	Spring dinner, House of Lords
18	June	Air Squadron (Aerobatic) Trophy, Old Warden
16	November	Winter dinner, Buck's

1978

6	April	Spring dinner, Mansion House
3	June	Air Squadron (Aerobatic) Trophy, Old Warden
22	November	Winter dinner, Boodle's

1979

13	March	Spring dinner, Fishmongers' Hall
2	June	Air Squadron (Aerobatic) Trophy, Old Warden
3	June	Air Squadron Flying Display, Old Warden
21	November	Winter dinner, Buck's

1980

29	April	Spring dinner, Royal Air Force Museum, Hendon
31	May	Air Squadron (Aerobatic) Trophy, Old Warden
1	June	Air Squadron Flying Display, Old Warden
13	November	Winter dinner, Turf Club

1981

13	May	Spring dinner, The Queen's House, Greenwich
11	July	Air Squadron Trophy, Old Warden
12	July	Air Squadron Flying Display, Old Warden
11	November	Winter dinner, Brooks's

1982

17–19	March	Visit to RAF Gutersloh
5	May	Spring dinner, Trinity House
10	November	Winter dinner, Boodle's

1983

24–26	March	Visit to RAF Brüggen
4	May	Spring Dinner, Armoury House
16	July	Air Squadron (Aerobatic) Trophy, Fenland
9	November	Winter dinner, Buck's

1984

7–14	April	Visit to Brazil
2	May	Spring dinner, Goldsmiths' Hall
26	October	Visit to Army Air Corps, Middle Wallop
14	November	Winter dinner, Rules

1985

16	May	Spring dinner, Royal Air Force Museum, Hendon
6	July	Air Squadron Trophy (Cadets), Old Warden
20	July	Air Squadron Trophy (Aerobatic), Audley End
21	November	Winter dinner, Household Cavalry Barracks, Hyde Park

1986

22	May	Spring dinner, Tallow Chandlers' Hall
5	July	Air Squadron Trophy (Cadets), Old Warden
18–21	September	Visit to RAF Leuchars
25–27	September	Visit to Epernay
24	October	Visit to Army Air Corps, Middle Wallop
19	November	Winter dinner, Buck's

1987

28	April	Visit to London air Traffic Control Centre
21	May	Spring dinner, Fishmongers' Hall
11	July	Air Squadron Trophy, Old Warden
17–19	September	Visit to RAF Leuchars
15–17	October	Visit to Daimler-Benz, Stuttgart
24	November	Winter dinner, Tower of London

1988

1–3	March	Visit to HMS *Illustrious*, Newcastle-upon-Tyne
29–30	April	Visit to Lotus and Ken Wallis autogyro collection, Norfolk
18	May	Spring dinner, Butchers' Hall
9	July	Air Squadron Trophy, Old Warden
28–29	September	Visit to RAF Brize Norton and RAF Marham
14	October	Visit to Brooklands Aerospace, Old Sarum
23	November	Winter dinner, Brooks's

1989

17	May	Spring dinner, Farmers' and Fletchers' Livery Hall
9	July	Air Squadron Trophy, Old Warden
26–27	September	Visit to RAF Kinloss and RAF Lossiemouth
14–19	October	Visit to Texas
10	November	Visit to Westland Group
22	November	Winter dinner, RAF Bentley Priory

1990

24	May	Spring dinner, Trinity House
8	July	Air Squadron Trophy, Old Warden
28	September	Visit to RAF Coningsby
22	November	Winter dinner, Turf Club

1991

26	April	London Heliport briefing, Blackbushe
9	May	Spring dinner, Goldsmiths' Hall
17	May	Visit to Brooklands
7	July	Air Squadron Trophy, RAF Cosford
27–28	September	Visit to RAF Scampton
25	October	Visit to Lamberhurst Vineyard
20	November	Winter dinner, Boodle's

1992

7–8	May	Helimeet International flying competition, Middle Wallop
15	May	Visit to Brooklands
20	May	Spring dinner, Watermen and Lightermen's Hall
12	July	Air Squadron Trophy, RAF Halton
14–19	August	Visit to Russia
25–26	September	Visit to RAF Shawbury
18	November	Winter dinner, Buck's

1993

23	April	Visit to British Aerospace, Warton
7–8	May	Visit to Aérospatiale, Marignane
20	May	Spring dinner, Armourers' Hall
11	July	Air Squadron Trophy, RAF Halton
5	September	Wallop Challenge flying competition, Middle Wallop
24–26	September	Visit to Epernay
8–9	October	Visit to RAF Waddington
24	November	Winter dinner, Brooks's

1994

20–3	April–May	Visit to Cyprus and Jordan
12–13	May	Visit to RAF Strike Command and RAF Odiham
26	May	Spring dinner, Cutlers' Hall
10	July	Air Squadron Trophy, RAF Benson
31	July	Vintage Motor Racing meeting, Silverstone
16	September	Gliding Day, RAF Bicester
24	November	Winter dinner, White's

1995

21	April	Gliding Day, RAF Bicester
31	May	Spring dinner, Fishmongers' Hall
22–23	June	Visit to RAF Cranwell
9	July	Air Squadron Trophy, RAF Benson
30	July	Vintage Motor Racing meeting, Silverstone
10	September	Wallop Challenge flying competition, Middle Wallop
16–25	September	Tanzanian safari
22	November	Winter dinner, Buck's

1996

9–10	May	Visit to RAF Brüggen
15	May	Spring dinner, Butchers' Hall
7	July	Air Squadron Trophy, RAF Cranwell
4	August	Vintage Motor Racing meeting, Silverstone
20–22	September	30th anniversary at Le Touquet
21	November	Winter dinner, White's

1997

24–25	April	Visit to Marshalls, Cambridge
15–16	May	Visit to RAF Wittering
22	May	Spring dinner, Royal Air Force Museum, Hendon
6	July	Air Squadron Trophy, RAF Cranwell
27	July	Vintage Motor Racing meeting, Silverstone
20–4	September–October	Visit to Pakistan
25	November	Winter dinner, White's

1998

15–17	May	Visit to Royal Yacht Squadron, Isle of Wight
26	May	Spring dinner, Goldsmiths' Hall
29–30	May	Visit to RAF Kinloss
4	July	Visit to Old Warden & Cambridge
5	July	Air Squadron Trophy, RAF Cranwell
26	July	Vintage Motor Racing meeting, Silverstone
20	September	Visit to Goodwood vintage motor racing meeting
26	November	Winter dinner, White's

1999

30	April	Visit to Imperial War Museum, Duxford
20	May	Spring dinner, Apothecaries' Hall
10–13	June	Visit to Isle of Skye with Royal Yacht Squadron
04	July	Air Squadron Trophy, RAF Cranwell
23–24	September	Visit to RNAS, Yeovilton
21–30	October	Visit to Jerez and Morocco
25	November	Winter dinner, White's

2000

4–6	May	Visit to RAF Brüggen
10	May	Spring dinner, Stationers' Hall
16–7	June–July	USA 2000
2	July	Air Squadron Trophy, RAF Cranwell
22	November	Winter Dinner, White's
7	December	Film Screening of USA 2000, ICA, London

2001

17	May	Spring dinner, Trinity House
31–2	May–June	Visit to RAF Coltishall
01	July	Air Squadron Trophy, RAF Cranwell
31–4	August–September	Visit to Venice
10	September	Parachuting with Red Devils at RAF Netheravon
21–23	September	Visit to Arnhem
21	November	Winter dinner, White's

2002

11	May	Visit to RNAS Yeovilton
22	May	Spring dinner, Skinners' Hall
5–8	June	Visit to RAF Valley and Isle of Man
7	July	Air Squadron Trophy, RAF Cranwell
16–17	July	Visit to Army Air Corps, Middle Wallop
3–4	September	Visit to Red Devils at RAF Netheravon
12–14	September	Visit to Epernay and Cognac
20	November	Winter Dinner, White's

2003

6–4	March–May	Visit to South Africa
21	May	Spring dinner, Savoy Hotel
19–21	June	Visit to RAF Marham
6	July	Air Squadron Trophy, RAF Cranwell
23–25	September	Visit to RNAS Culdrose
29	October	Film screening of Africa 2003, Royal Aeronautical Society
26	November	Winter dinner, RAF Museum, Hendon

2004

30	April	Visit to Imperial War Museum, Duxford
19	May	Spring dinner, Savoy Hotel
4	July	Air Squadron Trophy, RAF Cranwell
25–26	July	Visit to Cambridge and Great Massingham
10–12	September	Visit to St. Omer
24	November	Winter dinner, RAF Club

2005

25	May	Spring dinner, Searcy's
9–10	June	Visit to Isle of Man
18–24	June	Visit to Denmark and Norway
3	July	Air Squadron Trophy, RAF Cranwell
31–6	August – September	Visit to Sardinia
17	September	Mission Aviation Fellowship / Air Squadron fly-in, Headcorn
13–15	October	Visit to RAF Cottesmore
23	November	Winter dinner, RAF Club

2006

2	May	Spring dinner, Bentley Priory
16–18	June	40th Anniversary, Le Touquet
2	July	Air Squadron Trophy, RAF Cranwell
5–9	September	Visit to Poland
19–21	October	Visit to RAF Leuchars
22	November	Winter dinner, RAF Club

2007

20	March	Coutts Lecture: 'Concorde' by John Hutchinson
10	May	Spring dinner, RAF Club
9–14	June	Visit to Scotland
1	July	Air Squadron Trophy, RAF Cranwell
9–15	September	Visit to Tuscany and Lake Como
21	November	Winter dinner, Searcy's

2008

12	March	Coutts Lecture by Colin Prescott
26	April	Spring dinner, Le Touquet
25	May	Support Our Paras Day, Old Sarum
31–5	May–June	Visit to Ireland
29	June	Air Squadron Trophy, RAF Cranwell
12	July	Air Squadron (Aerobatic) Trophy, Compton Abbas
11	September	Wheels, Wings and Steam Day, Folly Farm
13–20	September	Visit to the Balkans
2–4	October	Visit to RAF Waddington
28	October	Coutts Lecture by Sir John Allison
20	November	Winter dinner, Cavalry & Guards Club

HONORARY MEMBERS

Honorary Air Commodore

1983   HRH The Prince Philip
        Duke of Edinburgh, KG KT OM GBE AC
        QSO PC

Honorary Life Members

2000   Marshal of the Royal Air Force Sir Michael
        Beetham, GCB CBE DFC AFC DL RAF

2001   The Lord Waterpark

Honorary Members

1969   Comte Frédéric Chandon de Briailles
        René Firino Martell

1972   HRH The Prince of Wales, KG KT PC
        GCB AK QSO

1982   Sir Thomas Sopwith, CBE FRAeS (d.1989)

1985   HRH The Duke of York, CVO ADC
        HRH Prince Michael of Kent, KCVO
        Colonel Ozires Silva

1989   Prince Friedrich Wilhelm von
        Hohenzollern-Sigmaringen

1994   HM King Hussein I of the Hashemite
        Kingdom of Jordan (d.1999)

1997   Air Vice Marshal Asim Suleiman,
        SI(M) SBt IS PAF

1998   General Nikolai Antoshkin
        Group Captain John Cunningham, CBE
        DSO** DFC* DL (d.2002)
        Charles Dobie
        Air Chief Marshal Muhammad
        Abbas Khattak
        Peter Nicholson, Commodore, The Royal
        Yacht Squadron

2000   General Michael E Ryan, Chief of Staff,
        United States Air Force
        Senator Ted Stevens

2003   Alex Henshaw, MBE (d.2007)
        Lt General R J Beukes, SD SM MMM, Chief
        of Staff, South African Air Force

2004   Basil Hersov DMS JCM LLD(HC)

MEMBERS OF THE AIR SQUADRON

Listed alphabetically.

The date refers to the year of joining. For other criteria, please see the Note at the end of this Appendix.

1966   Aitken, Group Captain Sir Max, Bt DSO
        DFC (d.1985)

1983   Allison, Air Chief Marshal Sir John, KCB
        CBE FRAeS

1974   Ames, Simon

2006   Andover, Viscount (Alexander)

1966   Annaly, The Lord – see White (d.1990)

1986   Argyll, The Duke of (Ian) (d.2001)

1966   Astor, The Hon Hugh (d.1999)

2006   Astor, James

1975   Astor, Michael (resigned)

1966   Bader, Group Captain Sir Douglas, CBE
        DSO* DFC* DL FRAeS (d.1982)

1990   Bagge, Sir Jeremy, Bt, DL

1976   Bagge, Sir John, Bt ED DL (d.1990)

1966   Baring, The Hon James (The Lord
        Revelstoke)

1968   Barraclough, Martin

1999   Bathurst, Admiral of the Fleet Sir
        Benjamin, GCB DL (resigned)

1991   Beetham, Marshal of the Royal Air Force
        Sir Michael, GCB CBE DFC AFC DL RAF

1988   Berry, Simon

1988   Best, Bob

1976   Bledisloe, The Viscount (Ben) (d.1979)

2004   Bloch, Dr Harold,

1995   Blois, Roddy

2005   Bondarenko, Lorraine

2005	Bondarenko, Viktor	1986	de Ferranti, Adrian	1995	Grandy, John (resigned 2005)
1980	Bostock, Air Commodore Simon, DL	1988	de Ferranti, Marcus	1995	Graydon, Air Chief Marshal Sir Michael, GCB CBE ADC FRAeS RAF
1975	Braybrooke, The Lord – see Neville (resigned 2008)	1991	de Ferranti, Mark		
		1967	de Ferranti, Sebastian	1989	Greenall, Dr The Hon Gilbert, CBE
1975	Bridport, The Viscount (Alex) (resigned 1983)	1966	d'Erlanger, Robin	1989	Greenall, The Hon Johnny, MFH
		1983	D'Oyly, Lieutenant Colonel Christopher, (resigned 1999)		
2004	Brun, Olaf			1970	Haig-Thomas, Flying Officer Anthony
		1970	Dugdale, Sir William, Bt CBE MC	2007	Haig-Thomas, Edward
1976	Cadogan, The Earl, DL – see Chelsea	1966	Dundas, Group Captain Sir Hugh (Cocky), CBE DSO* DFC DL (d.1995)	1977	Hall, Professor Edward, CBE (d.2001)
1992	Cameron, Lieutenant Colonel RM, Peter, MC			1984	Hall, William
1999	Camrass, Robert			1974	Hamilton & Brandon, The Duke of (Angus)
1989	Cavendish, The Hon Rory	1966	Eaden, David, DSC (resigned 1972)	1998	Hare, David, LLB (d.2009)
1966	Cayzer, The Hon Anthony (d.1990)	2001	Elwes, Jonathan	1990	Hine, Air Chief Marshal Sir Patrick, GCB GBE FRAeS (resigned)
1995	Cayzer, The Hon Robin (The Lord Rotherwick)	1973	Erne, The Earl of (Harry) (resigned)		
		1966	Everard, Anthony (Tony)	1994	Hoerner, John
2000	Cecil, The Lord Valentine	1992	Everard, Richard, DL (resigned 2008)	1988	Hogg, John (d.2003)
1983	Checketts, Squadron Leader Sir David, KCVO (resigned)			1994	Holloway, Group Captain Terry, FRAeS
		1966	Faulconer, Ivor (resigned 1982)	2008	Holman-West, Andrew
1976	Chelsea, The Viscount (Charles), DL (The Earl Cadogan)	2006	Folkes, Brigadier Richard, OBE ADC FRAeS	1966	Houlder, Professor John, CBE MBE(Mil)
		2000	Fopp, Dr Michael, FMA, FRAeS	1988	Howard, The Hon Alex
1966	Churchill, Winston	1993	Foyle, Christopher, DL FRAeS	2007	Hubbard, Ralph
2000	Clark, Tim			2005	Hutchinson, Captain John, FRAeS FRIN
1968	Clutton, Cecil(Sam), CBE (d.1991)	2000	Gainza, Maxi		
1966	Constable Maxwell, Major David TD (d.1985)	1966	Gardner, Richard (Jimmy), OBE DSC (d.1999)	1967	Kildare, The Marquis of (Gerald), (The Duke of Leinster) (resigned 1983) (d.2004)
2000	Cook, Nicholas	2004	Gavazzi, Egidio		
1983	Cook, Tom	1996	Gibson Fleming, James, DL, MFH	1966	King, Lieutenant Commander Osborne (Ossie), DSC (d.1995)
1977	Corbett, David	1989	Glenarthur, The Lord (Simon), DL FRAeS (resigned 2007)		
1985	Crouch, Derek (d.1989)				
1988	Curtis, Alan, OBE	1970	Gloucester, HRH Prince William of, (d.1972)	2001	Labouchere, Henry
1986	Cyster, Squadron Leader David			1977	Lamplough, Robert
		1998	Goschen, The Viscount (Giles)	1993	Leigh, Christopher
2006	Day, Catherine	2000	Gosling, Martin	2000	Leigh, Edward

1967	Leinster, The Duke of – see Kildare	1994	Norman, Sir Torquil, CBE		(resigned) (d.2009)
1988	Lindsay, Ludovic (resigned)	1997	Norman, Victor	1966	Sopwith, Thomas
1968	Lindsay, The Hon Patrick (d.1986)			1993	Spiers, Sir Donald, CB TD FRAeS
1993	Lindsay, Valentine	1995	O'Donnell, Carletto	2003	Spittle, Dr Margaret, OBE FRCR FRCP
1983	Liverpool, The Earl of (Eddie)			1990	Squire, Air Chief Marshal Sir Peter, GCB
2008	Loader, Air Chief Marshal Sir Clive, KCB	2004	Parkhouse, Nicholas, DM FRCS		DFC AFC DL DSc FRAeS RAF
	OBE ADC FRAeS RAF	2007	Partridge-Hicks, Stephen	1996	Stansfeld, Anthony
		1986	Pearson, The Hon Charles	1967	Steel, Anthony (d.1984)
1984	Macfadyen, Air Marshal Ian, CB OBE FRAeS	1994	Pegnall, Air Commodore Brian (resigned	2003	Steel, John, QC, FRAeS
1979	Macpherson, The Hon Ian, (The Lord		1996)	2000	Stinton, Air Commodore Julian, RAF
	Strathcarron) (resigned 2008)	2008	Perry, Dr Ian, FRAeS	2001	Stirrup, Air Chief Marshal Sir Jock, GCB
1998	Marshall, Michael, CBE DL FRAeS	1966	Ponsford, Ian (resigned)		AFC ADC FRAeS RAF
1996	Masefield, Sir Charles, FRAeS	2008	Ponte, David	1973	Storey, Thomas
1993	Mauleverer, Captain David, FRAeS FRIN	2007	Prescot, Nigel	1966	Straight, Air Commodore Whitney, CBE
1973	Mavroleon, Bluey (d.2009)				MC DFC (d.1979)
1988	McAlpine, James	1966	Revelstoke, The Lord – see Baring	1972	Strathcarron, The Lord (David) (d.2006)
1969	McAlpine, Kenneth, OBE DL FRAeS	2003	Rolls, George	1979	Strathcarron, The Lord – see Macpherson
1996	Meeson, Philip	1995	Rotherwick, The Lord – see Cayzer	1966	Strathcona & Mount Royal, The Lord
2006	Metcalfe, Jeremy	1986	Rothschild, The Hon Amschel (d.1996)		(Euan) (resigned)
1989	Mexborough, The Earl of (John)			1992	Suffolk and Berkshire, The Earl of (Micky)
1989	Milford Haven, The Marquess of (George)	1986	Salisbury-Jones, Raymond (resigned)	1985	Sutherland, Ian
1991	Montagu, Dru	1966	Salmond, Julian (resigned)	1967	Swire, Sir Adrian
2008	Moran, Air Chief Marshal Sir Christopher,	1989	Savage, Julian (d.1990)		
	KCB OBE MVO RAF	1966	Savile, The Hon Anthony	2006	Taylor, John
1986	Moss, Lieutenant Colonel Johnny, MBE	1974	Schroder, Bruno	1977	Tennant, The Hon Christopher (resigned)
		2001	Scurr, Dr James	1985	Thomson, Air Chief Marshal Sir John, GCB
1989	Naylor-Leyland, Sir Philip, Bt, MFH	1995	Scurr, John, FRCS		CBE AFC (d.1994)
1975	Neville, The Hon Robin, (The Lord	1994	Sharples, The Hon Christopher	1998	Thomson, Sir Mark, Bt
	Braybrooke) (resigned 2008)	1970	Shelburne, The Earl of (Charlie)(resigned)	2006	Torpy, Air Chief Marshal Sir Glenn, KCB
1983	Noel, The Hon Thomas	1999	Sheldon, Jamie		CBE DSO ADC FRAeS RAF
1994	Norman, Alexander	1982	Smallwood, Air Chief Marshal Sir Denis	1997	Townshend, James
2004	Norman, Casey		(Splinters), GBE KCB DSO DFC FRAeS (d.1997)		
1966	Norman, Desmond, CBE FRAeS (d.2002)	1966	Smiley, Colonel David, LVO OBE MC*	2007	Ussher, Christopher

2006 Vacher, Polly, MBE

1966 Vanneck, Air Commodore The Hon Sir
    Peter, GBE CB AFC DL (d. 1999)

1997 Vernon, Greville

1966 Verulam, The Earl of (John) (d.1973)

2001 Wake, Charles

2001 Walker, Air Vice Marshal David,
    CBE AFC RAF

1969 Ward, Gerald, CBE DL (d.2008)

1966 Waterpark, The Lord (Caryll)

2007 Wates, Henrietta (Mic Mac)

1982 Westminster, The Duke of (Gerald)
    (resigned 1995)

2007 Whitcombe, Susan

1966 White, The Hon Luke (The Lord Annaly)
    (d.1990)

1983 Wigan, David (d. 2006)

1982 Wigan, Michael (resigned)

1966 Wills, Philip (resigned) (d.1978)

1999 Williams, Robert (Tim)

1966 Williams-Wynne, Colonel John, CBE DSO
    (d.1998)

1974 Williams-Wynne, William

NOTES

1. The date shown is the date of joining.

2. Surnames are those on joining, so that if a title is inherited or bestowed later the member is shown under his or her name on joining, with subsequent title. Titles are shown in alphabetical order, with a reference to the earlier name.

3. Christian names are shown, with nick-name if known by such.

4. Initials of other names are not shown.

5. Academic achievements are not shown.

6. Business qualifications are not shown unless of an aeronautical nature.

7. Memberships of industrial associations and societies are not shown unless of an aeronautical nature.

8. Medical qualifications: general practitioners are shown as 'Dr', surgeons by fellowship of one or more surgical colleges.

9. Legal qualifications are shown.

10. Her Majesty's and Lord-Lieutenants' appointments are shown.

11. All military decorations for valour and service are shown. Second or third awards are indicated with an asterisk.

12. Masters of Fox Hounds are shown.

13. Honorary Members are not shown in the main list unless they joined as ordinary members in the first place.

14. The date of resignation or death is shown - if known.

15. RAF (Rtd) is now discontinued.

MEMBERS OF THE AIR SQUADRON
Listed by date of joining.

1966 Aitken, Group Captain Sir Max, Bt DSO
    DFC (d.1985)

1966 Annaly, The Lord (see White)

1966 Astor, The Hon Hugh (d.1999)

1966 Bader, Group Captain Sir Douglas, CBE
    DSO* DFC* DL FRAeS (d.1982)

1966 Baring, The Hon James (The Lord
    Revelstoke)

1966 Cayzer, The Hon Anthony (d.1990)

1966 Churchill, Winston

1966 Constable Maxwell, Major David TD (d.1985)

1966 d'Erlanger, Robin

1966 Dundas, Group Captain Sir Hugh (Cocky),
    CBE DSO* DFC DL (d.1995)

1966 Eaden, David, DSC (resigned 1972)

1966 Everard, Anthony (Tony)

1966 Faulconer, Ivor (resigned 1982)

1966 Gardner, Richard (Jimmy), OBE DSC (d.1999)

1966 Houlder, Professor John, CBE MBE(Mil)

1966 King, Lieutenant Commander Osborne
    (Ossie), DSC (d.1995)

1966 Norman, Desmond, CBE FRAeS (d.2002)

1966 Ponsford, Ian (resigned)

1966 Revelstoke, The Lord (see Baring)

1966 Salmond, Julian (resigned)

1966 Savile, The Hon Anthony

1966 Smiley, Colonel David, LVO OBE MC*
    (resigned) (d.2009)

1966 Sopwith, Thomas

1966 Straight, Air Commodore Whitney, CBE MC
    DFC (d.1979)

1966 Strathcona & Mount Royal, The Lord
    (Euan) (resigned)

1966	Vanneck, Air Commodore The Hon Sir Peter, GBE CB AFC DL (d.1999)	1974	Ames, Simon	1983	Allison, Air Chief Marshal Sir John, KCB CBE FRAeS
1966	Verulam, The Earl of (John) (d.1973)	1974	Hamilton & Brandon, The Duke of (Angus)		
1966	Waterpark, The Lord (Caryll)	1974	Schroder, Bruno	1983	Checketts, Squadron Leader Sir David, KCVO (resigned)
1966	White, The Hon Luke (The Lord Annaly) (d.1990)	1974	Williams-Wynne, William	1983	Cook, Tom
1966	Wills, Philip (resigned) (d.1978)	1975	Astor, Michael (resigned)	1983	D'Oyly, Lieutenant Colonel Christopher, (resigned 1999)
1966	Williams-Wynne, Colonel John, CBE DSO (d. 1998)	1975	Braybrooke, The Lord – see Neville		
		1975	Bridport, The Viscount (Alex) (resigned 1983)	1983	Liverpool, The Earl of (Eddie)
1967	de Ferranti, Sebastian	1975	Neville, The Hon Robin, (The Lord Braybrooke) (resigned 2008)	1983	Noel, The Hon Thomas
1967	Kildare, The Marquess of (Gerald), (The Duke of Leinster) (resigned 1983)(d.2004)			1983	Wigan, David (d. 2006)
1967	Steel, Anthony (d.1984)	1976	Bagge, Sir John, Bt, ED DL (d.1990)	1984	Hall, William
1967	Swire, Sir Adrian	1976	Bledisloe, The Viscount (Ben) (d.1979)	1984	Macfadyen, Air Marshal Ian, CB OBE FRAeS
		1976	Cadogan, The Earl – see Chelsea		
1968	Barraclough, Martin	1976	Chelsea, The Viscount (Charles), DL (The Earl Cadogan)	1985	Crouch, Derek (d.1989)
1968	Clutton, Cecil (Sam) CBE (d.1991)			1985	Sutherland, Ian
1968	Lindsay, The Hon Patrick (d.1986)	1977	Corbett, David	1985	Thomson, Air Chief Marshal Sir John, GCB CBE AFC (d.1994)
		1977	Hall, Professor Edward, CBE (d.2001)		
1969	McAlpine, Kenneth, OBE DL FRAeS	1977	Lamplough, Robert	1986	Argyll, The Duke of (Ian)(d.2001)
1969	Ward, Gerald, CBE DL (d.2008)	1977	Tennant, The Hon Christopher (resigned)	1986	Cyster, Squadron Leader David,
				1986	de Ferranti, Adrian
1970	Dugdale, Sir William, Bt CBE MC	1979	Macpherson, The Hon Ian, (The Lord Strathcarron) (resigned 2008)	1986	Moss, Lieutenant Colonel Johnny, MBE
1970	Gloucester, HRH Prince William of, (d.1972)			1986	Pearson, The Hon Charles
1970	Haig-Thomas, Flying Officer Anthony	1979	Strathcarron, The Lord – see Macpherson	1986	Rothschild, The Hon Amschel (d.1996)
1970	Shelburne, The Earl of (Charlie) (resigned)			1986	Salisbury-Jones, Raymond (resigned)
		1980	Bostock, Air Commodore Simon, DL		
1972	Strathcarron, The Lord (David) (d.2006)	1982	Smallwood, Air Chief Marshal Sir Denis (Splinters), GBE KCB DSO DFC FRAeS (d.1997)	1988	Berry, Simon
				1988	Best, Bob
1973	Erne, The Earl of (Harry) (resigned)	1982	Westminster, The Duke of (Gerald) (resigned 1995)	1988	Curtis, Alan, OBE
1973	Mavroleon, Bluey (d. 2009)			1988	de Ferranti, Marcus
1973	Storey, Thomas	1982	Wigan, Michael (resigned)	1988	Hogg, John (d. 2003)
				1988	Howard, The Hon Alex

1988	Lindsay,Ludovic (resigned)	1994	Hoerner, John	2003	Steel, John, QC FRAeS
1988	McAlpine, James	1994	Holloway, Group Captain Terry, FRAeS		
		1994	Norman, Alexander	2004	Bloch, Dr Harold,
1989	Cavendish, The Hon Rory	1994	Norman, Sir Torquil, CBE	2004	Brun, Olaf
1989	Glenarthur, The Lord (Simon), DL FRAeS	1994	Pegnall, Air Commodore Brian (resigned 1996)	2004	Gavazzi, Egidio
	(res.2007)	1994	Sharples, The Hon Christopher	2004	Norman, Casey
1989	Greenall, Dr The Hon Gilbert, CBE			2004	Parkhouse, Nicholas, DM FRCS
1989	Greenall, The Hon Johnny, MFH	1995	Blois, Roddy		
1989	Mexborough, The Earl of (John)	1995	Cayzer, The Hon Robin (The Lord	2005	Bondarenko, Lorraine
1989	Milford Haven, The Marquess of (George)		Rotherwick)	2005	Bondarenko, Viktor
1989	Naylor-Leyland, Sir Philip, Bt, MFH	199 1999	Camrass, Robert	2005	Hutchinson, Captain John FRAeS FRIN
1989	Savage, Julian (d. 1990)	1999	Sheldon, Jamie		
		1999	Williams, Robert (Tim)	2006	Andover, Viscount(Alexander)
1990	Bagge, Sir Jeremy, Bt, DL			2006	Astor, James
1990	Hine, Air Chief Marshal Sir Patrick, GCB	2000	Cecil, The Lord Valentine	2006	Day, Catherine
	GBE FRAeS (resigned)	2000	Clark, Tim	2006	Folkes, Brigadier Richard, OBE ADC FRAeS
1990	Squire, Air Chief Marshal Sir Peter, GCB	2000	Cook, Nicholas	2006	Metcalfe, Jeremy
	DFC AFC DL DSc FRAeS RAF	2000	Fopp, Dr Michael, FMA FRAeS	2006	Taylor, John
		2000	Gainza, Maxi	2006	Torpy, Air Chief Marshal Sir Glenn, KCB
1991	Beetham, Marshal of the Royal Air Force	2000	Gosling, Martin		CBE DSO ADC FRAeS RAF
	Sir Michael, GCB CBE DFC AFC DL RAF	2000	Leigh, Edward	2006	Vacher, Polly, MBE
1991	de Ferranti, Mark	2000	Stinton, Air Commodore Julian, RAF		
1991	Montagu, Dru			2007	Haig-Thomas, Edward
		2001	Elwes, Jonathan	2007	Hubbard, Ralph
1992	Cameron, Lieutenant Colonel RM, Peter, MC	2001	Labouchere, Henry	2007	Partridge-Hicks, Stephen
1992	Everard, Richard DL (resigned 2008)	2001	Scurr, Dr James	2007	Prescot, Nigel
1992	Suffolk and Berkshire, The Earl of (Micky)	2001	Stirrup, Air Chief Marshal Sir Jock, GCB	2007	Ussher, Christopher
			AFC ADC FRAeS RAF	2007	Wates, Henrietta (Mic Mac)
1993	Foyle, Christopher, DL FRAeS	2001	Wake, Charles	2007	Whitcombe, Susan
1993	Leigh, Christopher	2001	Walker, Air Vice Marshal David, CBE AFC RAF		
1993	Lindsay, Valentine			2008	Holman-West, Andrew
1993	Mauleverer, Captain David, FRAeS FRIN	2003	Rolls, George	2008	Loader, Air Chief Marshal Sir Clive, KCB
1993	Spiers, Sir Donald, CB TD FRAeS	2003	Spittle, Dr Margaret, OBE FRCR FRCP		OBE ADC FRAeS RAF

2008	Moran, Air Chief Marshal Sir Christopher, KCB OBE MVO RAF	1967	David Allan	2000	Mark Jefferies, ADV Jonathan Whaley
2008	Perry, Dr Ian, FRAeS	1968	Frances Macrae	2000	Mark Jefferies
2008	Ponte, David	1969	Bob Mitchell	2001	Not awarded (weather)
		1970	Mike Riley	2002	Not awarded (weather)
		1971	Roy Legg	2003	Gerald Cooper
		1972	Roy Legg	2004	Not awarded (weather)
		1973	Roy Legg	2005	Not awarded (weather)
		1974	David Perrin	2006	Mark Davies, INT
		1975	David Perrin	2007	Paul Tomlinson
		1976	Tony Smith (Tiger Club)	2008	Randal Hockey
		1977	Brendan O'Brien		
		1978	Alan Dix		
		1979	Barry Smith		
		1980	Roger Graham, ADV Nick Radford		
		1981	Barry Tempest, ADV David Perrin		
		1982	Barry Tempest		
		1983	Barry Smith, ADV James Black		
		1984	Richard Pickin, ADV Roger Graham		
		1985	Nigel Hall		
		1986	Nick Bloom		
		1987	Mark Jefferies		
		1988	Alan Wade, ADV Alan Wade		
		1989	Chris Kelleher		
		1990	Nick Bloom, ADV Alan Cassidy		
		1991	Tony 'Taffy' Smith, ADV Louisa Knapp		
		1992	Andy Legge, ADV Nick Wakefield		
		1993	Tom Cassells		
		1994	David Macdonald		
		1995	Nick Buckenham - Apprentices		
		1996	Stefan Kwiecien - Apprentices		
		1997	Alan Cassidy - Open		
		1998	Alan Cassidy - Open		
		1999	Nick Buckenham - Apprentices		

YEAR	REG	TYPE	WINNER
1970	G-AWDO	Druine Turbulent	Roy Watling-Greenwood
1971	G-AWEP	Gardan Minicab	Stan Jackson
1972	G-AVEY	Currie Super-wot	Kieth Sedgwick & Tony Eastelow
1973	G-BAAD	Evans VP-1	Richard Husband
1974	G-AXKH	Luton minor	Mike Vaisey
1975	G-BBJI	Isaacs Spitfire	John Isaacs
1976	G-BDAP	Wittman Tailwind	John & Tony Whiting
1977	G-BDHJ	Pazmany PL-1	Harold Jones
1978	G-BDWJ	Replica Plans SE-5A	Mike Beach
1979	G-BEVS	Taylor JT1 Monoplane	David Hunter
1980	G-LASS	Rutan Vari-Eze	Messrs Calvert,Foreman & O'Hara
1981	G-BJHK	EAA Acro Sport	John Kimber
1982	G-BFAS	Evans VP-1	Alister Sutherland
1983	G-RAFT	Rutan Long-Ez	Don Foreman
1984	G-BIYK	Isaacs Fury	Ron Martin
1985	G-PFAR	Isaacs Fury	Clive Repik
1986	G-FLIK	Pitts S1	Bob Millinship
1987	G-CWOT	Currie Wot	Don Lord
1988	G-BDME	Pietenpol Al Camper	David Silsbury
1989	G-BYLL	Falco F8L	N.Langrick
1990	G-BPRT	Super Emeraude	Nigel Reddish
1991	G-BDWM	Bonsall DB-1 Mustang	David Bonsall
1992	G-BSSK	Quickie Q.200	Robin Greatrex
1993	G-BRWV	Brugger Colibri	Joe McCollum
1994	G-LITZ	Pitts S1	Kevin Eld & Jenny Hughes
1995	G-GANE	Falco F8L	Stuart Gane
1996	G-BVSB	Minimax	Christopher Nice
1997	G-OCAD	Falco F8L	Clive Garrard, David Nowill & Gordon Blunt
1998	G-BVXE	Steen Skybolt	Trevor Reeve
1999	G-OJDA	Acrosport 2	David Almey
2000	G-ILSE	Corby Starlet	Steven Stride
2001		No Rally due to Foot & Mouth outbreak	
2002	G-IDII	DR107 One Design	Colwyn Darlow
2003	G-IIIV	Pitts S1-11B	Gary Ferriman & Rob Millinship
2004	G-SAZZ	Super Emeraude CP328	Derek Long
2005	G-ERIW	ZZ1 Flitzer	Rupert Wasey
2006	G-SIIS	Pitts S1S	Ian Searson

APPENDIX E
**WINNERS OF THE AIR SQUADRON TROPHY FOR
AIR CADETS
1985-2008**

APPENDIX F
**WINNERS OF THE SIR JOHN THOMSON MEMORIAL SWORD
1995-2008**

1985	Bedford Modern School
1986	George Heriot's
1987	Queen Mary's Grammar School, Walsall
1988	Bedford Modern School
1989	Judd School
1990	Birkenhead
1991	Adams Grammar School
1992	Monmouth
1993	Birkenhead
1994	Lancing
1995	Maidstone Grammar School
1996	Queen Mary's Grammar School, Walsall
1997	Maidstone Grammar School
1998	Dulwich College
1999	Maidstone Grammar School
2000	Maidstone Grammar School
2001	King's School, Grantham
2002	King's School, Grantham
2003	Victoria College
2004	Maidstone Grammar School
2005	Hampton School
2006	Maidstone Grammar School
2007	King's School, Grantham
2008	Maidstone Grammar School

Year	Name	School
1995	Ian Lakin	Queen Mary's Grammar School, Walsall
1996	Susan Mooring	Berkhamsted Collegiate School
1997	Lee Ahern	Wellington College
1998	Noel Rees	Portsmouth Grammar School
1999	Nancy Owen	Ryde School, Isle of Wight
2000	Angus Barr	Bridlington School
2001	Alex Vaughan	Bedford School
2002	Andrew McMaster	Royal Belfast Academical Institution
2003	Daisy Acres	Reigate Grammar School
2004	William Macdonald	Chichester High School
2005	Thomas Hansford	Robert Gordon's College, Aberdeen
2006	Nicola Clark	Colston's Collegiate School, Bristol
2007	Thomas Stratton	Maidstone Grammar School
2008	Ben Combs	Bromsgrove School

ACKNOWLEDGEMENTS

The author's special thanks go to Simon Ames, Martin Barraclough and Caryll Waterpark for the loan of documents, checking of the text, and much patient explanation of the history and ethos of the Air Squadron. Equally to Bruno Schroder for initiating and funding the book, Christopher Sharples for project management, picture research and financial support, Gordon Bain for his superb air-to-air photography, and Elizabeth Vanneck for the loan of Peter Vanneck's logbooks. Several people took me flying, and they deserve special medals: Martin Barraclough, Bill Hall, Anthony Kedros of the Flying Farmers Association, Henry Labouchere, Alex Norman, Casey Norman, Torquil Norman, David Ponte, Christopher Sharples, John Steel, Micky Suffolk and Tim Williams. Deep thanks also to James Baring, Jonathan Elwes, Maxi Gainza, Michael Graydon, Bill Hall, Terry Holloway, Torquil Norman and George Rolls for reading and correcting the manuscript; and to all the members, too numerous to list, who kindly gave their time, lent their photographs and shared with me the magic of their aerial adventures.

A.M.

The excerpt on page 119 is reprinted by kind permission of Michael Palin from his book *Himalaya* published in 2004 by Weidenfeld & Nicolson, an imprint of the Orion Group, London
Text copyright © Michael Palin 2004.

Air Squadron's major trips

▬▬▬	Russia 1992
▬▬▬	Pakistan and the Himalayas 1997
▬▬▬	USA and Alaska 2000
▬▬▬	South Africa 2003
▬▬▬	Norway and Spitzbergen 2005